Graphic Arts In The Twentieth Century

Praeger

Graphic Arts in

Wolf Stubbe

the Twentieth Century

40 color plates, 446 illustrations in black and white

Frederick A. Praeger, *Publisher*
New York · London

FREDERICK A. PRAEGER, *Publisher*
64 University Place, New York 3, N. Y., U. S. A.
49 Great Ormond Street, London W. C. 1, England
Published in the United Staates of America in 1963
by Frederick A. Praeger, Inc., Publisher

English translation
© Thames and Hudson Ltd., London, 1963
Library of Congress Catalog Number: 63-20968
Printed in West Berlin, Germany

CONTENTS

PREFACE

As it was plain from the start that any summarizing account of present-day graphic art would have to be tentative, this experiment was undertaken in the honest belief that it was an innocent one. For anyone concerning himself with the artistic events of his own times is constantly aware of the limits of his own powers of judgment, and he very soon comes to realize that, though highlights may perhaps be discerned, it is hardly possible to determine grades of value. Indeed, the very change in and probably also the broadening of one's own view are invigorating experiences, as one grows familiar with art previously unknown. Yet however ready one may be just to accept, the need for a kind of stock-taking keeps presenting itself, even if it is to occur with inadequate means. A need to "master" one's manifold experiences of new phenomena, to render oneself an account of what is really being touched in one's consciousness, and to see whether the bewildering hotchpotch of most varied sensations cannot after all be reduced to some kind of order and thus made easier to survey. That this need is legitimized, if on no other grounds, simply by its omnipresence becomes apparent time and again as people talk. Not just in the discussions of spectators experiencing something new but also, and still more distinctly, in the explanations given by creators of what they create. It is true that some artists are taciturn. The majority, however, have a view on what they ought and want to do — a view wholly committed to what is peculiarly theirs: the self-evident basic condition of all free creation, but also more or less a prerequisite for whoever seeks, in contemplating it, to give an account of what has just been produced. Today most artists — including the very ones who have made a decisive "practical" contribution to determining art's course — know how to express their aesthetic and philosophical opinions far better than did their predecessors. They are often great and intriguing theorists, and under the direct impact of their statements one can hold that these have the character of genuine commentaries and must therefore be seen as part of their maker's creative activity. With such autonomous reasoned explanations of autonomous actions it is undoubtedly a question of the most passionate and total commitment immaginable. Yet these highly personal verbal presentations of definite views on pictorial art are quite often endorsed by the appearance of the work produced, and thus help, like all relevant knowledge, to deepen the visual experience. If one must in any case set out from a fixed position, as one cannot stand above the present and obtain from afar a comprehensive prospect of what it yields, these committed views can, if one feels that a sort of correlation exists between them and the work of art, provide very useful information and direct the eye to what is essential.

An unclarified residue does of course remain. One can hardly check the authenticity of relations between word and work that are, so to speak, only felt. However, this element of imprecision is reduced if views can be assembled that are due to the efforts of many minds and approach a *consensus omnium*. Such deliberations guided to agreement over a wide area are particularly in evidence at the start of the graphic evolution here to be considered. Accordingly, they have been followed in comparative detail. But since the field in which individual opinions find general acceptance narrows the closer it gets to the present day, shorter references to different trends of thought have had to take the place of rather more lengthy expositions for the immediate present. As the diverse views on the nature and functions of graphic art are enumerated in their succession during modern times, its most recent history, full of decisions, also takes shape.

The one-sidedness of this essay is an inevitable result of all this. There can be no question here of giving marks, and so the mentioning of an artist is not to be equated with a value judgment. Rather it is a matter of citing examples, which as such do of course have their special weight. When choosing them the aim was as far as possible to eliminate judgment founded on personal taste. Just as far as possible. The fallibility of even a well-disposed will has a disturbing effect, and the achieving of a balanced assessment is jeopardized no less by the unavoidable limitedness of one's own experience. This assessment thus depends largely on which artists and which works the selector has seen. What it has been possible to study especially thoroughly within the compass of the accessible data of exhibitions, collections, sales, and so on, inevitably creates definite trends in the mind. The general valuation of a given artist does not remain without effect upon the individual, whether it induces him to agree with it or drives him into opposition. Experts on graphic art know about the power of suggestion wielded by the "provocative" offer on the art market. They see daily how various are the judgments even of really painstaking and naturally gifted connoisseurs, and witness the continual change in what one might call the public presentation of the artists. They know — apart from the artists who have "arrived" undisputably — how rapid is the succession in which ever different artists are put on display as being important. Little as this is to be lamented from the standpoint of the prospect it offers of what is going on in art, it still greatly hinders any attempt to establish a definite image of art today. From the point of view of the presentation, neither the ever necessary replacements nor the numerous deletions allow a conclusion to be reached. All this naturally applies less to graphic work from the first third of our century, but even as regards what may be held exemplary, its valuation is by no means free from movement.

Hence it has proved necessary to proceed not only as a summarist but also as a cataloguer, and to mention by name the artists who have become known to a fairly wide public, to be able to add to their dates a brief commentary, and above all to indicate literature that deals authoritatively with their works. The accompanying illustration is intended to show a work that exemplifies the graphic *œuvre*, and it is by no means always a late one. In assembling the material, Kurt Sternelle, whose collaboration through research and discussion the author recalls with gratitude, was often wholly dependent on exhibition catalogues. These were found to contain highly contradictory statements, which have as far as possible been clarified by comparison, further enquiry and careful thought. Here also it is a case of an attempt, felt to be a necessary one, at obtaining reliable information.

Joseph von Führich, 1832

Gustave Doré, 1868

Adolf von Menzel, 1850
Adolf von Menzel, 1877

Johan Berthold Jongkind, 1875
Charles-François Daubigny, ca. 1851

Edvard Munch, 1895

Max Klinger, 1884

James Whistler, ca. 1880

Camille Pissarro, 1879

Jean François Millet, ca. 1856

Edouard Manet, 1864

CONDITIONS AND FOUNDATIONS

The history of modern graphic art begins in those years after the middle of the nineteenth century when people first considered how the print could be raised to an independent art form. At a period like ours, which takes the independence of graphic creation entirely for granted, it is hard to understand these deliberations. In those days, however, making prints was largely a peripheral artistic activity, and this at a moment when people were everywhere speculating anxiously on the nature of the visual arts, on their currently appropriate function and their importance in everyday life. Even though in France great artists like Ingres and Delacroix were still masters of the field and enjoyed respect, it was generally felt with slight uneasiness that they were making no innovations, and all connoisseurs knew what was really to be expected of them. There was a growing feeling that a fresh start would have to be made, and people reflected on every aspect of artistic expression. They regarded art as something bound up with life, as an intensification of existence, or saw its true source in free phantasy. There were simultaneous tendencies to say yes and no to life, for the belief in progress and the power of science was balanced by resigned acceptance of a futile world that had become a self-regulating machine. No clear-cut spiritual trend could predominate at this period, so Malpertuy believed in 1844, because the nineteenth century was made up of the most diverse elements whose mutual attraction only led them to neutralize each other, a view that — for the future of art as well — was to prove correct.

But beyond these attempts to determine the position of the visual arts within one's own period, there once more hove in sight the problem of their forms, and it is at just such times that the graphic techniques are wont to be recognized as media that, properly used, can open up regions of expression shunned by painting and drawing alike.

To ferret out these autonomous artistic potentialities of the print and give them a part in the ensemble of pictorial techniques was the task of the hour, precisely because painting and drawing ranked far above print-making, and graphic means were really still only employed in the service of the former. As early as the eighteenth century, line-engraving in copper and etching, or else a combination of the two, was being used mainly to reproduce paintings — very graphic reproductions, it is true. Even when, later on, such intaglio processes were put aside in favour of woodcut and the new invention, lithography, these up-and-coming relief and planar techniques soon lapsed into the same subordinate dependency on painting and drawing, and, because of their ability to render the painted or washed original even more faithfully than intaglio, they sank completely to the status of a "black-and-white" art of reproduction, a kind of forerunner of photography, which would soon, and as it were logically, be invented. For woodcut, and even more lithography, make it possible — and in this they resemble photography — to reproduce tone and plane through unbroken areas of colour, whereas with line-engraving and etching they can only be inadequately paraphrased through parallel lines. At that period, the lithographer Nadar gave up this technique in order to create works of art by means of photography, since, in accordance with the taste of the times, his pictorial ideas tended towards compositions of tonal planes. To this end, photography was a more suitable artistic instrument than lithography, whose autonomous possibilities were not sufficient for Nadar's artistic aims.

The graphic medium's dangerous ability to reproduce the most varied originals — still both an advantage and a disadvantage today — did not on its own produce this weakness and self-surrender of the techniques. At the same time, graphic art at that date also lacked inward resistence. The brilliant use of lithography by the French romantics, when Géricault and especially Delacroix magnificently expressed their passion for movement in floods of velvet-black tone values, was a flowering of brief duration, as Delacroix ended his graphic activity in 1835, and around the middle of the century only Daumier went on being a great lithographer. Print-making so to speak negated itself at the start of the century, which means in neo-classicism. True artistic handling was intentionally suppressed in neo-classic graphic work. An impersonal, detached line glided along spiritlessly as a mere contour. It is significant that these twirling arabesque-like lines Page 7 (above) with their ornamental, calculated course — passing for the sign of a cool mind — created forms that could as well be reproduced by copper engraving as by woodcut, since the print of this abstract lineation did not reveal which method had been used. From the standpoint of artistic technique, it was thus a neutral line, which deliberately did nothing to cultivate the special character of each individual graphic medium. So far as specifically graphic effects are concerned, this widespread self-surrender as it were spontaneously promoted the tendency of the nineteenth century in its prime to look upon the graphic techniques solely as means of reproducing "real" works of art.

Nevertheless, all three graphic techniques had had their moment of glory during the early nineteenth century, and the history of the print in these decades is divided up into short periods marked by the temporary predominance of woodcut, lithography or etching. This will no longer, or only with many reservations, be the case in the age of "modern graphic art". Finally, woodcut took on a new lease of life when, instead of a block sawn plank-fashion, Thomas Bewick began incising one sawn across the grain. In his animal books published between 1790 and 1804, he showed that this end-grain wood-engraving was the proper technique for illustrations in printed books. In the hard cross-cut wood — boxwood was generally used — a sharply pointed instrument could plough thin white lines, with a manoeuvrability that had formerly been the prerogative of the etching-needle. Wood-engraving, in which the artist guides the burin to obtain white lines, makes possible extremely delicate work, so that purely linear inspirations can also be almost fully expressed. Increasingly displaced by copper engraving and etching since the end of the sixteenth century, book-woodcut underwent a renewal round about 1835 thanks to this new potentiality, which was not only realized to great effect in the extensive and often witty creations of the French illustrators around Gustave Doré, but brought with it a high tide of the art of woodcut in general. This was reached when Adolf Menzel managed in a few years to

Page 8 (*above*)

advance the development of xylography so far that it was able to render his drawings for Franz Kugler's history of Frederick the Great (1840—42) with complete fidelity in the cross-cut wood. Not only do these wood-engraved illustrations preserve Menzel's lines as the bearers of pulsating movement, but even the dark passages are now also resolved in the print into those areas of vigorous hatching with which the artist could turn planes into something lineal. Yet in his later illustrations Menzel comes close to the tonal woodcut, though certainly not through a free decision, but "for reasons of time", as he lamented. Thus his later woodcut illustrations look like tonal wash drawings: they increasingly lose the specifically graphic traits of a wood-engraving, and

Page 8 (*below*)

the very effective lines are replaced by indistinct *valeurs*. In France too, the rapidly multiplying advocates of autonomous graphic values complained that illustrational woodcuts looked like ink-blots beside the precise forms of the book-types. So it was generally regarded as a positive

Page 7 (*below*)

deliverance when in 1865 photographs were successfully printed straight on to the block, thereby making it unnecessary to draw on the printing-block. It was not "painterliness" in the broad sense but in the narrow one of a preoccupation with grey-black tone that deprived wood-engraving and lithography of their rank of pictorial means with intrinsic value, and reduced them to instruments with which to turn out reproductions.

One must picture this situation, hardly conceivable today, if one wishes to understand the efforts and ventures that soon began to be made to restore to the graphic techniques their artistic autonomy. An idea of the almost total extinction of independent graphic art can also heighten one's appreciation of the first results, still very faint in comparison with the strong features of more recent graphic work, produced by these bold endeavours. Energetically seeking to make line lively and variable, people in this hour of need remembered etching as it had been created by Rembrandt. What could etching in the spirit of its greatest master oppose to the listless weariness of limply swelling passages of tone? First of all, freshness and directness through a graphic animation of the whole surface. The emotion roused in the artist by an object or experience has the power to take on visible form in the lineal flow of the etched calligraphy. Such results naturally presuppose an independent act of graphic creation, in which the artist had to hit upon the motif spontaneously, as the only possible one, an act of free creation which no longer has anything in common with the difficult craft of those specializing in graphic reproduction. This was known from then on as a "painter-etching" and a distinction came to be made between original and reproductive graphic work. The creators of such original prints, who often, far from belonging to the "guild", were outsiders like the English surgeon Seymour Haden, called themselves *peintres-graveurs*. As far back as the eighteenth century collectors and connoisseurs of prints had thus designated etchers like Rembrandt and Ostade, as distinct from graphic crafts-men who worked after originals by others. It soon came to be perceived that it was to the *peintres-graveurs*, and them alone, that the real destiny of graphic art had been entrusted. Right at the start of the quarrel between the so-called specialists, who produced planes by mechanical, auto-matic means, and these *peintres-graveurs*, Bracquemond, a leading etcher of the Paris school, pronounced: "The specialists merely impose rules on the means that the painters have discovered."

Haden, the English surgeon mentioned above, who, guided by a certain congeniality, also made an important contribution to research on Rembrandt's etchings, took bare copper plates with him when visiting his patients, so that he could at once begin scratching the metal with his drypoint tool if he saw a suitable motif by chance. He first won recognition in 1858—60, when he was working together with his much younger brother-in-law James McNeil Whistler. Between the delicate furrow of a drypoint stroke and the deep trench of a line repeatedly bitten in by acid there lies an astonishingly wide compass of nuances; and if, like Haden and Whistler, one requires a line both to circumscribe forms and to represent the play of light and shadow, one can extract very much more from etched and drypoint lines than from those of a pencil. Such a range of variation between extreme delicacy and the most intense energy is only afforded by etching and drypoint, which in this respect leave drawing far behind.

Knowledge of this spread quickly. From 1866, William Unger, the founder of the Vienna school of etching, was already using the etching-needle instead of the burin for his copies of paintings. In so doing, he profited by the more ductile character of the needle, as compared with the burin's awkward heaviness. The etched line's rich possibilities of combination, responding to each delicate movement, allowed him to make, so Unger thought, more faithful translations of the values and warmth of the painted original than did copper engraving. But Unger never employed etching as an independent means of artistic expression, whereas his pupil Karl Koepping later never used the new etching technique to make a reproduction. For Koepping, etching and free creation were already synonyms. If a graphic artist ventured to copy by means of etching, the copied master's personality would envelope him like someone else's garment, he warned. In the societies for original graphic work now founded in many places, people at first still liked talking about tone. As though they had a guilty conscience owing to the new decision in favour of line, they kept affirming that etching would leave open every possibility of development for tone as well; at the same time, however, it would give the fullest scope to spontaneity in handling the tool. It was calligraphy that people wanted, and they saw the etching-needle as the instrument for achieving intentional, arbitrary, ebullient movement.

Here a creative drive was at work in graphic art that may be compared in all respects with similar impulses in contemporary painting. If, since Constable, the action of the brush no longer just helped to display plastic values on a plane, but, as a highly personal handling that broke up the picture-surface into lumps, flakes and dots, became the means of attaining hitherto unknown effects of colour, and if Delacroix made the whole paint-layer vibrate with the coloured traces

Page 9   of his spirited execution, Charles Daubigny now wanted to transfer his lively brushwork to the etching as well, and he therefore covered the entire surface of the paper with a congealed mass of lines. But, and this is also true of his paintings — though these do already betray the fleeting impression — one cannot yet really talk of impressionism in connection with Daubigny's graphic works. The objects are still composed in the last analysis of constant changes in the density of the tone. On the other hand, impressionist light-vibrations shatter and dissolve the forms in

Page 9   J. B. Jongkind's etchings. The seemingly effortless, quivering stroke of the "Bohemian", suggesting the rapidity of his execution and making visible the transitoriness of his impression, is a far more decisive instrument. Compared with this linear brio, Daubigny's needle seems inhibited in its movement, even though it is beginning to follow the impulse and express what the French call *la volonté*. Unconsciously driven to procure tonal unity, the artist still overburdens his sheet with an excess of contrasts. Impressionism's vibrant colourfulness is finally transposed to the black-white scale, and infused with light by the opulence of a variegated "chromatic" quality, in

Page 11   Camille Pissarro's etchings, through adding an extremely varied and delicate tonal effect by means of aquatint. After the first fleeting notation of the objects has been made with etching and drypoint, the plate is granulated by the salt aquatint method in repeated bitings, as a result of which the gradations from light to dark are constantly enriched. The first loose graining is thus overlaid at every new emersion in acid by increasingly dense accumulations of dots, locally determined according to the desired values of light and shade. Up to sixteen states can be followed in Pissarro's proof-impressions, and the whole range of the chromatically irradiated tone values

Page 12   on his canvases reappears in the greys of these prints. True, Pissarro's graphic art is descended from the etchings and lithographs of Millet. But if one compares Pissarro's sheets with the works produced by Millet about twenty years earlier, Millet's etchings show themselves to be still wholly determined by the dark tones. The forms are quarried from the chiaroscuro of an interior. With its wire-sharp strokes that often appear in dense parallel lines and its large expanses of white untouched by graphic work, Millet's technique has a pictorial aim entirely different from that of the impressionist method. It is able to be so simple because its purpose is to bring into being the monumentalized image of a simple, unassuming humanity of workers and peasants.

Whistler too soon developed his graphic technique into a means of presenting an impressionist range of vision in etching and lithography. So long as he was still working with Haden, and also when he was creating in 1860 the series of etchings with views of the Thames, he sought the significant, vivacious line. Later — above all in lithography — he pursued impressionist effects, the appeal of sketchiness. Scarcely inked at all, the stones have often printed only intimations Page 11 of forms. Floating silhouettes, elegant surface effects, and surprising "cutting" determine the appearance of the sets of Venice etchings that he produced in the 'eighties.

While this was taking place in England and France, and for a long time after, etching in Germany went on being essentially a method of reproduction, apart from Leibl's splendid efforts. Not until the 'nineties did the influence of Seymour Haden assert itself, particularly among the members of the Berlin society for original etching founded at that time, in whose works the technique developed by Haden out of the Rembrandt tradition became almost the sole means of expression. Later Max Liebermann tried to introduce impressionist light into his etchings, but only succeeded in doing so completely at the beginning of our century. The same forces that delayed the break-through of impressionism in German painting also retarded the emergence of new graphic forms. Again, it was by no means just a question of problems concerning form. As with all nineteenth-century art movements, this formally retarding phase of German art was decisively influenced by deliberations on what the message of the visual arts was really to be. Max Klinger, the one markedly original German etcher, who was active at the same time as the French impressionists, wanted to remain a graphic artist in the sense of somebody who describes with the etching-needle, contrary to the Frenchmen. He "narrates" in paragraphs and chapters by following the thread of a story with a series of engravings, interpreting his subject-matter in sets of prints, like Dürer and the old graphic artists. What is to be recounted has been pondered by Klinger in every detail beforehand and treated most minutely in preliminary drawings. When he then renders it by subtly combined and amazingly accomplished intaglio methods, the result seems more a reproduction than something issuing from the graphic process itself. Just as rich as the means employed — the burin, etching, drypoint, aquatint, mezzotint, and printing-inks in various nuances of brown and black — are the details fashioned with them. Klinger knows nothing about the accentuation of single elements of a pictorial statement through simplifying form or "leaving out" details. Not one word of the narrative is to be lost, and each outward event must be precisely recorded, each inward meaning established by allusions that cannot be missed. Naturally, he also shows some tendency to graduate the values of the separate descriptions and to emphasize the most important things he has to say. But the very profusion of novelistic particulars and the multiplicity of forms corresponding to it reduce the dramatic force by diverting and distracting the eye. Käthe Kollwitz recognized what was new in Klinger's graphic means Page 97 and tried to help them to achieve purer results. With her too, in the early works even more than the mature ones, symbolic statements disengage themselves from realistic descriptions. But at the same time subject-matter and formal means are moving together, and in like manner, towards a general statement whose simplicity of form and content approaches the universal significance of a symbol.

Page 10   Nothing other than human destiny is being broached when Klinger in his etching *Forsaken* places the figure of a woman before the vast expanse of the open sea: exposure, subjection to threat. That this is the true intention is again (and, as experience of present-day forms makes one feel, superfluously) emphasized by the "unnatural" demand made on a natural object: the cloud over the middle of the horizon is required to gather into a menacing fist. Only a decade later, however, Munch was able with an outwardly similar motif to create a pure visual symbol.

Page 10   In his etching *Woman*, universal significance probing beyond the here and now has been evoked and made clear, for there has been no attempt to define the indefinable. Objects intensified to the heart of their appearances contain assertions about a womankind unfolding like a flower, driven by sensuality, and mystically blessed — symbolic assertions that would inevitably at once be suppressed if, as with Klinger, detailed descriptions were to analyse the data of reality. Fundamentally this print by Munch is something quite unlike any previous etching. Both outwardly and inwardly graphic art was given an entirely different configuration in the closing decades of last century, and its changed aspect and new optical force were matched by a change of content. New themes, pressing forward strongly, availed themselves of fresh formal energy, and because of the desire to report on new experiences, form was required to produce hitherto unknown, immeasurably more powerful effects.

If one is seeking focal points among the graphic discoveries of these years rather than following the general progress, made in many small steps, of graphic development, it is above all in Manet's etchings and lithographs that one will spot authoritative decisions regarding form, and there one will discover far more references to the future than his own times could detect. That Manet's graphic works had no direct influence is not surprising in view of their very limited circulation, and the artist himself did not bother much about them. Manet still made etchings that, as *estampes de traduction*, reproduced his own paintings. Along with these, however, he was already creating *estampes d'inspiration*, prints that were genuine graphic works in the invention as well. But even contemporaries with a high regard for the painter hardly saw any difference between the respective graphic techniques of the two types, whereas it immediately strikes modern eyes, attentive first and foremost to the evidence of form, that with Manet each print is testimony to a special graphic method. This is more obvious in the earlier states of the proof-impressions than in the finished print, a fact that again is characteristic of an initial situation. As in his paintings, Manet sets out in his graphic works from the neutral tones, the big, unbroken dark passages, later displaying more and more the brilliance of his mature palette even in the black and white. Tonal aquatints and velvet-black chalk lithographs containing a distant echo of Goya's and Daumier's conception came first. But round about 1874 they were followed by a lithograph, still after one of his own paintings, with impressions of a race, in which the lines leading into Page 12 depth become lines of movement. Alongside them, the crowd of spectators appears as a distorted mass, as if seen from a galloping horse. Manet's friends felt that this print was not quite "finished", even though the sucking depth and the radiance of the light across the wide course demanded their admiration. "One divines more than one discerns", it was said, and people thought that what had found only indistinct expression would be made clearer by a subsequent state of the stone. But of course it remained at this one, first state, as in it the "intention" had already been "realized". A year later, in 1875, appeared Stéphan Mallarmé's translation of *The Raven*, a poem by Edgar Allan Poe, with illustrations by Manet. Manet did not call his illustrations to this book lithographs, as we no doubt would today. He still regarded a lithograph exclusively as something drawn on grained stone in soft, deep-black chalk, as had been the case with Delacroix and Daumier. Here, however, Manet used transfer-paper on which he had dashed off drawings with the brush in transfer-ink *(encre autographique),* and so he called these prints *autographies.* They display exciting forms that, as well as being recorded more swiftly and summarily than ever before, are also precise statements of something new. Though on other occasions he is often not entirely confident of his actual subject-matter, and sometimes borrows from works by others, in *The Raven* Manet presents one of those disturbingly illogical spiritual experiences that will not fit into the natural pattern of everyday happenings. This is perhaps especially noticeable in the print entitled *The Chair.* Here we have the tantalizingly meaningless thereness of an object that Page 21 at moments of great spiritual agitation somehow or other "strikes the eye". Alone in the empty light there stands a chair, and with mysterious power it forces us to look at it just as the raven's ominous shadow is flitting by. Later on Van Gogh too, will depict chairs that, like this one, are materializations of disquieting feelings.

Content and form: already then the one did not always follow directly on the other. Form sometimes had to wait patiently until it found its content, while content now and then tried out inadequate forms. Thus, while it can be said without hesitation that Manet produced the first colour lithograph in the modern sense of the term, there is still the question of why he applied this new colourfulness to making, with seven colour stones, a portrait of his painter friend Edmonde André as Punchinello. The theme did not take on a deeper significance until very much later, above all with Picasso. Previously the harlequin costume had been introduced into pictures like a fashionable dress. Meissonier, universally esteemed, always doing the right thing, painted several portraits showing the sitter as Punchinello. Manet's colour lithograph dates from nearly twenty years before the famous ones of Toulouse-Lautrec and appeared at a time — the year 1874 — when the production of chromo-lithographs, which are no pleasure to meet, was in full swing. Beset by countless chromo-lithographers whose sole task, lavishly and gladly performed, was to "duplicate" oil-paintings, Manet spontaneously hit upon the idea of using this enslaved process

Edouard Manet, 1875

to produce a light-coloured original work than even chromatically is wholly a lithograph. Just as it was necessary to call to mind the self-surrender of woodcut and black-and-white lithography in the mechanical reproduction industry, in order to see clearly the significance of etching during the 'sixties as the first medium of an original graphic art, it is only under the impact of chromo-lithography, with its dark hues dulled by the grey shadows of the black plate, that one can judge what new colour possibilities make their appearance in Manet's Punchinello print. If, on the other hand, its effect is compared with that of later colour lithographs, it literally pales, whereas at the time of its creation it was a colouristic miracle. Manet's print does not yet manage to do what the colour lithographs of Toulouse-Lautrec achieve with, as it were, polished ease, namely "get across" *(passer la rampe)*. It does not project itself buoyantly over the footlights into the consciousness of spectators to whom the colour print will soon present life as striking scenes on a very gay, very ingenious, and very amusing stage. We are back at the question of content.

By investigating the new lines of thought rather than by exactly following the time sequence of artistic events, we very soon encounter aspects of graphic art totally different from those that had previously been usual — at about this time, when the newly founded artists' societies were trying to restore to the print its lost autonomy by seeing that justice was done to line as an interpretable script and the bearer of movement, colour and brilliant light. The first medium to offer itself for this was etching. But woodcut and lithography soon reappeared, showing no sign now of their humble origin as slaves of the reproduction industry. Before long etching was once more back in the shade, although it would never again be quite so neglected as midway through the century, when only Meryon, Charles Daubigny and Charles Jacques knew how to maintain its vitality. It was nascent ideas about the meaning and substance of art that deprived etching of further prospects, just after it had been revivified. At a time when, despite all the respect felt for Delacroix, people had long ceased to share his view that the supreme task of the visual arts was to represent great historical events and deeply significant religious legends, and when scepticism regarding traditional subjects had grown to such proportions, because of the changes in religious and political opinion, that Bürger-Thoré could say in 1868: "...formerly art was for gods and rulers, perhaps the time is now coming when art will be for man...", many at first believed that the real future of artistic creation lay in representing landscape. Landscape as the whole area inhabited by man freed painting, so it was thought, from abstract and remote themes — the landscape that was being depicted by the new etchers of the Rembrandt tradition in all its aspects and its abundant vitality. People felt that such prints "concerned" everyone. But in this century of the most divergent views and notions, whose mutual antagonism was then already so evident that Malpertuy believed they would inevitably cancel each other out and that it was therefore no use waiting for one particular tendency to become dominant, the endorsement of landscape etching was naturally accompanied by very different conceptions of the true function of art, conceptions that to some extent, moreover, have remained influential up to our times.

Very soon the new realism, such as it was embodied in landscape subjects, came to be opposed by the opinion that realism should be rejected on principle, as it offered no scope for imagination and would therefore never be in a position to represent pure thoughts. New ideas and thoughts would, however, issue from the changed social order and crystalize into ideals, whereupon the artist would be bound to feel that giving these ideals a standard and binding visual form was what really made his activity meaningful. If anyone ventured to claim that the subject did not matter — since the beginning of the nineteenth century the doctrine of art for art's sake (*l'art pour l'art*) had been in existence — it was basically only a protest against historical and religious themes. For, as in all his ancestors, there lay hidden in present-day man an idealism leading him to the real values. Hence it was necessary to depict the ordinary person of today in accordance with his fundamentally good nature. Jean-François Millet acknowledged these views within the compass of his art. He tried to show humble folk credibly in an attitude that made apparent what was felt to be "true" human greatness, independent of time and outward status. The clever way he used his deliberately simple etching technique was particularly suitable for this. But what may have seemed authentic in looking at his creations could very easily become doubtful at an impartial consideration of the contemporary reality. Here there were no clearly defined values, and yet, as Emile Zola saw it, the artist was to use his talent to help the society of this period surmount the given state of obscurity and contradiction. For it was out of this general uncertainty that the valuable creative individual, a unity in himself, developed in a continual interchange of challenge and substantiation. But through directly expressing the unity of the creative individual, the artist mastered the chaos of reality with its manifold values. The multivalence of phenomena was thus the actual condition of artistic activity, inasmuch as it left it to the artist to establish values for each particular occasion by his creative act. Such a view denied art a universally binding moral duty, which to many seemed its essential point. It is striking how far this conception approximates to that of impressionism, which also recognizes the thing perceived as the starting-point of artistic representation, but has this phenomenon changed, through the action of the artist's temperament, in favour of a formal beauty, each ideal concept being eliminated at the same time.

There remains the individual, at once acknowledged and left in the lurch. Answerable to himself alone and entirely self-dependent, he is able to establish artistic values solely by virtue of his own peculiarities. It was a necessary consequence of this view that from now on, which means from about the middle of the nineteenth century, "modern" and "anti-traditional" were synonyms. Having talent thus means being marked out by an exceptionally intense power of reacting to the hum-drum life that everyone lives. To make the impact of reality optically

Page 12

convincing as the concentration of individual experiences requires distinctive forms opposing the dullness of "nature". Here again the graphic medium proved highly suitable for giving expression to the artist's inward participation in what he saw, to the intensity of his most personal experience — a literally downright "posterly" expression. It was at this point that, partly because of the new urge to experience life intensely and pushfully, the modern poster first appeared. There now came into being that form of picture, soon to become a kind of Art for All, which obtains its autonomy solely from freshly employed graphic means and is therefore only conceivable in graphic terms. The poster became possible when the chromo-lithograph, the oleograph of unhappy memory, had been turned into an original graphic creation and thus exalted to an independent work of art. Colour effects such as the hour demanded could not be achieved with oils, so it is very understandable that a few avowedly modern artists soon made the autonomous colour lithograph their most characteristic vehicle of expression.

Henri de Toulouse-Lautrec was one of them. His art, however, cannot even be thought of apart from the poster — the poster in the modern sense with its tyrannical shrieking, through which it brands advertisements and slogans of the city directly, aggressively and impetuously on the retina even of those who just glance at it. Given the poster's violent optical impact two questions at once posed themselves to the period. Was the poster, since it aimed to woo and therefore always had a seductive quality, a deliberate allurement, in the drawing and colour, unable to be a work of art as well? And if so, is not then the new painting as a whole, with its strong, showy colours, non-art? Behind such much-debated questions there still lay the old idealist view of art, and an intelligent man like Maurice Talmayr, writing for the *Revue des deux Mondes* in 1896, could observe with a hint of resignation: "One hardly ever finds morality where there is art and one never finds art where there is morality . . . , nothing characterizes the nature of the poster better. It has issued from the spirit of our life. The poster is indeed art and, what is more, just about the only original art of this era." In any case, art has since then shown itself to be a match for the hubbub of the street. Artistic expressions of an evil vitality, often created by the artist for the sheer delight of it and unburdened by any ideal or moral concept, Toulouse-Lautrec's alluring Page 43 posters for the erring, demonic and at the same time trivial world of Montmartre — that skin disease of city houses, as some apostrophized it with a shudder — were felt to be direct and honest *vis-à-vis* the "life". The fact that this wicked city world was introduced with just that exhibitionistic loudness with which it obtruded itself appeared as a kind of adequate pictorial presentation of this modern vitality.

From the standpoint of content too, the entire production of Toulouse-Lautrec and his circle has something of the poster about it, and thus complies with the wishes of its times. The subject had to renounce all lofty spiritual pretensions; it had to be boisterous and frivolous, which meant full of movement, and to attract attention as it were automatically. Life, or more precisely modern

Henri de Toulouse-Lautrec, 1893

life, was being referred to, and art had the task of making this genuine, unmediated life percep- Page 45
tible even when it had gone astray, though not of interpreting it. This new frame of mind tolerated
neither the unburdened cheerfulness of an incident full of poetry, like those the eighteenth
century was able to depict, nor the oppressive weight of a tragic event, like those often represented
in neo-classic and romantic art. Edgar Degas, who, in spite of taking great pains over the graphic
technique and producing some delicate etchings as well as a number of lithographs that are
astonishing above all for their subjects, was not basically a graphic artist, struck up the new
pictorial melody, which then, transposed to a slightly different key, turned up again and again
in the graphic work of the so-called late impressionists. The melody is that of a relentless,
exciting realism, which, far from gaining its effectiveness from the choice of subject alone, does
so from the way this subject is seen as well. What people had hitherto overlooked (and probably
had not wanted to notice), now caught the eye. Art discovered an abnormal décor and also the
strangeness of its previously disregarded actors. Not without reason, Degas held the view that
half of city life, and the most agreeable half at that, was spent by artificial light. One no longer
ignored ungodly places but deliberately sought them out, because they were focuses of an
unadorned, though dangerous, vitality. People liked best to visit those pleasure haunts then known
as *cafés-concerts*, since there one came across every species of a humanity that, with an animal's
instinct, had made itself a slave to life's temptations. And it was precisely this animal confidence
of victory displayed by a lower world that the artist, yielding fully to his own individual sense
of life, noted in, say, the nonchalant swagger with which robust *filles* brazenly struck an attitude
or, as with Toulouse-Lautrec at the Moulin Rouge, in the pounding entry of a girl dancer dressed
as Pierrot and her challenging, provocative gestures. With his posters, Toulouse-Lautrec tempted
people to take part in this life — a life that was anything but noble and fine, and that, for its
part, enthusiastically approved these enticing sign-boards, as in them it saw itself intensified
and delightfully exposed. Art and life were completely bound up with each other for Toulouse-
Lautrec, in the sense that here was a special kind of art for a special kind of life. The content
of his artistic posters, thanks to which his reputation as an artist rose higher and higher after
1891, is entirely realist. But what a realism! Here again, an artist was meeting a general requirement of his times. Castagnary formulated this in 1863 with a pronunciamento to the effect
that the spiritual object of a new and necessary realism must be to embody life pictorially at its
most intense. If the artist pressed towards this goal, his temperament would by that very action
become free, concluded Castagnary, and, far away from records of stale facts, the creator would,
following this route, attain his true artistic personality.

Many decisions had to be made in order to characterize pictorially the very features for whose
sake people were venturing to explore this newly-discovered world. The crowdedness of the
city's multifarious life was already made apparent in the composition. A scene that, because of

Page 25 the cramming of the space, cannot be properly surveyed — a new visual experience, this — becomes "clear" if the artist puzzles us with a close-up of some large form which, since it cannot be taken in as a whole, is hard to identify, so that, from overlapped coiffures, scrolled heads of double basses reaching into the picture, lamp globes thrusting into the foreground, or Jane Avril's reticule in Toulouse-Lautrec's poster for the Divan Japonais, the direct impact of pure, non-representational forms is obtained. No longer is a scene arranged according to the inner importance of those taking part. The main character gets moved to the side; and if, as so often, a theatrical presentation is being depicted, the artist does not place himself "correctly", which means in the middle before the proscenium arch, but takes up his position somewhere towards the side, so that through the picture's composition one gets a sense of the strangely curved ground-plan of an auditorium. For the real aim of the pictorial statement is not to describe the performance as a physical fact but to impart the feeling that in the artificial atmosphere of the social game of "theatre" one is experiencing a special exhilaration. "Up-to-date" motifs would not on their own make the new theme really new. This is only done by the dispassionate gaze with which the subject is considered, without the latter knowing, if it is human, that it is under observation — by the "intimate" look, in this sense. Daumier's figures still show traces of that ordered beauty of composition and movement developed by the Renaissance and Baroque. Degas, Toulouse-Lautrec and Jean-Louis Forain no longer even see in their dancers the canonical gestures of movements perfected by the choreographer. Workaday poses of bodies wearied by their job describe the existential intensity of a ballerina far more thoroughly when they are represented with those new graphic means whose range and possibilities of application were now being tested until they could be used with confidence.

The maximum optical effect, necessary for characterizing a life that, like the night life of a city, was stimulated by every kind of artificiality to a condition of strained over-intenseness, could only be achieved with a minimum of strong formal means. Delicacy and the blending of hues, as oil-painting sought them, would be of no effect in this case: no more than a few colours were used and as far as possible primary ones. If mixed colours were unavoidable, they had to be made up of only a small number of elements, so that one could take in these elements optically at the first glance. It was now that the effect of "artificial" colours and the heightening action of artificial light were discovered. The colour lithograph too was increasingly freed from the graduations of shade of chromo-lithography, which had resulted in a grubby tonal effect. Artists Page 47 restricted themselves to a few strongly coloured planes, and then ensured that as far as possible these areas of colour did not blanket each other, since, instead of fusing, the colours of a litho-graph overlap transparently and therefore appear a trifle dead. More thought was now given to the harmony of a simple colour ensemble than to intricate combinations of nuances. A mere contrast of cool and warm hues often had to realize the forms that had previously been modelled by muddying patches of shadow. But it was precisely this simplicity of means that called for a true artist. The new strength in the colour, the gaiety and crude, chalky brightness were felt to be the expression of a new emotional attitude to life, an attitude that, making itself apparent on every hand, would soon reject unqualified acceptance of mere vitality and give hearty approval to what was forcefully "natural" and wholesome. In his book on colour lithography André Mellerio wrote in 1898: "Now that we have built the great boulevards, we want light to stream into our homes. Science itself proclaims cheerfulness to be a state of spiritual health that can even become a means of bodily healing. When it does not borrow anything from painting, the colour print undoubtedly goes very well indeed with our plain furniture made of natural wood and no longer hidden under compo and gilt."

Page 49

If one takes 1885 as the date at which Toulouse-Lautrec hit upon his "proper" form after initial impressionist experiments, one finds that for the works he did in water-colour, body-colour and pencil at this time he used both Van Gogh's excitedly swirling lines and Degas's comparatively orderly areas of parallel strokes. Depending on the subject and what he wanted to express the artist inclined more towards the one or the other model, and there is no denying that this instability in the choice of artistic means withheld from such works the ultimate expressive power characteristic of his later prints. Only in the print is Toulouse-Lautrec's true form fully realized, and only there does the way of conceiving the content that alone fits his mentality become clear. At the close of the century the graphic processes had once more come to be such a completely autonomous instrument of pictorial creation that crucial pictorial ideas of the period could only be expressed by means of them. With Toulouse-Lautrec it was first of all, that is from 1891 to 1893, the posters, those "feuilles nées en souffle de l'actualité", those seductive representations that life seems to have penetrated with its air stream as it went roaring by.

There is no need here to go into detail over the way Toulouse-Lautrec later evolved a wholly independent technique that, deviating from the common course of experiments in graphic expression, increasingly freed his lithographs from the aggressiveness of startling linear images and the weight of unbroken planes; and the way he perfected a new method whereby he sprinkled the colours on the planes as a fine drizzle of varying density. It is only the essential features that require presenting, and Toulouse-Lautrec played such an essential part in establishing them, above all with his earliest prints, that his name was to stand here for a general development.

NEW GRAPHIC FORMS AND THEIR PICTORIAL THEMES

In the meantime, then, graphic art had taken on unexpectedly different aspects. It had discovered hitherto concealed formal means and with them achieved a capacity for expression that allowed it to take an interest in new themes — indeed, that sometimes, as in the hands of Toulouse-Lautrec, made it the sole vehicle for particular ranges of statement. Woodcut and lithography returned to the fore, after the asceticism with regard to colour, still prevalent midway through the century, had been most vehemently renounced in both these techniques. So unfamiliar was the strong colouring of the new colour lithographs that people immediately reproached it with being too harsh to permit artistic expression. But the decision had long since been made, just as every aspect of later graphic development was already beginning to show in the last two decades of the nineteenth century.

These graphic forms and colours, which are very different from the appearances of reality and indeed come close to abstract arabesques and colour harmonies, served a new realism at the beginning, though a realism pulsing with the beat of a peculiarly agitated temperament. It was noted with astonishment that for decades only country life had been considered remarkable and worth depicting. Life, people now saw, was to be truly experienced in what was insensitive and uncomfortably aggressive about the forms of urban existence. Very soon it became obvious that contemporary graphic art reached far beyond a Manet's experience of city and street, and that in the new prints not only the "here" of an interesting location but — and this above all — the "now" of something observed at that very moment by that very artist was becoming highly important. Everything that now happened in graphic art as regards form was connected with this intention. The new forms were to a large extent partly determined by late impressionism — for a start by the liberation of pure colour in mature impressionism when the shadows turned violet ("violet mania" to those who liked to brand it as a morbid degeneration); but also by Seurat's efforts to indicate the third dimension without piercing the picture plane, through a surface development of his pictorial means, and to combine linear structure with pure colour. There was also the influence of the Japanese woodcut, which had first reappeared at the 1862 World Exhibition in London. What is significant is that it was consciously noticed and made use of at all. Already then people knew very well how to distinguish between copyists, who reproduced particular Japanese woodcuts more or less faithfully and more or less badly, and those artists who obtained suggestions and endorsements from Japanese graphic art for what was already present to their mind's eye: a simplification of the design and reduction in the number of colour blocks, say, or manipulations of the tension between the "void" of the white surface where the paper remained unprinted and the paper's partial covering of flat unbroken areas of colour or a black silhouette. Or else hints on how one could produce an equivalent to plastic values merely by juxtaposing warm and cool colours. But above all on what the distribution of the forms, especially a distribution over the surface that was unexpected because unrelated to the intrinsic importance of the objects, could achieve in the way of artistic impact. Exhaustively studied and confidently used by all graphic artists at the period, *mise en page* could also be learnt from Japanese prints. Beyond this, people found out from them that slightly modified forms introduced into another ensemble could completely change their meaning as receptacles of a content or signals of a message, the very phenomenon that had already cropped up many times with Toulouse-Lautrec. It was to appear more and more often the nearer artists got to the present-day use of the graphic media. The colours of Japanese woodcuts are heightened in late-nineteenth-century prints, which only seem to be related to them, and their surface-tensions made even greater. In conception too, these new graphic works differ fundamentally from their Oriental models. For whereas the Japanese woodcut is a sort of heraldic "fixing" of a preshaped, ritualized life, European artists want, with similar formal principles, to leave life to a large extent untouched, a life experienced quite directly and realizing itself promptly in the here and now.

But these new factors that have just been mentioned are accompanied by a new application of line. Here again Toulouse-Lautrec provided the authoritative example when he gave contours the job of establishing with one and the same line solid body and movement in space; or when he endowed the edges of floor-boards — it could also be the diagonals of benches in a dance-hall — with an uncanny spatial dynamic, and made them rush into an emptiness that causes agoraphobia. His lines often abruptly ignore the course one would expect them to follow; they are determined by constantly changing impulses. The irritating interruptions subject the beholder to a *puissance de choc*, and this now became an accepted instrument of art, which, no longer wanting to obtain beauty from linear arabesques, produced disturbing effects with great creative intelligence for the sake of the force of the expression, of "getting across". The new motifs, chosen and changed by new expressive aims, provide all the prerequisites to the effects of line described above: form and content are truly identical in this art.

However richly faceted later graphic work appears and however different are the pictorial resolves made only a little while after this, it is necessary to examine thoroughly these first decisions and discoveries of "modern" graphic art, and to investigate the new connection between form and content. For, in their essentials, all future artistic problems have already been sketched out here. Pictorial means and areas of expression were already entering those relationships whose carrying capacity would be tested again and again in the coming development: form and the intensification of reality, form and the transformation of reality, form and transcendency. Could it be that a form freely handled and relieved of the object gave direct answers to questions regarding which artists who enquired indirectly of reality remained in the dark?

Since the moment when the developed technique of artistic print-making was able to secure graphic work the status of an independent art category, and when graphically autonomous expression could be achieved not just through the vitality of the line but also from the graphic process as such, graphic methods have been used for fundamentally differing purposes. On the one hand, to bring into being works of art with an entirely new look, and on the other, not of course to make reproductions of works from other categories, but to give up independent effects in so far as the artist merely endeavours with the help of these methods to reproduce "something drawn" by him. This second procedure results in prints that are really multiplied drawings and therefore graphic in the sense of being purely linear in conception. It is of the essence of the highly adaptable lithographic process that it is generally used for obtaining many examples of a drawing. Etching turns out to be far less docile in this connection, for only through a time-consuming application of refined drypoint and etching methods did people succeed in making facsimiles of drawings, before the invention of lithography. How hard it was to achieve this aim with woodcut-technique is shown by the pains that Doré and Menzel had to take in order to train the xylographer to render faithfully the drawings they had made on the block. In the future as well, and right up to the present day, many artists would regard graphic creation to some extent as a form of drawing whose results did not appear on just one sheet but in a considerable number of "impressions". However, the majority of those producing graphic works would henceforth look upon print-making as an art that, though related to drawing, was none the less of an entirely different kind.

And as it too occurs for the first time in these years, mention must also be made of something that, while apparently only concerning the details of its reproduction, can quite often have a decisive effect on a print's appearance. This is the more or less far-reaching collaboration of the printer, which, when things turn out well, becomes the beneficial help of a friend. Odilon Redon, the sensitive lithographer of the most delicate nuances, spoke of this relationship as a marriage, by which designer and printer ought to be bound. The printer Auguste Delâtre, regarding whom the exacting Haden said that Rembrandt, had he still been alive, would have given him all his plates for pulling, held courses at the South Kensington Museum. The publisher Pellet, who issued Toulouse-Lautrec's *Elles* set in 1896, did all he could to ensure that the colour came out clearly in the print. It is true that others, such as the printer Clot, tried to intrude far too much upon the artist's inward decisions. For this reason, one talked in France less about original graphic work than about prints of the *peintres-graveurs*, which was meant to signify that these works were indeed thought out by the artist himself and intended for printing from the start, but that their production was not exclusively due to him. And so it has remained. Up to the present time, there

Page 45

have continued to be, along with graphic works produced simply and solely by the artist, prints to which others have contributed to a greater or lesser extent.

Every kind of application of the graphic media was open to artists in the last decade of the nineteenth century, and hardly anyone objected when graphic art struggled forth from the privacy of the portfolio and sought to thrust its way into the visual field of open, public life. It had, and people accepted the fact, so changed its means that, having started out as something calm that could be read rather than something one could take in at a glance, it finally presumed to poster-like aggressiveness. Only in posters? Or was another application of these decorative optical signals possible, as well? After the riot, a new ordering of these all too freely squandered elements already suggested itself purely with regard to form, and it was surely natural to put these elements together as easily surveyed ornamental ensembles so that they might symbolize a kind of spiritual order. Like the elevated language of poets, forms "lifted out of" reality and stylized as ornament can become vehicles of statements explaining the worlds within and advocating the purity of spontaneous feelings. The ornamental and the symbolic can be brought into a very favourable constellation, out of which there then appears what in mere unannotated descriptions of life, even when they are heightened in the extreme, never allows itself to be revealed. It is such potentialities that those decorative works produced in France by Maurice Denis and Félix Vallotton immediately after impressionism and just before expressionism try to realize. The same tendency is shown by the graphic works of Burne-Jones, William Morris, and the late Pre-Raphaelites in England, as also by the prints of the artists of the Art Nouveau movement, known in Germany as the *Jugendstil*. In them a poetic beauty that readily invites cheap exploitation aims at obtaining symbolic effects with pure colours, unbroken planes and lines full of a noble *élan*. Félix Vallotton's forceful woodcuts, entirely built up out of black planes bordered by gently drawn-out contours, certainly exerted a powerful influence on the handling of form in this graphic art whose neo-romantic content here and there still brings to mind the unburdened lightness of impressionist subjects. Yet even though the far-reaching independence of the form, the emphasizing of the lines and the unconditional recognition of the energy of life — so that *Jugend* (youth) seems to be its only valid phase, justifying it as a whole — identify this art as something belonging to its times, it is easy to understand today why very soon after its prime around 1900 Art Nouveau was already regarded as unimportant — indeed, as an error of taste. As an error of taste, because its way of stylizing all forms by means of decoratively waved lines was easy to copy, and feeble hangers-on exploited it to obtain cheaply attractive effects. In the sphere of subject-matter as well people soon found distressing the continual vacillation between a forced youthfulness, the cheerful fairy-tale with a background of symbolism, and an ironic, flippant diablerie. Before long they came to loathe these themes, which, moreover, gave scope to an unreliable and not very fertile power of invention. Very soon Art Nouveau's shortcomings really did outbalance the important things it had to say, and determined the general verdict on this style, which, very aware of itself, intruded upon public life in newspapers and exhibitions, positively inviting

Page 67 criticism. Today people are more just with regard to its genuine, great achievements. It is now realized that the basic idea of Art Nouveau was quite incompatible with the very earnest, repeatedly expressed, austere conception which from the start was at the root of the styles replacing it, and which underlies the utterances of expressionism in particular. We have recaptured a clear view of the triumphant beauty of many Art Nouveau forms, and recognize that they influenced nearly all the great graphic artists of the end of the last century and the beginning of ours.

Gauguin's zincographs, such as the one showing Breton washerwomen (1899), are certainly inconceivable without the decorative graphic discoveries of Art Nouveau. The same is true, though
Page 34 to a lesser extent, of his later woodcuts. But the very fact that one has to spell this out to oneself and does not very readily accept it is a sign of the totally different spirit in Gauguin's works. In Art Nouveau the "message" is much too easily pondered and served up in the expert play of cleverly prepared forms. With the virtuosic pointedness of their forms and conception, the creations of Art Nouveau sometimes come very close to caricature. It would be terrible, because basically quite impossible, to think of caricature when looking at Gauguin's woodcuts. The un-committed elegance that found its goal and resting-place in aestheticism had no part to play in the future of graphic art. Think of what Munch does in his woodcuts with the wavily combed
Page 53 linear tresses of line-laden Art Nouveau! How little originality there is, on the other hand, in Nolde's early fairy-tale woodcuts, which as regards both the handling of the form and the spiritual attitude of the content are still wholly Art Nouveau in character! Yet shortly after this, Nolde will be entirely himself, not through any fundamental changes in the forms but through the
Page 35 replacement of drollery, the genus to which these fairy-tale scenes belong, by a demonism that is the fruit of inner compulsion. So, while acknowledging the great beauties of Art Nouveau and its formal importance for Gauguin, one can already see that he was heading in a completely different direction from the fact that, with the simplification of his forms and the regularization of his lines in lithography and woodcut, he ventured to express peculiar ideas that would have an effect in the future. For to him art was "une abstraction", which meant that its forms could not be observed from nature but, nourished by the imagination, had to be invented. Even the early lithographs from Brittany, drawn on zinc and running from 1889 up to the first Tahiti journey in 1891, are not "landscapes" in the old sense but evidence of an *idéeisme*. Their titles indicate subject-matter of universal validity. Here in these lithographs that at first are still related to paintings he has done himself, Gauguin remains entirely a draughtsman, though a draughts-

Paul Gauguin, ca. 1899

man with the water-colour brush who still has a knowledge of effects very different from that of mere lines. Even on the sheet that, following Poe's poem, shows the fisherman dragged by the maelstrom into the depths, the flow of the colours running from the brush is comparatively undynamic. In return, somewhat frayed, somewhat irregular planes take shape everywhere. They give the picture a peculiar optical ambiguity. Our attention is attracted anyway by a strange effect due mainly to the unusual organization of the planes. Surfaces of the most diverse objects run into each other, constituting curious non-representational passages, and so contribute a third, non-rational element of compelling formal power to the general appearance of the print.

This formal principle was therefore already active in Gauguin's graphic work before he developed under the influence of Maori wood-carving a woodcut technique in which, it is true, the basic principles of "modern" woodcut became apparent almost without any transitional phase. One knows that Gauguin was seeking "primitiveness", though not in the undisguised vitality of the immediate, city environment but in the faith and behaviour of distant "savage" peoples and in their way of looking at things. His two journeys to the South Pacific were not just a flight from Europe. They also have something of the home-coming of a man who had already searched for the archaically savage quality among the peasants of Brittany and found it to be truly real to him. Gauguin's woodcuts of 1894, memories of Tahiti, are evocative illustrations

Emil Nolde, 1906

of a mythology that, by virtue of his own inner certitude, the artist read into the life of the South Sea Islanders. In so doing, he observed, when looking at Maori idols, what amounted to signs long known to him. As early as 1889 he had already as it were recognized these cult images at an exhibition of Aztec sculpture, and become convinced that: "The greatest error is the Greek one, beautiful as it may be." Something of the "barbaric" carving on totem-poles now passed over into his woodcut style. The prints reflect the roughness of the exotic wood-carving and the "untidy" way in which the material of Oceanic sculpture is presented. On the island Gauguin worked the block with an ordinary gouge, because, so it is said, he lacked the special tools of the woodcut artist. He let the grain print too — again, of course, the grain of wood sawn plank-fashion. There is also a "barbaric" quality about his method of printing. He took the proofs without a press and inked the blocks only lightly and unevenly, so that irregularities also appeared in the impression, which is what he wanted. Moreover, out of the block for the second version of *Manao Tupapau*, he later made, by overcutting, a relief from which good prints could of course no longer be pulled: thus close to one another were woodcut and sculpture for Gauguin. In this manner, and by contrasting large areas of black and white, he created the myth of a primitive Arcadia. This myth reveals itself more earnestly and convincingly in the severe medium of Gauguin's rough woodcuts than in his paintings, whose enchanting loveliness now and then eclipses

35

it. However melodious the flow of the contours may be, and however near his drawing may therefore come to Art Nouveau, with these contours a theme quite inconceivable in Art Nouveau is presented. These beautiful lines no longer spring from the beautiful gestures of figures, but accompany visions statuesque in their calm. They merely ensure that the remote, mysterious shapes are attractive to European eyes — eyes which at that time had already found pleasure in the gracefully flowing lines of Indian sculpture and the stately rows of Egyptian figures. Forms from Indian and Egyptian art exerted very much more influence upon Gauguin's style than those met with on the unfamiliar islands. From all these heterogeneous elements, from its own interpretation of the world, from the formal vocabulary of its present, and from experience of the collections of Indian and Egyptian art, there sprang into being the homogeneous truth of Gauguin's graphic work.

In his earliest woodcuts, the work of the burin, which draws faint, delicate lines, is still very extensive compared with that of the gouge, which produces irregular patches of white. It should not be forgotten that Gauguin's painter friend Louis Roy pulled most of the impressions from blocks that were too heavily inked, so that the fine white lines were covered by printer's ink. Gauguin is said not to have appreciated very highly the prints of his co-operative friend; their inert blacks reminded him too much of linocuts. The new impressions taken from ten blocks by Gauguin's son in 1921 undoubtedly render the artist's ideas, projecting a relatively large number of individual graphic forms, better than do the prints of Louis Roy. For Gauguin only became the immediate forerunner of the expressionists with his last woodcuts. These are chiefly cover designs for a satiric periodical, a *journal méchant*, of which the artist published only a few numbers, in 1899. He called it *Le Sourire:* "Hommes graves, souriez, le titre vous y invite." In Page 34 these cover woodcuts, the little white furrows hardly contribute any longer to the print's general appearance, which really depends on the now considerably larger areas of empty white space. From small patches of black there now spring just a few, but crucially figure-forming lines, which are printed from energetically cut reliefs. Above all, they run round the human nudes along paths so strongly reminiscent of the lineation of expressionist woodcuts that one would believe Gauguin's cover designs to have been their models, if one did not know that these designs were printed in only very small numbers and, going almost unnoticed, were largely wasted.

Soon it was recognized that Gauguin had produced a new form for the woodcut to suit a new content. People liked stressing that woodcut, which had previously come to grief in the *savoir* of highly accomplished professionals, had been restored by him through "naivety" to new undreamt-of life. Odilon Redon's lithographs could not have been characterized in terms of such a playing-out of new forms against the conventional ones of the "trade", as they still contain Page 59 all the masterly *savoir* of professional lithographers. None the less, Redon's prints are not comparable with any others made since the invention of lithography. They come closer to earlier lithographs, as did Gauguin's woodcuts to those of his predecessors, but they are as apt to express Redon's intention as were the woodcuts for Gauguin's Oceanic myth. Redon did not oppose the great craftsmen of his day. His prints are as polished as theirs — indeed, they even excel the products of the lithographic studios in the rendering of values through a black-grey-white scale that develops in the most delicate graduations. What appears in Redon's images is also found in reality, but, and this is crucial, real things now appear in unusual relationships, because this reality is intended to transcribe dreams — *songes* — in which Redon has glimpsed the origins of existence. Presenting new subject-matter was for him as well the main part of his artistic mission: the spiritual room of impressionism had too low a ceiling, was "trop bas de plafond". Independent of each other as regards proportions, because their size depends only on their spiritual importance, elements of reality — an eye, a flower, a flower-eye, heads, or even a whole figure — spread over the picture surface, their arrangement dictated solely by the inner meaning of the dream. Something comes into being, as a whole, that is totally different from compositions under the command of real space, something that Redon himself called a "composition lumineuse". Thus Redon was in no wise a literary artist, any more than Chagall would be later. Shocked that the hitherto unseen had been laid open to the eye, his contemporaries dubbed him a frustrated man of letters, since he wanted to give life to unreal creatures, something only the poets could do. Yet Redon was certainly no *littérateur*, even though he enjoyed a close friendship with Mallarmé and Huysmans; for instead of lining up along the thread of a story, his phantasies evade words. Inexplicable views of objectively definable phenomena contain allusions to what is unknown and ultimately closed to sight. This way of placing "la logique du visible au service de l'invisible", this Redonian way of suggesting the invisible with things comprehensibly visible, will from now on into our times be found again and again among graphic art's principles of creation.

Thus, as a whole comprising content and form, the print strikes a new note with Redon, despite the fact that his lithographs still retain many features of a drawing. Under the impact of Redon's ideas and handling of form, one cannot help thinking of James Ensor, who twenty years later

Page 51

also developed a phantasy world, but one of entirely different appearance; with Ensor too, there are no prints that can only be thought of as prints, but lithographs like red-chalk or coloured-pencil work and etchings like delicate slate-pencil drawings — drawings extremely lively in their structure of lines whose thread-like curliness and delight in angles and bends can in fact only be exacted from the bitten line. Yet Ensor probably comes to mind above all because he likewise hears the call of another world, a world more ghostly and morbid than the "surreal" spaces from the depths of existence that Redon hints at. Though more haunted than possessed of intimations, Ensor too belongs to that circle of modern graphic artists who experience the enigmatic directly, who light upon what has not hitherto been found and, through an individual symbolism, make the unknown known.

Together with the complete, sensorially stressed devotion to the present world, there was, then, as complete a surrender to a supernatural one that at the same time always reveals features of a highly personal inner world. With their obvious propensity for rendering transcriptive signs, the graphic processes now lent themselves to the representation of this inward domain no less adequately than they helped, with a plane fashioned as in a poster, to make visible the special complexion of some experience of the outside world.

It was above all to this realm within the psyche of the creative being that German graphic art turned, when, in expressionism, it burst into a bloom only to be compared with its florescence at the time of Dürer. The graphic works of Edvard Munch with his very personal interpretation of existence were therefore both a stimulus and a sanction for this flowering. At the moment Page 57 when Toulouse-Lautrec was capturing in posters the violent intensity of Parisian life, Munch — who went to Paris in 1889 — was introducing into etchings and lithographs, whose forms clearly show the influence of the Paris school, motives that do not appear any less "real" than Toulouse-Lautrec's, but are seen with quite different eyes. Eyes of the soul whose perceptions are coloured by the anxieties, troubles and misgivings of Munch's sensitive psyche, eyes that see in reality Page 53 what, as vague, neurotic feelings, cannot be defined with words and can only be hinted at "between the lines", as also happens in the plays of Munch's fellow-countryman Ibsen. But Munch, younger by a generation, could now, with a vigour scarcely inferior to the energy of Toulouse-Lautrec's effects, make visible what disquiet, trepidation, jealousy and morbid notions signify as vital forces. It was now that the theme of "anxiety" appeared in the visual arts, and the inward destiny Page 55 of a love-affair: attraction, growing apart, jealousy, ashes. States of soul are embodied, just as the forces of nature are personified in myths. Something of Van Gogh passes over into Munch's forms of expression, as far as excitement is concerned, except that with Van Gogh excitement is mirrored in the happenings of nature. Something of Toulouse-Lautrec appears in Munch, in so far as he is dealing with present-day life, only that for Toulouse-Lautrec the present is also what can be understood, and excludes the incomprehensible and mysterious. But it is precisely the incomprehensible and uncanny that is always of the present in Munch's graphic works: death around the sick person in the early etching from the mid 'nineties, and — pictorialized shortly after — the ineluctable end even of the most organic, most real relationship of love, or the great uncertainly beyond the grave. In this way, death as a spiritual phenomenon is transferred from the emblem to the our-worldly event of dying, and it is interpreted from this standpoint, together with the small, uncomfortable incidental feelings of civilized people, in a lithograph laid out with broad passages of flat wash: *The Death Chamber*. Prints like *The Death Chamber*, of 1896, or *The Cry* look like planar woodcuts, but they are lithographs just the same. The contours of their big black areas have the decorative flow that is also displayed by their lines, which recall Van Gogh's undulations. In this ornamental aspect, they bring to mind the black-and-white work

Edvard Munch, 1897

of Félix Vallotton and its closeness to the stylized, decorative poster. It was thus logically in keeping with his new subject-matter that Munch now opted for the woodcut, which with its Page 39 more severe forms opposes to the softness of the expanses of wash, unsuitable for such themes, hard contoured areas of white colour, and enlivens the calm continuity of the washed silhouettes by means of jagged and flickering empty white spaces, such as the gouge produces. With this very sharpening and "angling" of the forms, Munch goes far beyond Gauguin's woodcuts, heading in the direction of later cutting methods, and in so doing breaks his last ties with Art Nouveau. For him, making a woodcut is now anything but the reproduction of a drawing and, chromatically too, the effects of his woodcuts are fundamentally different from those of a water-colour. Munch it is who inks the block, with its lively relief, in a manner particularly suited to the character of the wood, doing so with specially chosen colours in such a way that the prints acquire colouristic Page 55 effects inaccessible to paintings. Different in its results, but similar as regards the principles of handling, is the change in his etching technique. The very large format, which has really out-grown the portfolio, already brings his mature etchings near to the woodcut that makes its impact on the wall. Deeply bitten lines, forming string-like, palpable ones in the print, and vigorous areas of tone secure for Munch's etchings effects in a category different from that which had previously been valid for etching and which had, however, been determined in its essentials by drawing. If Toulouse-Lautrec conquered new themes for pictorial art, his achievements undoubtedly had the support of first steps taken by artists who preceded him. Munch, on the contrary, followed only his own inward compass as regards subject-matter, though in the technical field he learnt much from the methods of the graphic artists around Toulouse-Lautrec. Just as with Toulouse-Lautrec, the ultimate meaning of his motifs is clearer in the prints than in the paintings. It is as if all the graphic discoveries made at the end of the last century were brought to an editorial conclusion in his *œuvre*, and as if this was also felt to be the case by the young graphic artists after the turn of the century; for however different their subject-matter may be in detail, in one way or another they all remember the work of Edvard Munch.

Toulouse-Lautrec, on the other hand, had no real examples to give the expressionists. From their point of view, his prints appeared decidedly "old fashioned"; and yet, in the last analysis, Munch as a producer of coloured graphic works stems from Toulouse-Lautrec. Moreover, the creative activity of the one is connected to that of the other by a basically identical desire: the desire to achieve something forceful. With Toulouse-Lautrec it is the startling expression of a city's vitality, with Munch a compelling transcription of anxiety, distress and mental torment, or else a heightened presentation of injured human dignity. If one wants, deliberately simplifying, to indicate the pictorial attitude of expressionism, one may safely quote the words often repeated by Van Gogh: "s'exprimer plus fortement!" ("express yourself more strongly!"). Here the stress is as much on the "self", on the egocentric intention of talking about one's own concerns, as on the desire to make these statements emphatically. Today there can no longer be any doubt that, as it set off with revolutionary *élan* after 1905, German expressionism outdid contemporary French art in many respects. Its urge to confess is far stronger, and whereas at the time Van Gogh meant technical freedom and brilliant colour to the French, for the Germans he was the embodiment of passion, of eccentric ecstasy and of a martyr-like paroxysm of the soul. Whereas Gauguin seemed all linearism and sublime decoration to the French, the Germans experienced through him a determination to achieve lyrical primitivism and expressive colour.

Henri de Toulouse-Lautrec, 1892

Henri de Toulouse-Lautrec, 1896

Pierre Bonnard, 1896

Edouard Vuillard, 1899

49

James Ensor, 1921

Edvard Munch, 1896

Edvard Munch, 1896

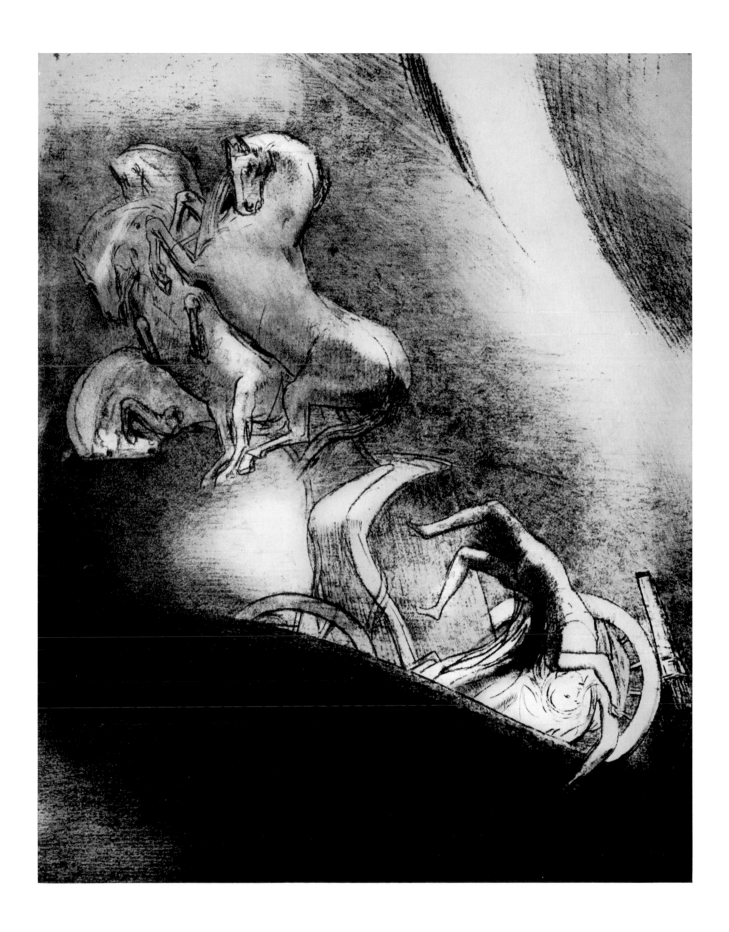

Odilon Redon, ca. 1895

Emil Nolde, 1906

EXPRESSIONISM

It is significant that, unlike French graphic art, German expressionism developed in addition to the colour lithograph the colour woodcut, training it until it could punch home the new colour effect with a powerful fist. And just as Van Gogh wanted to express love through the "marriage" of two complementary colours, or the thoughts behind a brow through the colourful shimmer emanating from it, so Kirchner endeavoured to make manifest the force of femininity and Nolde undertook to portray a landscape's melody of fate in violent colours that are deliberately un-natural because set over reality. As at the time of Toulouse-Lautrec, excitement and "high signal level" again characterized graphic art, but they served a new programme, which the ex-pressionists proposed with an affirmatory gesture, often setting forth their opinions in manifestos.

Back again too was the concept of an ideal, for art was once more required to tell of human qualities. Given this duty, it reached far beyond itself, since, in the last analysis, the object was with its aid to renovate the whole of existence and to determine and perfect the "coming religion of the mind" (Marc). The turn away from impressionism is evident. No longer was it a question of abandoning oneself with joyous consent to superficial excitement, just as pleasure in general seemed to be covered with the stain of materialism. Honesty, the old requirement, took on a new sense. Being honest now meant seeing what was genuine in the spiritual and social life of the present, and thus perceiving how true emotional values choked beneath social conventions and humanity suffered under a bad social order. The artist was only completely honest when he gave direct expression to the emotions that his soul felt particularly strongly because of its artistic sensibility. As these were violent emotions, they had to be enounced with all one's strength, screamed out if necessary, so that none of their vitality should be lost. From the expressionist justification of artistic activity a programme was thus developed that in principle strongly recalls that of Zola's day, when the special mentality of the creative being was likewise charged with establishing values in the otherwise unappraisable chaos of contemporary life. Now however, in expressionism, it was not a question of the attitude of those with artistic perception towards the contradictory phenomena of existence, but solely one of the individuality of the artist's spirit. Only the creator's personal capacity for experience counted, and extreme subjectivity alone could lawfully transact artistic business.

The failure of people to appreciate this new conception and the burden of their unaccustomed task drove the young artists to look around for others of like mind, and to form groups. But it is significant that a definite model was no longer set up to be copied, as it had been with the

Lukas-Bund of the Nazarenes shortly after 1800, and that no rule was now formulated for art. Instead, the individual artistic outlook alone decided the matter. "Everyone belongs to us who portrays his creative impulses honestly and directly", announced the *Brücke* programme, which, printed from wood-blocks by Kirchner, appeared in 1909. The *Brücke* group had developed out of an alliance of four young architects — Heckel, Kirchner, Bleyl and Schmidt-Rottluff — who rented an empty shop in Dresden-Friedrichsstadt as a joint studio. They felt sure that a turn inwards was necessary, a turning away from the outside world, though not in order to seek the extra-human absolute, but to investigate one's own emotions and express them alone, without disguise. To make the object represented a mirror of psychic agitation — that is what these young artists regarded as the special task through which pictorial art could help in its own way to uncover the true sources of a life worthy of mankind. They had faith in the psychological expressiveness of form and colour, and were convinced that the intensity of the emotion would also determine the level of their creations' artistic value, if only they were able to express this intensity. Borne up by strong feelings, they created with a violent *élan*, which worked itself out in an impulsive action decisively affecting the look of their representations. In this way, the emotion as well entered the picture-structure, from which it was relayed to the spectator, communicating itself to him in accordance with its specific character. A wish and a belief, this, that distinguishes the expressionists from the fauves, who were active in France at the same period. For though the latter also conceived life as a basic force of the temperament, they saw it being co-ordinated and harmonized through rational activity. German expressionism has rightly been called a stressed romanticism. It was also romantic in so far as it had retained youthfulness from the *Jugendstil*, and the youth of the artists who exalted it to a programme undoubtedly counted amongst its preconditions.

The inevitable point of departure for expressionism was reality as presented to the eye, the formal situation in the outside world. For the nature and power of the emotions whose vibratings determined the artistic impetus can only be inferred from the degree and character of the distortions of the real objects, and from the heightening or altering of the colours in relation to those of the true optical phenomenon. How could the graphic techniques help offering themselves as an extremely clever means — so that it is possible that expressionism and the beginning of modern graphic art appear at first glance actually identical? The severe woodcut process, which grants the artist only a relatively limited range of formal elements, proved specially suited to extracting from reality a highly forceful complex of forms harmonious in themselves; and precisely because the graphic handicraft restricts the variety of the forms as compared with painting's possibilities, the separate expressionist artists managed to formulate their own particular attitude towards man and the world more individually in their graphic than their painted works. However strongly and surely, and without reservation, the woodcut technique was simplified by the *Brücke* artists, even a cursory glance at once reveals the author of the, as a rule, resolutely primitive planar composition of one of these prints.

Page 73   Ludwig Kirchner gave the woodcut a new outward form, and in spite of his creative process driven by excitement he was quite clear about these formal innovations of his, with the result that he was able to explain them in detail in an article for *Genius* dating from 1921. It cannot be said that Kirchner arrived at his own forms under the influence of Dürer's woodcuts, since what filled him with enthusiasm at Nuremberg was significantly not the prints but the actual wood-blocks by Dürer that he saw. Munch's woodcuts were far more important to this almost pathologically sensitive being, tormented by neurotic moods. A born graphic artist, he made all his prints himself, and, with colour woodcut, further developed the method used by Munch, so that ultimately a woodcut conceived wholly in terms of colour, without a block for the lines, was produced by overprinting from several pure colour blocks (in up to ten operations). In woodcut, which he called "the most graphic of the graphic arts", he — like Gauguin and Munch — naturally did not follow the procedure of the old masters around Dürer, who had a vigorous linear image printed on the sheet from "relief-lines" left on the block. Instead he proceeded from unbroken planes, but these he enriched in frequently varied, always essentially graphic ways. Often the planes peter out raggedly at the edges, adding splintery effects that stress the medium's woody character to the static blackness of these confidently disposed planes. Groups of black lines settle on the white ground, just as, vice versa, pencils of white lines penetrate into the black areas. In prints made on absorbent paper, the black of the unbroken planes is graduated as far as grey, and the wood's elastic compliance is used to make one conscious of the depths of the block, dug up with the gouge and hence animated like a relief, in the print as well, through a delicate flecking. One sees that Kirchner felt the possibility of working at a wood-block for a long time without, as in painting, jeopardizing the direct impact of the result to be a special artistic potential of woodcut. Like Gauguin's, his woodcuts contain forms that have the power of securing independent optical effects that are unrelated to the subject — he called them "hieroglyphs" — but that, if properly distributed on the sheet, still evoke forms from reality. In the process, these rich arrangements of lines and planes never lose the essential features that take into account the interests of the content, since the artist confidently proclaims his message through a free treatment of the proportions of things: heads are often stressed by being made "too big". Lithography, a technique that like etching allows him to make direct records, also becomes with Kirchner an autonomous graphic medium quite independent of drawing, thanks to a remarkable continuity in the rise and fall of the values and to lines that in their consistence turn to account the delicate complexion of the printing stone's surface.

In the realm of content, Kirchner's graphic work comprises two domains that, only in appearance mutually exclusive, correspond to the dual tendency of the expressionist programme. On the one hand, man in his creaturely splendour and autonomous dignity, symbolized in the nude or when tied up in the basic facts of existence: among the prints with symbolic themes may be counted the sets of woodcuts illustrating Chamisso's *Peter Schlemihl* and Petrach's *Triumph of Love*. On the other, man harassed and endangered by the immediate facts of present-day life in prints that purely as regards theme and in their vitality recall Toulouse-Lautrec, but in which one can also perceive criticism, according with the changed intentions of a later generation of artists, directed at conditions that were not conducive to the sanctity of the soul and the dignity of man as defined by the expressionists.

Such motifs from city life and the urban landscape are rare in the work of Erich Heckel, as Pages 75, 77 they do not belong to his true range of subjects. Heckel is the calmest of the *Brücke* artists, and it is not rebellion but sympathy that leads him to make pronouncements. His figures have nothing aggressive about them and live withdrawn lives, enveloped in their submissiveness towards fate and the scheme of the universe. With him, woodcut as well as lithography performs the paradoxical feat of expressing in a loud voice the taciturn states of soul of those who are lost in thought, peacefully happy, or, now and then, composedly gay. The vigorous appearance of these prints, produced by their planarity and concentrating of the black-and-white values, usually goes with a representation of something fragile and tender that stands in contrast to the forceful aspect of these prints. In his elongated contours and the slight bends of his otherwise ruler-straight lines, together with the acute-angled intersections of this contour and line work, Heckel goes back to pictorial principles that already in mature gothic procured an expression and gesture for emotion, pious assent and inspiration. The artist's feeling for line is expressed most directly in his drypoints, but it is also apparent in his lithographs, although here he does not give up tone values.

Karl Schmidt-Rottluff's work probably comes closest to people's idea of expressionism as the Page 83 style of the most direct expression of strong inner agitation. "Barbarity", something that would have ruined the intense yet at the same time very spiritual utterance of Heckel's creations, is developed by Schmidt-Rottluff into the real operative element. His woodcuts provide an example of this with their clamping together of hard-edged patches of black, the extensive reduction of internal drawing, and the uninterrupted flow of elongated contours. It is especially in Schmidt-Rottluff's *œuvre*, including the etchings, that the importance of exotic figure art for expressionism becomes particularly evident. The impressiveness of the appearance of exotic cult images — felt by Kirchner as early as 1904 before the Palau (Indonesian) wood-carvings in the ethnographical museum at Dresden — the incomprehensibility of what is involved with the unfamiliar, became important hints for Schmidt-Rottluff in his attempts to make representations of things encountered at the present time optically significant. Accordingly he set about producing strange and daring combinations of portrait and cult images, especially in woodcut. In the woodcut series *Kristus* (1918), frenzied ecstasies and fleeting visions are at last successfully transmuted into the powerful optical effect of stiff, angular images. Risky ventures such as these were not undertaken by Max Pechstein. His talent lies rather in overlooking difficulties and in finding without let or hindrance a solution that is unburdened by weighty significance and hence very accessible. It is not surprising that he was the first member of the *Brücke* to win recognition, and that above all his clever and easily understood graphic works have opened many people's eyes to the intentions of these artists.

Not wholly without reason, Emil Nolde is usually associated with the *Brücke* group. Yet if one considers the matter chiefly from the standpoint of the crucial spiritual and technical discoveries made in the graphic sphere, one is bound to see Nolde primarily as an individualist of genius. It is true that the "real" Nolde first came fully into action at Dresden around 1907, when the artist became acquainted with the *Brücke* group, to which he briefly belonged. At that date he was already forty. Moved by different expressive aims and, with a sound instinct, mindful of not exposing his peculiar gift for too long to alien influences, Nolde very soon left this group, especially because two characteristic tendencies of his talent separated him from its members. In the first place there is his marked feeling, reminiscent of the old Dutch landscapists, for the great operative forces of nature, a feeling certainly rooted in his country home under the restless skies of a flat northern region; but there is also his inclination to create often impishly ludicrous phantasy images, which as it were issue from the realm of the bogies and the world of second sight. Demoniac drollery, which — still in the garb of innocent fairy-tales — we already meet in the earliest woodcuts, appears in the etchings of 1906 with an earnest claim to being, even if not, it is true, a serious world, one that is none the less undoubtedly there in the background of existence. Now even his — never jocose — humour is moved by a passion that in Nolde the man quite often turns into violent religious emotion. However convincing Nolde's woodcuts may be, especially through his exploiting of the embossed effect of a block, the special features of his creative gift still come out most clearly in his etchings and lithographs. His graphic pictorial ideas are always determined by painterly conceptions. Nevertheless, Nolde the graphic artist seems a different person from Nolde the painter. Something essential would be missing from the picture if one excluded his graphic work. An elementary artistic reasoning power, less apparent in his frenzied paintings, is clearly active in many of his prints. Moreover, in his etchings and lithographs alike, Nolde is a high-grade technician. He develops both media from processes for duplicating drawings into purely graphic arts whose autonomy is fully marked with his personal stamp. Just as early drypoints still adopt the script of drawings, so one still notices in the transfer lithographs of 1907 the softly wiped tracks of the wash-brush. In the mature etchings, which he knows how to convert, through often reckless planar bitings, from drawings into bearers of powerful, solidly dark tone values, Nolde is able to express convincingly his feeling for wind, weather and cloud, as, for example, in the sets showing the port of Hamburg with its soot-steeped clouds and the

Page 84

Page 79

Page 60

Page 88

turbulent processions of its waves ploughed up by ships. However, the late lithographs finally expand this raw tonal effect of the mature etchings into a magnificent orchestration of colour, with which both Nolde's landscape and his natural leaning towards what is passionately humorous, excitedly religious and ecstatically emotional attain a visual clarity that in its distinctive character stands out as much from the graphic constitution of German expressionism as Nolde's mentality remains distinct from that of his contemporaries. The hounding urge to seek new possibilities that overcame Nolde when in 1913 he was first able to collaborate in a lithographic studio, and that led him to make entirely new and impressive discoveries, reminds one of the crucial stimuli received years later by Picasso in Mourlot's lithographic studio at Paris. Now Nolde worked Page 81 directly on the stone and, often giving up lineal frameworks altogether, produced that series of thirteen big lithographs which, composed of purely chromatic planes and lines, count like Kirchner's colour woodcuts among the noblest testimonies to the splendour of German expressionist graphic art. If the term had not gone out of use, one could characterize these new graphic artists much more appropriately as *peintres-graveurs* than their predecessors. For with the latter the reference to painter was only intended in the sense of someone who invents freely, whereas now it is a question of people who really do paint in the strictest sense of the word, though they are painters who, as the second half of the concept affirms, at the same time remain wholly within the graphic medium.

Ernst Ludwig Kirchner, 1906

Ernst Ludwig Kirchner, ca. 1908

Ernst Ludwig Kirchner, 1918

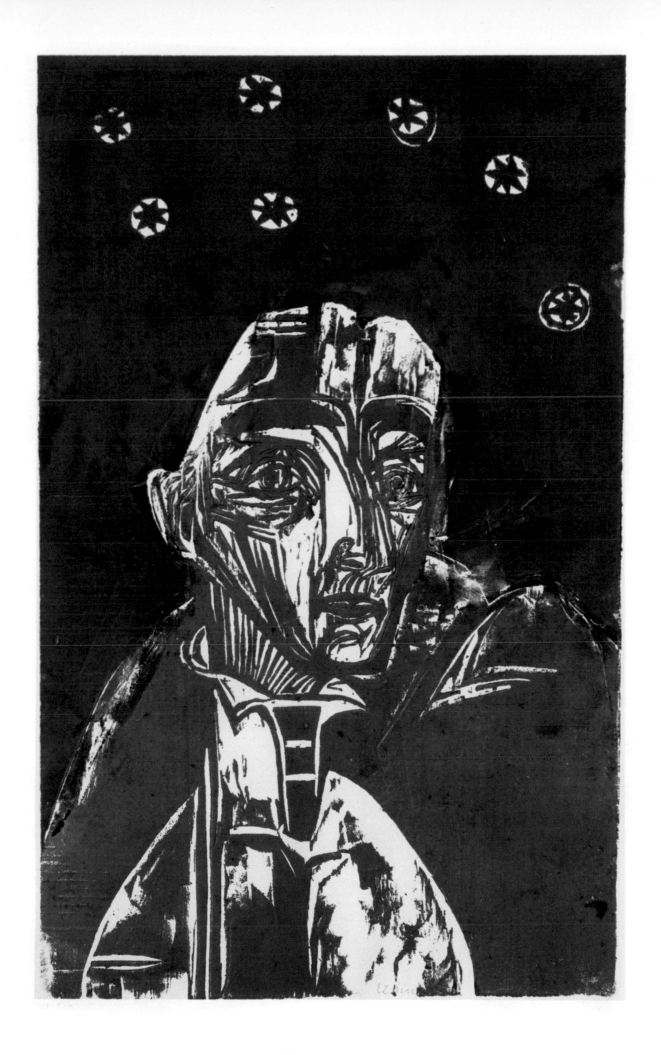

Ernst Ludwig Kirchner, 1919

Erich Heckel, 1910

Erich Heckel, 1912

Emil Nolde, 1926

Karl Schmidt-Rottluff, 1918

Max Pechstein, 1917

Erich Heckel, 1915

Ernst Ludwig Kirchner, 1922

Karl Schmidt-Rottluff, 1920

Emil Nolde, 1910

DECISIONS ALONGSIDE EXPRESSIONISM

Setting out from the print and its materializations in modern art, we inevitably pass again and again beyond the limits of the schools and styles, and see what is individual. This procedure would be "erring" if we really wanted to impose an orderly pattern on the graphic events of the most recent past. It seems to us — and this has been stressed time and again — that such an ordering is more possible in connection with the basic concepts, the general ideas, the thoughts, let us say, on what commissions art has to discharge, than with the final result in the separate works. For it is certainly not just an intellectual conception and a will directed by it that are at work in these results, but also those imponderable creative forces which only appear to us in their effects and whose possession we call artistic talent. Just as there are phenomena in modern graphic art that arrange themselves in groups, so do many other products of recent graphic activity offer any orderly pattern the resistance of what is vital and alive.

If the etching method with an extended or, more accurately, a new use of biting effects, etching that includes aquatint work and scratchings on the surface of the plates with the drypoint "pencil",

Pages 106, 107 was passed on to the *Brücke* artists by Nolde, it was Otto Mueller who, as a trained lithographer, inspired them to make lithographs. The soft graininess of his crayon lines and the gentle expressive quality of his subdued colours seem entirely appropriate to what Mueller represents over and over again with their aid: images of a humanity close to nature yet strangely homeless and unsettled, from the world of the gypsies. In their shyness and reserve, Mueller's nudes recall the figures of Gauguin, and one also notices in them influences from Egyptian art. Indeed, more frail and asthenic than Gauguin's Tahitians, they are even closer to Egyptian models.

Having just considered these very refined and very graphic treatments of the stone, one will

Page 94 perceive particularly clearly Corinth's totally different use of the litho crayon. For with Corinth it is still always a question of a drawing — one undoubtedly seen in a most painterly fashion, but which none the less obtains the very modern violence of its appearance and much of its life

Pages 100, 101 from the powerful strokes of the calligraphy. Likewise, Oskar Kokoschka, who has made few woodcuts, is almost exclusively a lithographer in the graphic field, and must be regarded in his prints above all as a draughtsman, if one wants to do him justice. True, he produces linear inventions of a very independent kind. With its characteristic eddies and interruptions of the flow, his impetuous handling is able to convert the torment and turbulence of a soul into significant signs.

During and also after the movement's prime, many artists were called expressionists even if their work showed but few links with the general idea of expressionism. Christian Rohlfs, for

Frans Masereel, 1933

instance, was placed near the expressionists probably just because, after coming to grips with many styles even as an old man, he let his work enjoy the benefit of that general reduction of form and colour through which expressionist works obtained their strong visual impact. Almost twenty years older than even Nolde, the eldest of the expressionists, Rohlfs handled the graphic Page 105 means in his own very independent way. Even in his late woodcuts put together out of large forms there still remains something of impressionist light. For solid forms, too, have with Rohlfs a tendency to "dissolve", to be irradiated by a supernatural light. Now and then his prints recall batik designs in the colour as well. Their forms floating in an indeterminate fluid medium are obtained by a process unrelated to the expressionist techniques, chiefly by inking the block unevenly, an operation that, judged by the rules of the guild, is just as "irregular" and daring as the working methods of the expressionists.

Karl Hofer's underlying artistic idea likewise has only relatively little in common with expressionist aims. It is obvious that the strong impression made on him as a thirty-year-old by the pictures of Cézanne affected all his later work. Building a strictly ordered, clearly arranged construction of figures with a few broad strokes, Hofer at the same time adds a contrasting active element to this classically calm structure of his lithographs. His figures, physically so tranquil, Page 96 undoubtedly acquire something of expressionist aggressiveness through the forceful representation of the expressions on faces marked by terrors and anxieties.

To make optically perceptible the nature and strength of the emotions pressing up to the surface from the depths of the soul, a radical change in the graphic tools and methods had been necessary. The deliberate alienation of graphic art from drawing proved to be a condition of giving it the characteristics of a new, specific instrument. Yet this greatly altered use of graphic techniques certainly did not yet mean that the earlier application, nearer to drawing, of the graphic means had now exhausted its possibilities and would have in any case to be replaced by the new methods. There were still artistic talents capable of demonstrating new subject-matter by employing the old Page 104 implements. With Max Beckmann the decision was different for each technique he used. Whereas he handled woodcut as a matter of course in the way developed by Gauguin and Munch—probably because woodcut had at that time really been born again and become quite unserviceable in its old forms — his etching technique stayed essentially in the tradition founded by Klinger. The fact that within these limits it underwent crucial changes resulted from the new aims it was now intended Page 102 to express. But Beckmann's etchings always remain — and the same goes for his lithographs — above all linear graphic creations, despite quite a number of tonal effects delicately applied with the drypoint "pencil". Much with Beckmann is really script, the record of his pronouncements, guided by reflection, on the phenomena of existence: energetically delivered pronouncements, of course, but no uncontrolled release of powerful emotions in the sense of expressionism. His Page 103 etched and scratched linear images simply contain all dimensions of an active, passion-driven existence, where there is no comment or classification in accordance with a pre-established scale of values. The jostling planes and very exactly plotted lines of his woodcuts often suggest individual forms that in the way they have been chosen from the totality of appearances make one feel, through their symbolizing power, the terrible force of life.

Page 99 On the other hand, the art of George Grosz develops hitting power from the very fact that it adopts a definite attitude, that it is opposed to the "ruling class". For ethical aims and immediate tasks such as these, pure drawing, bitterly malicious caricature, is the predestined means. The sharp line characterizes and exposes the evil nature of each individual phenomenon; it drags it out and, what is more, distorts it in accordance with the indictment, thus achieving a special classification that other employments of the graphic means would inevitably pass over. Grosz is, to be sure, an alarming draughtsman. Like lampoons, his lithographs in line spread invective against social conditions and complaints about the dreadful cruelty of a mankind blighted in its soul, whose drives have been reduced to greed and perversion.

War, want, brutalization of the feelings, the horror of the trenches, and the misery of impoverished cities are the subjects of the extremely conspicuous announcements in the etchings Page 98 and lithographs of Otto Dix. The evil vitality, disregarding even death, of many of his figures recalls Toulouse-Lautrec. With the aggressive colours of the lithograph and the lines often lying tangibly on the paper like solid poles, active elements of a purely graphic kind are included in his essentially "draughtsmanly" creations. Alfred Kubin, nothing but a graphic artist, keeps, in the graphic sphere, to pure drawing. Thus Kubin is a graphic artist in the literal sense, an artist, that Page 98 is, who describes with the indian-ink pen his themes from a world haunted by chimeras and beset by strange things, and who records his drawings on litho stones, thereby securing for them a wide diffusion as single prints or book illustrations.

As in that of sculpture, Ernst Barlach occupies a special place in the graphic field among his Page 95 contemporaries. With him, it is a question of woodcuts and lithographs. Sometimes given lively rhythms by a brisk alternation of white and black planes, the former appear much more independent *vis-à-vis* drawing — as is natural to their technique — than do the latter. It was only in his early lithographs, above all the first prints for his drama *Der tote Tag*, that Barlach tried to wrest autonomous possibilities from the process of printing from stone. Later he employed the litho crayon as, so to speak, a double of the broad-grinded charcoal that was all he used for his mature drawings. The lithographs are consequently involved in the artistic decisions and show the qualities thanks to which Barlach's drawings take such a prominent place in his pictorial and poetic *œuvre*. For the most part, these lithographs issue from creative deliberations that the artist ran through repeatedly in charcoal sketches. Indeed, there are times when, with the amount of "perfecting" that the ideas have thus undergone, their lithographic final form appears less lively than the preparatory drawings.

la Modersohn-Becker, ca. 1900

Lovis Corinth, 192

Lovis Corinth, 192

94

Ernst Barlach, ca. 1916/17
Ernst Barlach, 1912

Karl Hofer, ca. 1930

Käthe Kollwitz, 1920

Alfred Kubin, 1920

Otto Dix, 1922

George Grosz, 1915

Oskar Kokoschka, 1921

Oskar Kokoschka, 1918

Thusfs (18)

Max Beckmann, 19

Max Beckmann, 1946

Max Beckmann, 1923

Christian Rohlfs, 1916

Otto Mueller, ca. 1915

Otto Mueller, 1927

3 Schafe in weil 1948

Ewald Mataré, 1948

Gerhard Marcks, 1926

Otto Pankok, 1936

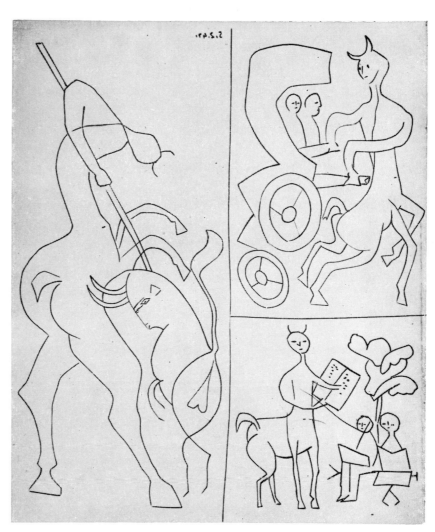

Pablo Picasso, 1947

Pablo Picasso, 1948

112

Pablo Picasso, 1949

Pablo Picasso, 1959

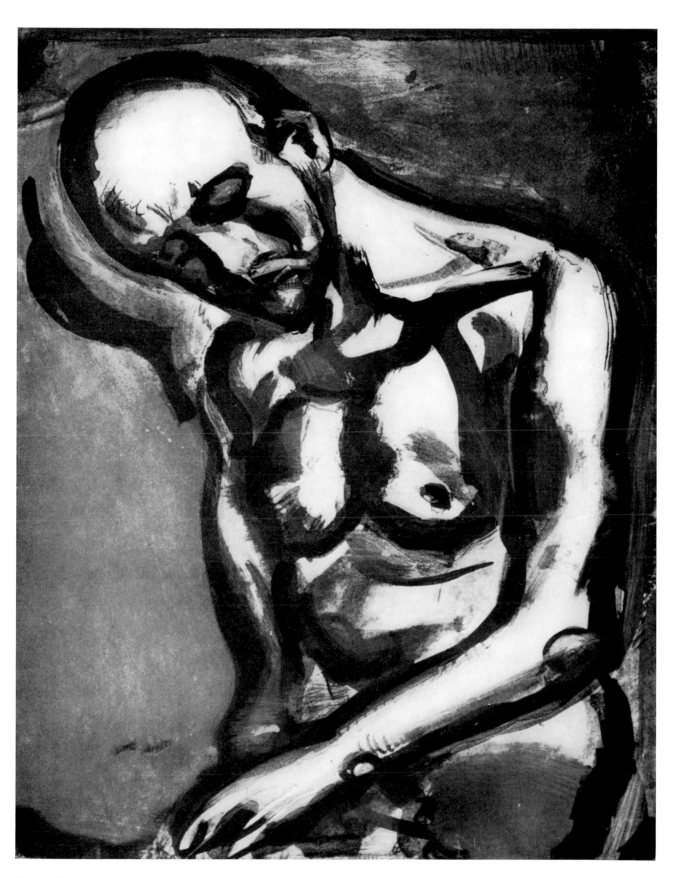

Georges Rouault, ca. 1925

Georges Rouault, 1926

Marc Chagall, 1956

Marc Chagall, 1953

Marc Chagall, 1926

120

Marc Chagall, 1948

Robert Delaunay, 1909

Maurice de Vlaminck, ca. 1906

Henri Matisse, ca. 1945

Henri Matisse, 1929

Henri Matisse, 1927

Raoul Dufy, 1930

André Derain, ca. 1927

Dunoyer de Segonzac, 1930

Alberto Giacometti, 1957

Jean Carzou, ca. 1958

Bernard Buffet, ca. 1958

Giorgio de Chirico, ca. 1930

Carlo Carrà, 1924

Giuseppe Viviani,
1937

Giorgio Morandi,
1927

116/200

CAMPIGLI 57

Massimo Campigli, 1957

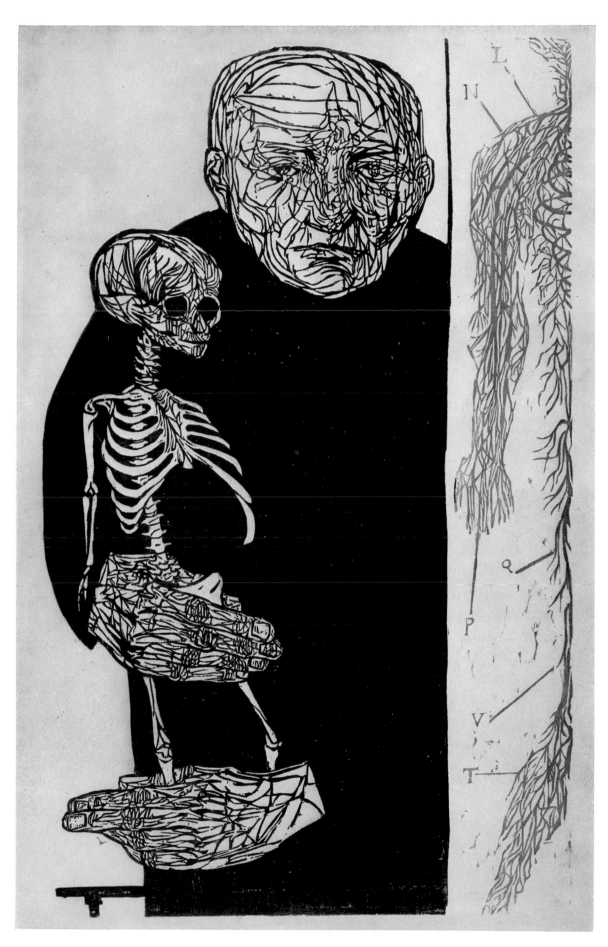

Leonard Baskin, 1952

Misch Kohn, 1959

Mauricio Lasansky, 1947

Antonio Frasconi, 1949

Ben Shahn – Leonard Baskin, ca. 1954

NEW ASPECTS OF THE OBJECT

During the last decade of the nineteenth century, and again at the beginning of ours, in the period before the First World War, pictorial ideas were developed everywhere and artistic decisions made that still form basic postulates for creation. If thoughts had previously centered chiefly on the question of using new formative means to increase a picture's expressiveness, one could convey the most important aim of the now completed deliberations with Braque's words: "refraîchir la vision" (to renovate the appearance of the picture). Really, the problem of the motif was now often solved, both in German and, though differently, in French art, by referring to the requirements of the picture's intended look. If one is prepared to call a group of connected thoughts a theory, then theories regarding art and artists have constantly escorted modern graphic art along its path. Certainly deliberateness and reflection must, save in the case of a few artists who create purely instinctively, accompany artistic activities just as they do others, though this artistic deliberateness is to be understood as a setting up of criteria for determining value rather than as a kind of aesthetic statement of accounts. Such audits, markedly beautiful in their intellectual structure but also of great importance as objective reports on the pictorial events of the time, are, for example, Kandinsky's book *Uber das Geistige in der Kunst*, brought out in 1912, Gleizes's and Metzinger's *Du Cubisme* of the same year, Klee's *Schöpferische Visionen* of 1920, and the same artist's *Pädagogisches Skizzenbuch*, published as a Bauhaus Book in 1925. Everywhere, in following these trains of thought, the artists come up against the question of the expressive possibilities of forms. All, as they deliberate, light upon a cardinal problem of creation. Inevitably they have to confront the question of whether art is now as ever bound up with representing more or less accurately the phenomena of reality. They pose this to themselves because they have become convinced through experience and experiment that representation (i.e. producing an illusory space on a surface by means of perspective constructions, and stocking this space with apparently three-dimensional objects) provides no path towards the new visual range that has now become necessary.

The suggestions for new aspects are radical in varying degree. The cubists in France, for whom the most important thing was to intensify the perception as such, still went on busying themselves with real objects. Through adding together in a single picture different ways of beholding, through a simultaneous presentation, that is, of, say, the front, side and top views of an object, as also through a reduction of the appearance of this same object to elementary forms from solid geometry, like the cube, the parallelepiped and the cylinder, there came into being a sort of heightened realism, in which physical solidity depends on a visual presentation unconnected with reality: on the very multiplicity of views that, in one and the same picture, split up the data of the objects, as they, the data, issued at any particular moment from the given fact, unavoidable in reality, of a beholder — a thing beheld. This procedure offered many hints on how to organize picture surfaces, hints that were to have a great influence particularly on graphic art. Moreover, cubism, such as it was developed from 1907 to 1914 by Pablo Picasso, Georges Braque, Juan Gris, Page 169 and, in an individual way, also by Fernand Léger, provided new possibilities of development for graphic art, which shortly before had come to grief in the fauves' endeavours. Fauvism, whose mainstays were the young painters Henri Matisse, André Derain and Maurice Vlaminck, continued, as it were, an element of Gauguin's creative practice: the intensification of colour. All those artistic decisions of Gauguin's which had enabled him to express his *idéeisme* were given up. There remained an aesthetic of flat areas of intense colour, an aesthetic that, free from all ideological reflection, was without "bagage symbolico-humanitaire". To impose order on the Page 126 strongly coloured picture surface was certainly the aim of the fauves, but this ordering derived its laws solely from decorative considerations. Yet a decorative arrangement of strong colours hardly offered a springboard for graphic art, which has to do with the linear elements. Matisse himself soon missed the power of a contour on the unrestrainedly vibrating colour areas of the fauve pictures, and so reverted — in his graphic works, as well — to the wholly individual form of the line drawing, in order to find again a lineal scaffolding for his pictorial ideas. As early cubism, making use of everything to achieve the "thingish" quality, drove back colour, which had prevailed almost unconditionally in fauvism, for the benefit of form, pure graphic art too was again given plenty of scope. Rejecting as they did the "panthéisme impressioniste", these ideas with which cubism re-established the plastic importance of the thing — in impressionism still only represented by the colour values of its appearance — had crucial consequences precisely in the graphic field: in the first place, owing to the structure of the picture surface newly won by cubism, but above all because in mature cubism there existed close together an abstract union of forms and the appearance of things built up from elementary forms.

However, the proposals for new pictorial aspects that were made in Germany almost at the same time, together with the demand that the artist should confine himself exclusively to an abstract union of forms, went even further than those of the French cubists. Strictly speaking, it was only one artist out of a like-minded group, Wassily Kandinsky, who sagaciously and fearlessly drew these ultimate conclusions. Looking back across what is now half a century, one sees clearly that these artists who came together at Munich between 1909 and 1912 prepared the way into the future. After a picture by Kandinsky, they called their group the *Blaue Reiter*, and published an almanac under the same title in 1912. They differed from one another even more than did the *Brücke* artists: Franz Marc, whose creative activity was guided by deep moral con- Page 147 victions, from Alexei von Jawlensky, a highly gifted colourist who worked instinctively; or, in spite of their having the same speculative ability, Kandinsky, say, from Paul Klee.

Most of the *Blaue Reiter* artists had already arrived round the turn of the century in Munich, which at that date, being a centre for new experiments with forms of artistic expression, had become the focus of the German Art Nouveau movement *(Jugendstil)*. The boldly decorative arrangements of ornamentally stylized forms, fresh in colour, that were common in the Munich school certainly helped to make the young artists see there rather than anywhere else opportunities for developing further their new pictorial ideas. In the works of the young Kandinsky, the closeness to *Jugendstil* is clearly apparent. Around 1906 Kandinsky and Jawlensky approached the aims of fauvism when they laid stress on a planarity emphasized by means of colour. Now what distinguishes the creative intentions of the *Blaue Reiter* fundamentally from those of the fauves is due to the group's attitude towards the problem of content. The Munich painters worried incessantly about what meanings would have to fill the new forms in order that the formal and chromatic power acquired with the latter should be counterbalanced in the intellectual sphere. With the fauves, on the contrary, there were no such deliberations, so that, while still in the middle of the experiment, their intellectual leader, Henri Matisse, perceived with discomfort that the strong optical claim of his paintings did not really suit their subject-matter, and he resolved to be a "herbivorous lion" no longer. He now devised the motifs of *joie de vivre* and optimism that were to characterize his mature work. In this sense of obligation towards the intellectual significance of content, the art of the Munich painters continues that of the Dresden *Brücke* group. Only in this sense of obligation, though, for as with the forms, *Blaue Reiter* subject-matter differs completely in the nature of its implications from the kind of content that the *Brücke* sought. And just as through its formal vocabulary, the art of the painters united in the *Blaue Reiter* group also determined the future by — at least in principle — bindingly fixing the sectors of possible fields of expression to which art should henceforth confine itself, for, despite all the variability of the expressive forms they championed, the *Blaue Reiter* artists were at one in rejecting the expressionist idea that art is solely an utterance of the most personal feelings. The title of Kandinsky's book *Uber das Geistige in der Kunst* intends also to refer to the absolute element in what is purely mental. True, art will from now on pledge itself still more resolutely to transpose what is indistinct in the realm of reality to a sphere of vividness that can be established by the picture and the picture alone; but it will no longer be states of the soul that are to be made visible. "Abstract" art, as people then called a world of form and expression that Kandinsky, after long, systematic and reflective experiments, had introduced into the pictorial domain through "the separation of nature and art", is a name that most probably originated chiefly in the idea that this art abstracted from the object. Right from the start, how-

Heinrich Campendonk, 1918

ever, a contributing factor was undoubtedly the idea that, as with the abstract concept, the subject-matter of this art was not presented sensually, but only through "signs".

Although the artists of the *Blaue Reiter* produced far fewer graphic works than those of the *Brücke*, and also did not come nearly up to the expressionists in developing new graphic techniques, the print still provided them all with an extremely useful means of formulating their new expressive aims. Kandinsky and Franz Marc both found their way to new structures earlier and more completely in the graphic field than with other techniques. Already in the fifty-six woodcuts of 1913 with which Kandinsky accompanied his poetical work *Klänge*, the "stylization" of the forms approaches the limits of what is recognizable, releasing effects that hold the spectator even if he has not yet taken in the figurative content. Thus, the picture-structures demanded by Kandinsky already seem to be hinted at and anticipated here as a mere constellation of "*Klänge*" or "sounds". Structures, therefore, that, because their composition is not determined by something narratable, have to forego specific communicatory properties, and instead are intended to evoke in the beholder an unparticularized response, which is precisely what Kandinsky meant by "*Klang*". To him the word signified a harmony that was also the criterion of something complete and perfect: the complete cosmos as well as the complete picture, since both had arisen from catastrophes "that out of the chaotic roaring of the elements in the end create a symphony". The four lithographs, four woodcuts and four etchings of the album *Kleine Welten*, compiled in Page 181

146

Franz Marc, 1912

1922, look like a kind of summary of all the formal methods with which, continually varying them, Kandinsky tried to display such an absolute lying beyond our illusive world. With the vigour of the lines, patches and colours, Kandinsky wanted to make visible his revelations as he had experienced them through nature as a whole; his subject-matter strives for the eternal and objective, since "the eternal and objective rings through the time-bound, subjective soul of the artist". This subject-matter also seeks, however, to encompass the true being that can never be aesthetically defined through interpreting the separate phenomena of reality, but only through a deeper, undivided experience of nature. Kandinsky's *Kleine Welten* series is thus the first great and bold attempt to render pictorially a kind of aesthetic experience of the cosmos. It also precedes many similar experiments in that it not only aims to show how abstract qualities appear less elusively in what is non-figurative than in what is figurative, but at the same time tries to make it clear — through a set of compositions most diverse in their formal character — that abstract form is more variable, richer in content, and more comprehensive than representational. The graphic techniques proved useful for the first experiments in this direction inasmuch as their forms — especially planes of colour — were able to look purer, more impersonal than those described with the brush: possibilities that Kandinsky knew how to use to the utmost above all in woodcut and etching. In other respects, however, it was not necessary for his formal conceptions to win new effects from the graphic processes.

Lyonel Feininger, 1918

Franz Marc likewise wanted to reveal an absolute that, situated far above immediate reality, cannot be perceived in our world objects. Apart from the purely formal aspect, what places Marc in the *Blaue Reiter* circle is his "attempt to make the world itself speak, instead of our souls excited by the image of the world". The thing that, in a way, marks him off from Kandinsky is this conviction that "world" can only be made to speak through itself. The artist's devotion to reality is noticeable even in his latest woodcuts. It began with the close observation of animals, an observation that, however, is already marked in the early colour lithographs by the way it exposes the essential form of an animal's body or even the main factors in a beast's movement, the basic phenomenon in creaturely behaviour. Marc's pictures of that date already present us with the whole genus in one animal rather than a definite individual creature. This devotion ends with the representation of the *Fate of Animals*, the preordained share of an animal's soul Page 183 in the ups and downs of cosmic events. As a means of eliminating the inessential and of making clear the eurhythmic flow of a beast's contour as well as the lineal movements in its surroundings, Marc uses a planar woodcut technique that opposes energetically coursing black lines to unbroken areas of black. The degree of abstraction in such prints is much higher than in Marc's paintings. If early woodcuts still show a fondness for curves that is not so far from Art Nouveau, Page 147 the stroke-power of the lines as a symbol of creative forces and, correspondingly, a cubistic hard-

148

Lyonel Feininger, 1920

ness of the forms constantly increase in the late works: the crystalline quality stands for a higher material reality.

Just as one can say that in prints like these, which transcribe the primeval forces of the cosmos or acts of devotion before the powers of creation, Franz Marc stands between the *Blaue Reiter* and the *Brücke,* so the works of Lyonel Feininger approach the ideas of French cubism, above all with respect to form. The analysis of objects into elements easy to define in terms of solid geometry and the gradually attained fusion of volumes and space into a prismatic formal unity had led in France to a completely changed structure of the picture surface. A new method had been found of representing spatial and plastic relationships on this surface without the use of perspective. In the effort to submit to the two-dimensionality of the picture surface, the sculptural forms had by degrees been flattened, and had largely relinquished their spatial values, finally entering into a planar union of almost abstract forms. There remains a planimetrically determined picture structure, as in the lithographs and etchings of Juan Gris and Georges Braque from these years, a structure whose compositional framework, supporting the pictorial effect, was largely independent of the forms of objects. Robert Delaunay adds a new experience of space to such constructions, which — like all cubist products — never give up their last links with figurative art, in spite of being far removed from reality. His prisms, closely packed together in the cubist way, grow transparent. They thus once more obtain spatial values for the composition, despite

Page 169

its being cubistically crowded with things, and at the same time provide an equivalent for phenomena of light. With Feininger, who knew Delaunay well, the sense of space is also very strong, and with him too, this impression depends on a new experience of space that he pictorializes by cubist methods. When Feininger depicts in woodcuts his beloved landscapes and towns from along the Baltic coast, or else the villages of Thuringia, one can make out what are positively portraits of objects he has come upon, portraits of churches, bridges, or moles, for example. Nevertheless, such references remain in the sphere of mere allusions, because the purpose is not to assemble them in an illusionistic manner, but to define pictorially a very modern experience Page 148 of amplitude and cosmic openness of space. What has today become the avowed aim of many modern artists, namely to translate data and forms from the physicist's interpretation of the universe into visible signs, is thought to be already present in Feininger's highly impressive woodcuts. Up-to-date concepts of physics, such as lines of force, vibrations in the ether, matter as a product of "vibration nodes", but above all the idea that all phenomena lead back to a dynamic primary element and can be regarded as variations of it, prove amazingly fertile with Feininger as suggestions for previously unknown — at least in the graphic sphere — forms with which to pictorialize landscape. Feininger conveys this idea of the universe as etherial happenings, as a complex of dynamic events, by means of an artistic technique that in general is bound to seem especially unsuited to this type of communication. It is the "achromatic" technique of the planar woodcut, forming with extremely opaque planes and lines as hard as rods. The resistance that this eye-slamming method, which records signs for the permanent and immovable rather than the etherial, offers to Feininger's particular expressive wishes, is, however, developed by the artist into his most essential creative factor. Today one might say that this is exactly what makes Feininger's woodcuts suggest the world is an immaterial power-field through which rush streams of energy; its pictorialization forces the artist to "estrange" the woodcut technique he has deliberately chosen. Feininger's woodcuts are among the most persuasive results of employing form in cubist ways. These applications, truly bound up with things, are treated by the mind of a very individual artist in such a fashion that they let themselves be used for motifs diametrically opposed to the still-life images of cubism. Such woodcuts do not, of course, allow Feininger to employ Delaunay's transcriptions of spacelight through an interflow of diaphanous prisms, though it is true that he uses these methods in his lithographs.

As always in the history of recent graphic art, tidy arrangements do not stand up to the diversity of individual decisions. Should Paul Klee be mentioned now because he belonged to the *Blaue Reiter* group, and because he later developed at the Bauhaus the pictorial and philosophical beginnings of the *Blaue Reiter*, which was broken up and destroyed by the First World War (Macke fell in 1914, Marc in 1916)? Or, both on chronological grounds and because cubist experiments would henceforth remain — especially with Klee himself, for example — more or less perceptible everywhere, should one first talk about the graphic art of cubism? About the fact, therefore, that the increasing tendency of cubist forms to flatten out greatly suited the graphic processes, including those that involve colour? What one first thinks of in this connection is probably Braque's graphic work, as to a certain extent it has gone on accepting cubist axioms right up to the present day, doing so precisely in its "attachements au sujet" and rejection of abstract art. Together with Picasso, Braque developed the aesthetics of cubism, whose simultaneous presentation of different aspects of the object he retains even in his less programmatic and far more lyrical works from after 1930. And just as already in his opening phase, when still a friend of the fauves, he rejected "the excesses of their colours", so he has gone on evolving in his late colour etchings curiously broken tones in broad areas over which he lays representations made up of nimbly running line work. One also thinks of Juan Gris, who became the leading representative of cubism's late, synthetic phase, in that he started with the organization of the picture surface and only then defined the objects, reifying the abstract as a second step. However, the communication between picture and beholder was certainly not intended to consist just in the latter's being stirred by the noble decorative arrangement of the forms. Juan Gris sought to add to his synthetic surface organization relations between seeing and experiencing of a different nature, by admitting, as Braque did, letters and writing into the union of forms. With this, the complex of the aesthetic connections between what has been created and whoever takes it in embraces another formal experience, which establishes an extra link. The spectator must also "participate" in the picture by taking in such forms, which, because of the need to decipher them, invite him in their special way to look.

Page 171

Page 169

In this connection the names of Picasso and Léger spring to mind, but a moment's reflection makes it clear that both these artists proceed from assumptions other than those mentioned so far. Picasso's attitude is determined by his continual searching and the incessant changes in his decisions regarding form, while a different relation to the object underlies the works of Léger.

Independent and yet roused by diverse stimuli, Paul Klee marked out his artistic provinces across whose borders no one else has been able to force their way. His circumspect awareness of what had happened in art and what was happening now — a striking characteristic of many artists of genius — enabled him to find in the depths of time, as also in his own present, technical tricks and spiritual trends that took on the rôle of catalysts bringing about the concretization of his intentions. A crucial co-determinant of Klee's earliest graphic creations was the work of some of those masters to whom graphic art owed its new independence. Redon must be given pride of place here, but also to be mentioned are — approaching the present — Ensor, Stuck and Kubin, just as — from the distant past — Pisanello the draughtsman. The fact that it was Pisanello with his subtle yet metallically exact way of drawing whom Klee had before his eyes when in 1903 he made his etching *Virgin in a Tree* is explained by Klee's outstanding sense of line, apparent in all his graphic works.

As regards technique and the rendering of form, the first etchings, produced between 1903 and 1905, are extraordinarily punctilious. In an almost old-masterly fashion, the contours are first bitten as continuous lineal paths and then later the interior forms are elaborated with hatchings of short lines, in the course of which Klee's inventive power at once proves its worth through the way the ludicrousness and irony of his grotesque subjects — *Two Men meet, Each believing the Other to be of higher Rank,* for example, or *Senile Phoenix* — leads to forms that, despite their severe and detailed finish, remain conspicuously ironical and unsolemn. The precise, quattrocentist use of line (Pisanello) of the first etchings disappears in later lithographs. They retain, however, general refinements thanks to which they recall Redon's prints, even though at the same time they leave many results to chance, thereby including specifically modern effects. The etchings of 1913 and 1914 acquire a density in the forms that gives rise to the artist's tussle, concluded at Paris itself, with the compositional problems of cubism. Klee's well-known hint that his picture titles are only intended to be "comparatively like" can also be applied to the form. Cubist in general appearance, these etchings are none the less quite independent with regard to content and the individual forms. In the print *Little World*, a principle of figuration that would not be fully played out until Dubuffet seems already to have been anticipated in 1914: out of a disorderly conglomeration of patches and lineal structures, outlines of masks, hands and flowers are scratched. Only very late etchings have once again a similarly dense surface, for it was round about 1914 that line finally became the principle bearer of messages wholly connected with Klee as an individual. Its use in etchings and lithographs Page 185 is determined by well-weighed communicatory aims, though the order to make realistic statements does not hinder it from developing entirely free expressive gestures. Applied in scant strokes, as thin as spider-thread and often rather isolated on the surface, it is deliberately made to look like the line in drawings by children and the insane, for the simple reason that Klee, proceeding in a manner that parallels their direct, untrained creation, wants not really to define form and content, but only to suggest them. All this leads to that unburdening of the appearance which is also the plastic equivalent of the cheerful irony with which Klee obtains for the world of the picture new poetic possibilities and an untheatrical romanticism freed from the weight of over-simple feeling. Such creations and their special task are very graphic in the original sense, which means, for one thing, that, compared to expressionist works, they are mostly very small. They have rightly been called "magic epistles". Regarded generally, Klee's graphic art occupies in each of its components, from mere technique to the spiritual beginnings, an extreme position *vis-à-vis* expressionism. In accordance with its underlying nature, it strived to get back from the wall into the portfolio. Its aspect avoids strident brutality, and, as a light, delicate fabric, has nothing of the poster about it. Its contents certainly do not claim to have in any sense absolute validity and to be able to derive from this validity the right to make demands of any kind at all. On the contrary, it brings home the ambivalence and doubtfulness of all criteria and keeps suggesting, with romantic irony, the ambiguities and many-sidedness of appearances. With this cast of imagination Klee stands at the centre of modern sensibility. Yet in contrast to its forms the fascinating character of the subject-matter of his works has found scarcely an echo in modern graphic art. This is undoubtedly because his peculiar ability, furnished with a marked taste for new possibilities of expression, to combine poetic imagination and pictorial conception is an essentially personal endowment. He is linked to the *Blaue Reiter* by his intention of referring through pictorial interpretations to the universal active elements that determine all appearances. For to Klee the world is not fully formed and so not the one and only world. Representing it in the "form-ends" just reached at the time cannot be the task of an art whose business it is to produce a kind of optical projection of the cosmic forces. In this sense, it creates parallel to nature. Hence, line too no longer has the task, with Klee, of being a sort of script that can be read as the expression of states of soul. What it "writes" is rather paths and directions of forces and operative elements. Space likewise is not interpreted by the artist as a stable vacuum in which different objects are placed, but as a mobile development of depths by means of, let us say, precisely and lucidly drawn "space diagrams". His lines nearly always make what is static active. They do not feel empowered to describe a given fact, something concrete, and appear as "abstract" signs in so far as they refer to spatial tendencies and general flows of movement, but also mark trends of thought and planning, of wishing and willing. Here lies the significance, too, of the direction arrow that often finds itself inscribed in the loose net of lines. It does not "embody" but "indicates", gives the direction of a transient movement or of outer and inner tensions. "The father of the arrow is the thought: how can I reach my goal?"

Where it is not a question of mere imitation one can seldom point out direct influences from Klee in graphic work of the present time. Yet no one has produced more indirect effects on modern graphic creation than he. As a single whole isolated by its unrepeatable originality, principles of his pictorial activity have to a large extent determined the general artistic attitude of today. His prints have taught people to regard as obligatory for graphic art a different form of looking that has more in common with reading, and his very timely search for a new, unexpended vision made him recognize the creative power of form and thus led him to a creative principle — not of course one used by him exclusively — that has increasingly become a very dominant factor in present-day artistic activity. It is not what Klee brought into being, namely the enchanting and very clever ironic fantasy, that appears again in more recent graphic art, but the method of presenting a thought through suggestion and evocation instead of an explicit pronouncement.

Art Nouveau, fauvism, expressionism, cubism, *Blaue Reiter*, the questions regarding the range of artistic communications, and the attempts, closely bound up with these questions, to make the unutterable evident by way of the visible, lie like a system of pictorial thought behind all that is now manifesting itself in graphic form. They are acknowledged as binding, heeded as possibilities, condemned as deviations, and thus assert themselves, through their recognition or rejection, in every decision made by modern artists. From the sum of the pictorial results of the first decades of our century, it emerges that, despite the wealth of art-theories, manifestos and much reviled isms that accompanied artistic activity during these years, individual decisions again and again, and by no means in scattered cases, prevailed. A prototype of the absolutely free approach to the rules and claims of the programmes and schools is Pablo Picasso. In early judgments on his work, we therefore witness the absurd event of the complaints ordinarily made about intolerant theories and formulae suddenly changing into the reproach that Picasso disavows his own work and is not true to himself. As do all the other processes used by the artist in creating, the graphic aspect of his protean production bears out his resolve never to copy himself and the determination with which he establishes the postulates that are necessary for setting to work his creative forces and that have been concisely formulated by him in the remark: "I do not seek, I find." For a long time the graphic techniques served Picasso merely Page 111 as another kind of drawing, and later on they have been sporadically used in this sense, above all during the phases of his evolution dominated by that genuine classicism which is characterized formally by drawings with the purity and sensuous power of an Ingres — drawings that the artist disseminates in the form of line etchings and lithographs. There are such drawing-etchings from as early as between 1900 and 1906, during the "blue" and "rose" periods, though the run of their lines still accords completely with that of his contemporary calm and melancholy paintings, which in their turn — and this applies to many of Picasso's late paintings as well — are emphatically linear in character. Slight distortions, with which accurately plotted lines lengthen the figures and make them angular, give these scenes from the life of the *saltimbanques* the austere charm of reticent, controlled feeling. In 1916, when, after long, systematically con-ducted cubist experiments, Picasso was seized by a new delight in reality and devoted himself for the first time to a "classicism" of Pan-like vitality, this technique completely attuned to the lineal image was again adopted and long retained, both as etching and as lithography. Its wide-ranging lines pictorialize chiefly a lyrical basic theme of his work, centering on motifs that involve a calm, sensually stressed juxtaposition of people, one of whom seems deeply affected by the existence of the other: the artist by his model, the waker by the sleeper, the companion holding the mirror by the woman adorning herself. They are compositions that will be varied once again in the most recent lithographs and linocuts, and that, in their poetic power issuing entirely from pure visibleness, at times remind one of those pictures by Titian which the great Venetian called his *poésie*. Etchings of similar form, dating from 1927 and 1930, constitute sets to go with Balzac's *Le Chef-d'œuvre inconnu* and Ovid's *Metamorphoses*. Cubist elements already announce themselves in a woodcut of 1907, and the artist runs through them in etchings that are impetuously lined, vigorously hatched over, or etchings given planar effects with tonal bitings of the copper.

From such experiments, Picasso won the ingredients for later graphic creations of pronounced visual clarity and challenging aggressiveness, in which forcefulness and drama determine his themes instead of lyrical tenderness. Thus, for representing ecstatic movements, as when he announces the oath of truce between man and beast in his bullfight prints, or for formulating angry complaints against war and murder, Picasso employs in his etchings and lithographs these shapes obtained from the hard, splintery structures of cubism, so as to drive what is horrible into the consciousness via the shock produced by such "formes désagréables". With its flat, ragged forms, alternately black and white, *Guernica*, the terrible "counter-image" of human misdeeds, makes the fullest use of graphic possibilities; and in the etching series *The Dream and Lie of Franco* there are four prefigurations of the great picture. In all these various pictorial statements, the graphic means, even though used most effectively, again and again follows the discoveries made by the artist while painting or drawing. Not until rather late did Picasso train all his intense, choked-back feeling exclusively on the graphic medium as such, when, in the course of a few months of the winter of 1944, he produced over a hundred lithographs at Mourlot's lithographic studio. Ever since then new provinces have been open to the litho technique — regions that earlier it had seemed impossible to enter. Often in many variations, the most diverse themes — portraits, animals, still-lifes, circus scenes — take on ever different appearances in the planar lithographs. The no less bold than unexpected combination of collage and print that Picasso risks when he cuts out outline forms drawn or done in wash on litho transfer-paper, sticks what he has cut together on a new sheet, and only then transfers it to the stone; the covering of the stone with picked paper; the building up of a composition from representational and purely abstract forms (such as the lines ending in dots); the remarkable scraping technique; the combined use of wash and opaque white on transfer-paper — all these devices and many others bear the mark of a brilliant artistic resourcefulness directed by an instinct for invention. The most characteristic feature of Picasso's special kind of working processes is, however, his persistent exploitation of such technical factors as only lithography has to offer. With their help, he achieves something that could be called a derivate of the original pictorial invention. By lithographic methods, he engenders richly branching lines of descent of a family motif. Even one single litho stone proves extremely tolerant about the artist's desires for change, a permissive-

Page 113

ness that he makes the very most of, in order to produce variations on a basic theme. Yet Picasso is often not content just to continue with a particular way of varying, for variants of a different character suddenly appear desirable to him. At this moment, he makes an impression on transfer-paper of the result hitherto obtained on the first stone, and conveys it to a new one. This means that two stones now allow the theme to be modified according to the most different tendencies. Thus, in the eleventh state of a stone, Picasso hits upon the variation *Theme expressed* Page 112 *only through Lines;* or, in the eighteenth, he presents as an exact union of pure lines and planes what began in the first as an amorphous clouding made up of loose areas of "wash". The colour linocuts done in 1956—60 and collected together as a set of forty-five prints seem like a résumé of the most essential themes — those really close to the heart of the artist, whom Daniel-Henry Kahnweiler called "the most human of humans". Meanwhile it is quite evident that, though Picasso has time and again abruptly dropped what he has come to regard as fully investigated, Page 115 this ceaseless trying out of different expressive possibilities is not an end in itself, but a means of finding increasingly far-reaching forms of expression that are able to communicate the growing sensitivity of his visual experiences. Old themes, new forms: accordingly, the new colour lino-cuts add a new component to the old themes of human relations, the bullfight, and an anti-Winkelmannian, orgiastically vivacious Antiquity. In a technically most simple way, these prints composed of a few areas of colour provide a direct graphic equivalent for light. Cut into sharp strips by Venetian blinds, it falls on the bodies of wakening women, streams with Mediterranean intensity over those ecstatically dancing children of nature, the fauns, panisks and nymphs, and dazzles the eye with its reflections in the sand of the arenas, so that a body and its shadow can now hardly be distinguished from each other. Digging out the same block in several phases and inking what remains of the surface on each occasion with increasingly dark tones, Picasso sometimes outlines in his linocuts black nucleal forms with light, colourful bands. Or else he impresses over an expanse of solid black covering the whole sheet a white lino-block in which he has previously cut those lines that, since no white body-colour is laid on the black along the path of these incisions, are to appear black through the overprinted area of white. An effect of white, trickling lines of light similar to that in the colour linocuts is thus produced, since, in the course of printing, the white ink was squeezed up to the edges of the dug-out grooves, concentrating there into fine, brightly gleaming lines that, so to speak "by accident", graphically transfer the brilliance of the light to the contour of a body. In this way, the sky above the blissful countryside of ancient demigods is agitated by curving lines of whirling light. In the bullfight prints the contours of man and beast change, to the eye dazzled by the glittering sand, into mazily curving lines whose supple course describes the elasticity of those in combat. The lively waxing and waning areas of colour and black, however, make the beholder feel the frenzy of the fight by subjecting him to a strong sense of optical malaise. Looking at them, the eye is no longer able to make out — as can happen in the agitated space of reality, too — whether the impression of the movement just completed still clings to the retina or whether it already perceives what is happening right now, since one is not certain where the flickering, tightly inter-wedged colour areas are still intended as solid bodies glittering in the light and where only as patches of transilluminated shadow. Many "accidents" in these prints and their simple technique, accidents that Picasso has swiftly seized upon and turned into new effect-producing elements, make such linocuts particularly convincing certificates of the artist's credo: "I do not seek, I find."

Cubist formal decisions automatically turned our thoughts to Fernand Léger. The winning back of the volumes and the restoration of the object by cubist methods instinctively made one think of Léger's violent treatment of form, although it is easy to see that cubist structures are only at work in his creations as a contributive factor. Léger's objects, as he evolved them after his contact with the cubists, account for their exactness and their solid-geometry clearness chiefly by the fact that they issue from the formal reservoir of the precise, hard-stamped, smoothly polished components of machines. The critic Louis Vauxcelles, to whom both fauvism and cubism owe their names, which he intended derisively, dubbed Léger a *peintre tubiste*, on the model of *peintre cubiste*. Only later did the human figure too become a machine-turned object. Yet, at the same time, Léger's pictorial aims are entirely different from those of the cubists. In grouping his things or bodies reduced to elementary forms, he does away with all logical objective relations and avoids letting the presence of one object explain that of another, as it would in a normal picture-subject (water and ship, say), where the separate features are fitted into a rational continuum dependent on the motif. With Léger, on the contrary, the ensemble firmly sees to it that the objects remain largely independent. Instead of being reduced to part of a whole, they acquire an impressive phenomenal force "simplement posés dans l'espace" — a force that even men and animals obtain through this process of "objectification", which also includes making them completely free from emotion. For Léger's forms, compositional methods of a very individual sort are necessary, ones quite unlike those of cubism, which after all still enable a large number

Page 173 of things to maintain paraphrastically the over-regimented cohesion of a still-life. His arrangements of emphatically contoured objects accented with very forthright, signalling local colours allow the lithograph to display an armorial chromatic splendour, so that, as a bold mosaic of colour areas radiating the most vigorous colouristic harmonies unrelated to the real hues of things, it attains an orchestral sonority. From such "sounds" liberated in this manner, the way leads to the non-representational "sounds" of abstract creations. The free arrangement of the components of things, an arrangement, that is to say, which releases objects from the contexts into which they usually find themselves bound according to their immanent meaning and purpose, and which thereby also frees them from the rôle of being supports or properties for narratable subjects, already gives them an aspect comprising expressive forms that, while they do not pictorialize logically definable statements, contain universal features of experience. Thanks to such aesthetically effective components as these, Léger's use of forms has a share in the plastic experiments of the present day.

While these experiments with an autonomous graphic art were being made, great draughtsmen were still active who deliberately employed the graphic technique as a means of realizing their linear conceptions. In France there was above all Henri Matisse, who as a painter, too, did not Pages 125, 126 develop plastic form towards a conventional three-dimensionality through patches of shadow and perspective effects, but obtained plasticity from what was essentially two-dimensional with thin, circumscribing lines, so that the vegetal heaviness of his spreading volumes do not burden the floating appearance of his pictures. The extreme economy in the line work of his etchings and "lino-scratchings" make them very easy indeed to take in with the eye. This effortless winning of delectable visual experiences goes together with the sense of calm, purity and sumptuousness that Matisse was able to preserve for his own pictorial world in a world of terror and despair. Delicate, mobile lines settle only in light, frugal arabesques on the sheet, whose undisturbed whiteness is transformed in a way discovered by Matisse into graphic light — a brightness that, together with the shapes of body and face, unceasingly confirms that living is a joy and makes in every print the inspiring paraphrase of a big "yes". Similarly unburdened by harassing problems and, like an ancient nature-poet, entirely devoted to the beauties of creation, Dunoyer de Segonzac transmits all the freshness and buoyancy of his pen drawings Page 130 to the lineal images of his etchings. His extreme delight in working has enabled him to produce an extensive corpus of graphic works.

Italian artists found very independent ways of drawing in the field of graphic art. In the empty spaces of disquieting perspectives, Carlo Carrà builds objects and figures out of dry, Page 135 impersonal strokes, and thereby gives to his etchings the enchanting power of his paintings. Only in the deliberate stiffness of the line could one compare Giorgio Morandi's etching to Page 136 the graphic work of Carrà, for it is different in all essential features. Fine parallel strokes abstaining from any calligraphic tendency spread over the sheet an intarsia made up of blackish, deep grey, and soft grey areas. In their intermeshed construction, one reads very serene, very impressive texts about unassuming landscapes and frugally ordered meals, and one experiences in such themes and representations the calm persuasive power that can be won a total rejection of everything showy. With similar graphic means, Giuseppe Viviani intones themes of quite another Page 136 sort. They call for a different manner of composing, as they do not bother about the relative size and actual correlation of real things, but, with a slight surrealist tendency, group what gives them pleasure and stress what seems important to them: a glove, a fig, a little lace shawl, with a duck, and a charming bit of junk in the shape of a plaster Pisa cathedral with its leaning tower.

The progressive development of the graphic techniques opened up a new field of action above all for the sculptor's drawing. Always highly individual, the sculptor's drawing could now, whether it was a first idea or a carefully pondered design, turn into something autonomous, if "extras" of a graphic kind, such as backings of colour areas or a richly varied elaboration of the line, were added to the original lineal image. For his woodcuts and etchings, Henri Laurens takes over from collage the inclusion of calm planes of colour in what he has drawn, so that, like a distant echo, they shall intensify the conception of form that his thin-lined drawing evokes in an extremely gifted way. Differently again, Ossip Zadkine translates cubist sculptures in his lithographs by colouristically stressed planes and conspicuous systems of beams built up from vigorously directed lines, while, on coloured backgrounds enclosed by colouristically accentuated frames, Marino Marini builds, in unmistakable drawings out of broad, angularly broken strokes, figures whose joints are often kept pliant by means of circles looking like swivel pins. Alberto Giacometti's etchings and lithographs appear almost identical with his frail drawn sketches, for his prints too content themselves with a few space-indicating lines that seem more like co-ordinates for pinpointing the figures, and replace the density of figure masses by clearly determined positions.

Among the great graphic artists of the present, Georges Rouault in his lifetime and Marc Chagall appear independent of illusionism and the demands of abstract art alike, yet they derive from the expressive potentials of both operative factors suiting their particular pictorial ideas. In the use he has made of the etching process, Rouault stands no less alone among contemporary graphic artists than, with his themes and views, he does in the art of our times as a whole. In an original manner, he transplants the solemn chromatic gleam of medieval stained glass (the artist was apprenticed to a glass-painter and restored medieval windows), and the lights welling up from its opaque darks, to his big etchings, whose representations also seem to have a religious colouring, although they adopt none of the old legendary subjects. But the everyday wretchedness of prostitutes and clowns and the usual imperiousness and injustice of the "mighty" mark in a novel way the weary and heavy-laden figures which Rouault lines up as a train of forcefully obtruding visions in prints to which he gives strange titles with undertones of myth. The great series *Réincarnation du Père Ubu* (created in 1927), *le Cirque* and *Miserere et la Guerre* (first published in 1948) group graphic images of heads, bodies and night landscapes that not only in the coloured realizations but also when printed in black-and-white achieve the magic power of painted glass. Ceaseless technical experiments and untiring work on the separate plates, which were often developed through many states, have finally arrived at magnificent visual effects by means not practicable for others. Rouault first had a heliogravure made after one of his wash compositions by photo-mechanical methods, but then worked the reproduction plate over so

Page 195

Page 200

Page 201

Page 131

Pages 117, 118

completely that only scattered traces of the reproduced wash drawing remained. In other respects, the plate now bore a stamp wholly determined by the artist's spontaneous action with scraper, roulette, file and glass-paper. Sometimes Rouault also made broad bands over the plate with brush and acid, working into the metal these cane-like lines that recall the leads of medieval stained glass.

Ma Vie, his autobiography, published in 1923, is full of the very peculiar experiences that Chagall had while growing up at Vitebsk in the bosom of his pious, artistically sensitive family. Mental images from these early memories still besiege the mature painter and determine his work, setting it apart from everything contemporary, even though his thoughts on art's new tasks led to questions and answers regarding form that were similar to those that arose then for all progressive artists. Thus Chagall's forms certainly follow the directives of the times, which means that, with him as with other contemporary *avant-gardistes*, boldly drawn-out contours and strong colours bring expressive emphasis into the general look of etchings and lithographs. But in Chagall's case, the expression aims at the intenseness of a dream, achieves poetic concentration, and has nothing to do with the programmes and postulates of the true expressionists. With regard to the world and art, Chagall has views quite different from theirs: "My pictures are just arrangements of mental images that haunt me, I do not understand them." The fact that comprehending and precisely formulated requirements are not involved already distinguishes his art from expressionism. Nevertheless, its own domain is laid open by emotional forces — forces that, responsive to what is sensuously charming, present themselves as an ample capacity for love, an unlimited sensitiveness to the felicity of colours and forms, of movements and melodies in painting and print. Chagall very quickly found the graphic means he required, first using them in 1922—23 at the age of thirty-five. Later on he was to change them in many respects, but even in these early drypoints and lithographs of compositions with which he accompanies the very strange and moving account of his Russian childhood, his self-discovery, and his beginnings, one meets the characteristically elongated contours and the free distribution, recalling Redon, of bits of objects and parts of living bodies over the entire picture surface. Delicate as it is, the line, here the medium of a very refined and pure form of etching, secures the expression almost single handed. In comparison, the dark, soft-grained lithographs still remain duplicated chalk drawings. During the same year, 1923, many differences appear in a second long series of illustrations, which Chagall created in Paris. Again it was a question of a work very closely connected with him — almost as closely as his personal memoirs: Nikolai Gogol's *Dead Souls*, which the artist had chosen himself. Something unfamiliar is confided to us in these etchings. A rich, strange world full of irony and hidden meaning — one that leaves the exhausted thematic material of contemporary illustrations far behind — approaches us through that arbitrary formal synthesis of Chagall's which has been called "poetic-objective". From the outset, technical problems caused the artist no difficulties: etching, aquatint and drypoint were all used by him with unerring instinct. Not much later, this time at the suggestion of the art-dealer Vollard, he began considering and making experiments for a set of illustrations to La Fontaine's *Fables*. A first draft in colour proved impracticable and was given up. Thereupon, making a fresh, determined start, Chagall completed in the course of the three years 1927—30 that long series of prints whose remarkable biting technique calls to mind the first golden age of pure painter-etching. For drypoint is used only very little and aquatint not at all, so that the endlessly graduated tone, the painterly chiaroscuro, is achieved almost entirely through varied biting. Thereby, the etchings retain a mysterious transparentness, nowise dulled to dark opacity, and it is possible, in this loose-textured medium, for an osmosis of the forms to occur that almost makes "objectively" credible what is undoubtedly there in Chagall's dream phantasies: the fusion of the bodies of man and beast, the interchangeableness of all manifestations of the vital forces, permutations and metamorphoses of man and woman, plant and thing. If the French line-engravers of the eighteenth century bring out the lessons of these ancient-cum-modern fables in an amiable, straightforward way, here it is the metamorphic world of forms at their legendary sources that Chagall, living there himself in his dreams, makes manifest. A manifold convertibility of what is material and corporeal, past, present and future, just as is the peculiar form of Chagall's experience of the world. A decisive metamorphosis of the artist's graphic technique already announced itself in the *Fables* etchings through a kind of auxiliary process that he used for a number of impressions from the series: he added body colours to many prints with his own hand, limiting himself to a few crucial spots on the printing surface — real colouristic "points of impact". However, the most powerfully expressive work among the sets of illustrations, *La Bible*, was again produced wholly and adequately by monochrome etching. True, the forms change, the figures grow more monumental, the contours more concise, and the composition clearer to the eye. What has been embedded in Chagall's memories of his youth as pious sensibility, now, in the Bible prints made between 1931 and 1939 with the remoteness of the sources of these recollections, becomes something objectified that resembles a confession. Work on the Bible was interrupted by the artist's emigration to the United States, and not until 1956 did he complete the remaining images. Now, in America, colour manifested itself most forcibly in the graphic works as well, a logical step in the progress of Chagall's general development. Perhaps his acquaintance with the colour-etcher Stanley W. Hayter induced this decisive resort to the colour plate. Though preceded by sketches in gouache, the thirteen colour lithographs with scenes from four *Arabian Nights* stories are still genuinely graphic in the sense that colours with this pungent effect are reserved for the print, the medium of the poster, alone. As

Page 119

Page 121

vehemently as if they were meant for a poster, Chagall's litho colours are, however, because of their harmonization, able to reveal to our astonished eyes the unreal pomp and artificial splendour of Oriental worlds of romance.

All the prints that Chagall, back in France again, has designed and printed since then have also been lithographs. The early themes now give way to circus motifs and visions of a mysteriously inspirited world above the roofs of Paris. They are by turns transcribed as loose, planar black-and-white variants and as supernatural bursts of colour whose magic fire burns both more richly and more softly than is the case with the lithographs conjuring up the *Arabian Nights*. Once more, prints appear with Bible figures and stories (1956), this time eighteen of them and in colour. Only very recently has an entirely new series of subjects entered Chagall's work, with the creation of a set of big colour lithographs. These painting-like prints Chagall's work, with the creation of a set of big colour lithographs. These painting-like prints garland the enchantingly natural love-stories of the shepherd and shepherdess Daphnis and Chloë from that late-antique novel by Longus which has been illustrated time and again since the eighteenth century. Yet it is precisely when one looks at the formal solutions found by Maillol or Bonnard for such illustrations that the autonomous value and intangibility of Chagall's pictorial world become clear. *Arabian Nights*, Bible and antique merge in its homogeneity, and provide the most varied themes, which, however, all change into the special material of the Chagallian world of illusions, through which float weightless elements of reality. Just as Chagall's art raises an imperative claim to uniqueness in the very extensive provinces of its thematic conceptions, so it remains unmistakable within the narrower compass of what is purely graphic. Its lines curving away beyond the requirements of a corporeity articulated in the antique manner define contours that have a peculiar power of suggestion. Once again, as at the time of Toulouse-Lautrec, this graphic art found a previously unknown coloration without which potentialities of the print — discovered by Chagall — could not have been realized.

Around the middle of our century, graphic art not only took on new aspects thanks to the then young generation, but also received new stimuli from some artists belonging to the older generation born just before the turn of the century. What distinguishes their work from that of those still standing at the start is the markedly individual character of the forms developed by mature artists as a result of many experiments. One has only to think of the prints made by Picasso after the Second World War or of the colour lithography begun by Chagall in the 1940's: two consummate graphic pictorial worlds possessing absolute independence. Or else one calls to mind Joan Miró's wholly unmistakable printed work, whose earliest evidence did not appear till after 1930, and whose first climax came a decade later still, in 1944 to be exact, with the *Série Barcelona*. Since then, the graphic production of the Spanish artist, who was born in 1893 near Barcelona, has grown to about four hundred etchings, lithographs and woodcuts, and belongs to the vast and unequivocal findings that point to an emphatically intensive and extremely complex creative performance by the graphic arts midway through our century. With his aversion to the conventional, illusionistic panel painting and preference for a radical planarity, Miró exemplifies, as it were in his person, one of the reasons why the print is generally regarded as a medium suited to the times. It offers superlative opportunities for producing absolutely plane forms. Thus the surreal pictorial world of Miró is distinguished from the fantastic one of Chagall, still partly bound up with reality, by its total elimination of all signs that could indicate spatiality. Though Chagall's forms do not for the most part dwell on our earth, they still always remain in the sphere of a reality that, even if magically heightened, is three dimensional. Miró's *personnages*, on the contrary, come from another world and fashion themselves out of "weightless" signs, which, however, become compelling and importunate through an unambiguous, cheerfully ironical or even malicious reference to the real world. All the same, these signs charged with significance kept themselves hidden away for a very long time. After much searching, the artist finally brought them out of concealment and introduced something of them into his paintings in 1924, though he placed them in surroundings where they could not yet live unhindered. Not until the drypoint series *Black and Red* did they find themselves in that world of mere ciphers for possibilities of things which is appropriate to them. This did not happen before 1938. Chagall found cubism useful as a means of giving his private visions a secure optical basis. For Miró, Klee's linear conversions of the concrete, the discoveries of surrealism, and Picasso's figures constructed from bone-like *formes désagréables* were directional beacons to help him determine his own course. Everything is there in the fifty black-and-white lithographs of the *Série Barcelona*: the human, animal and vegetable grotesques composed of wandering lines and animated contours. For the most part, this "sign work" comprises pure line, though some planes do occasionally blacken over as if they lay in shadow. One can clearly recognize male and female *personnages* by the attributive addition of significant ciphers, and from time to time one also sees, chiefly by the dangerous serration of tooth-work, that it is a case of a wickedly snappish creature.

Still content with signs lithographed in black, in 1948 *Album 13* brought a new association into the cheerfully cheeky game. Movements now accompany the forms, or rather both combine as a single unit and are therefore indivisible. They turn the whole picture surface into something like a field of force. This is not true to the same extent of the single lithographs that followed very soon, and are composed of a few coloured forms jumping up at one most gaily. As with all their predecessors, the mark of their graphic nature is still a rigorously maintained planarity. Whether it is a question of colour or of black-and-white, they are set forth in two-dimensional areas, bands or lines. Shortly after this, however, the surface character of Miró's graphic work changed, first in two sets of colour etchings from 1952 and 1953. Miró now

Page 177

recalled the experiments he had attempted in the New York studio of the colour-etcher Stanley W. Hayter. Hayter, the great systematizer of the etching techniques, has been the Page 177 inspiration and teacher of many modern artists, since, with his experiments, he anticipated graphic methods craved more and more strongly during the last decade. Up till now, etching had counted for little, colour etching being wholly regarded as a medium with aesthetically dangerous shortcomings, on account of its colour applications that easily shade into deadness and, moreover, cannot always be accurately registered. Yet however clean of colour and paper-light the visual effects of the modern colour lithograph may be, the ink coating of these surface prints, just because it is flat and even, binds itself so closely to the support that printed matter and paper become virtually identical in the general appearance. There is not the slightest hint of a texture, and the physical character of the printing substance does not make itself perceptible through traces of any kind. The second basic possibility of graphic creations, namely that of affording tactile as well as visual sensations, was thus completely excluded in lithography. Very recently, however, this second potentiality of printing techniques has been increasingly recognized and exploited in novel pictorial prints as an effective means of obtaining a different, no longer strictly graphic quality. Even Miró has now largely stopped depicting *personnages* and their world as irrelevant as it is full of meaning, and devotes himself mainly to presenting effectively the graphic material itself. The ability to produce textures and place colours one over the other in layers is among the special features of intaglio printing and hence of etching. Compared with earlier compositions, Miró's brilliantly bitten and printed etchings in the two coloured sets are positively "depopulated", but in exchange their surfaces are enriched by interesting granulations and diverse relief and hollowed-out features, as well as several interpenetrating beds of colour. Occasionally, elemental formations appear as white blanks in the bright ensemble of the variously presented colouring substances, because their shapes were protected on the plate with coatings of asphaltum, so that acid baths could not get at the areas occupied by them. They were thus left as the topmost, plain areas of a plate other-wise bitten in all sorts of ways; and if this plate was overspread with printing-ink and then cleaned, even a gentle wipe exposed its smooth metal again, whereas the ink remained caught in the etched hollows. Under the strong pressure of the roller, the paper was pressed into the hollows filled with ink, so that, in the impression, the coloured parts appear on paper that has risen up, and hence stand out slightly in relief. Continuing the game, Miró sometimes also approaches his forms from the opposite point of view, as when, using the same plate, he does not print the colouring on the sheet from the hollows, which means the etched areas, but from the inked heights. Thus, the bitten parts remain uncoloured while the hitherto bare *"plateaux"* are now carefully inked so as to obtain a print with little pressure from the roller. In this way, a reverse, almost "negative" image of the same basic composition is produced. Like many modern graphic artists, Miró often readily follows his impulses as they seize him in the course of technical creation, and new pictorial ideas burst forth thanks to this instinctive way of acting that is independent of the artist's directing will.

Within the bounds of strictly graphic procedure, everything is tried in the late work, including lithography with nimbly circulating crayons, a combined action of results achieved lithographically and by etching, and also certain effects such as embossing produces. But Miró never attempts that crossing of the border risked by younger artists when they build the provider of the print out of heterogeneous kinds of material. He has often made it plain, however, that he, like them, is concerned with the effect of the artistically worked material: "In my view, the material must be rich and powerful, so that it immediately leaps to the beholder's eye, even before he has had time for reflection." Joan Miró, like Klee a poet with pictorial signs that affect us through a direct call without communicating a logically definable message, found in Paul Elouard's alignments of autonomous linguistic elements a word poetry that has a similarly random and suggestive effect. Poet and graphic artist, working together for years, in their book *A toute épreuve* produced out of the integration of letterpress areas and woodcuts that unison which comes from the combination of two different forms of artistic experience in a single, many dimensional whole. Completed in 1958, the work was printed by Lacourière with a hundred woodcuts. The signs appear to be conditioned by the text, which, for its part, looks as if it has been called forth by them. As the most freely mobile of forms, these signs hover round the type with a weightless colourfulness that is reminiscent of transparent watercolour hues and was obtained through repeated inkings of the wood-blocks cut by Enrico Torno at Barcelona, and through a corresponding number of printing operations. Descriptive passages in literature from the past invite the reader's imagination to form self-consistent mental images, to which illustrations generally do violence. Today's pure verbal creations and linguistic discoveries, on the other hand, achieve unsettled, freely wavering moods to which paraphrasing signs like those of Miró add new aspects without at the same time meeting the resistance of definite (conceptual) orientations. Graphic art's earliest province, the illustrated book, has now found, with the fundamental change in literary and pictorial forms, new tasks that it can accomplish more perfectly and purely than when subject to the former preconditions. But it has also become something other than a book with passages of reading-matter interrupted by pictures that relate these texts over again.

Among the artists who have gone on being stirred by new ideas at a mature age, and who, though born by the end of the last century, have continued to give graphic art new aspects in the middle of ours, Rolf Nesch has come closest to the younger graphic artists as regards technique. Even if it is true from a purely chronological standpoint that Nesch anticipated present-day working methods by using printing plates with bits of metal placed on, soldered to, or worked into them (as early as about 1934, he was producing so-called "material pictures", which, having served as "printing-blocks", were promoted to the rank of independent picture), the artist thereby in no wise set himself at the head of a long line of copyists. For like that of Chagall and of his own exact contemporary Miró — Nesch was born in 1893 at Oberesslingen — his graphic work is inimitable in all its richly varied facets, and stands independent and separate amid our period's graphic modes of expression. Though he placed himself in the front line from the start as far as technique is concerned, Nesch proceeded at first from thematic material that is closer to older, expressionist graphic art than are, say, the early pictorial ideas of Chagall — not to mention Miró. Even since the complete change that this initial pictorial world of Nesch's has undergone, its origins are still active. They fully determine the special character even of the artist's more recent graphic work, whose subjects still comprise landscapes, incidents with a dramatic or other emphasis, or a strange, adventurous, grotesque humanity. Nesch is besides an outstanding craftsman, who undertakes every operation himself. He received his first instructions at Davos in 1924 from Ernst Ludwig Kirchner, who was an excellent printer and pulled his impressions himself. These early works, produced at Hamburg, may bring to mind Nolde's magnificent harbour etchings. Likewise, the aquatint series *Karl Muck and his Orchestra* of 1931, with its vehemently silhouetted figures and instruments and its deliberately ludicrous monumentality, makes one think of those plates on which Nolde etched his mysterious world of beings from the hidden reaches of existence. True, the effects are even more forceful with Nesch, and the technical experiments are quite intentionally made perceptible. Tirelessly varying his technical processes, the artist keeps giving himself new chances of finding what seems valid and right to him. It is characteristic of his partiality for "material pictures" that a plate inadvertently bitten right through gave him the idea in 1925 of including among his formal ideas the effect of the paper swelling through the hole in the plate during printing. Only a year after the orchestra views, which, though making a violent impact on the eye, were still produced by traditional — if strained — intaglio methods, a series of bridge pictures made its appearance in an entirely new manner. To call such works prints is merely to indicate the most general principle of their technique: their true nature can only be conveyed by describing their plates. These "plates" are the first examples that no longer just consist of a flat piece of metal — even though it is still so multifariously worked — but comprise structures with a plate as their foundation, on which other, smaller, variously shaped plates are laid, tin solder is dripped, or wire is twisted. Additional elements made of punching sheets, wire gauze and pieces of zinc (the latter possibly bitten in their turn or worked with the drypoint "pencil") do not only print — that is, do not just pass on the ink spread over them to the paper; they also stamp the sheet more or less vigorously. The graphic images obtained from plates inked directly or with rollers are Pages 188, 189 thus supplemented by the shadow-trapping effects of relief printing. Constantly making new decisions, the artist applies the inks to these metal structures in such a way that every impression receives a new colour-scheme and so becomes a monotype, a unique image. One day he may decide to regard the "plate" itself as a fully valid work of art. Frontier regions between the artistic categories now show themselves to be areas of new pictorial effects. So new technical findings not only call forth ever different technical discoveries, but in the end have results going far beyond them: graphic art quite simply changes. For, by means of these techniques, Nesch now creates wall-size compositions made up of several connected prints, which, pulled from tone and line plates, present monumental images in colour-variants that are always different. In 1936 appeared the *Herring-fishing*, in 1941 the *Sebastian* and the *God the Father*, and after 1951 the tragic portrayal of the reindeer being massacred wholesale — creations grouping up to six plates in order to print over a surface about ten feet long. Even if the fresh, gaily sonorous colours of such big, graphic-cum-sculptural pictures can be realized solely through these methods developed by the artist from graphic procedures, they still have nothing in common with the shrill, violent colours of graphic art deriving from Toulouse-Lautrec. They are new and independent, like Nesch's graphic works as a whole. Since the Second World War, the artist has begun to lay colouring and shaping elements loosely on the plates so that they can be shifted about, thereby forming variants of the composition. He also keeps open the possibility of obtaining new themes from separate components of different sculpture-prints. Sometimes Nesch comes via such manipulations very close to the most recent use of form — namely, when the reality of the pictorial world conceived is so to speak identical with the reality of the chosen medium: when, for example, the veil before an old lady's face is represented with the aid of the reticulation of wire gauze. Nevertheless, this occurs — like everything with Nesch — in accordance with an entirely personal desire for expression, and thus owing to different intentions from those that lead younger artists to realize such metamorphoses. Only when taking the most general view of it can one regard Nesch's production as a sort of connecting link between expressionist and the latest graphic art; for in each individual work it stands alone and establishes wholly autonomous values.

In the wide regions about the line of demarcation between fashioning that is meant to represent objects and an independent creating of form, the most varied expressive values for graphic art are to be found. Their aspects depend in principle on how far the shapes are removed from mere descriptions of objects. Whether the artist wants to make the reference to real phenomena an explicit one, whether he is more concerned with a far-reaching assimilation of forms found in reality to abstract shapes, or whether he wishes to add purely abstract forms as an alloy to a figuration bordering on reality, such decisions have a vital influence on the result. From the various degrees of tension between artistic expressive form and real appearance results the picture's character as an illustration simply portraying the referent or as something prompting one to make associations, to form pure mental images that lead beyond what is seen to inward perceptions. How far such a work, which also aims to gain expressive operative forces from among the data of reality, is able to control bindingly what is called up in the imagination depends on the artist's power and is crucially determinant of the artistic significance of what has been produced. With inferior creative power, it can easily happen that the tension between a theme embarked on and the freely chosen formal structure attains degrees leading to implausibilities. The distance between real appearance and artistic form may be so great that a spiritual particularization of the theme is no longer present, and one can no longer believe in a possible characterization and interpretation of the subject even via association. There exists a genuine no-man's-land between representational and non-representational art.

Juan Gris, 1921

Georges Braque, 1909

Jacques Villon, 1951

Georges Braque, 1955

170

Georges Braque, 1948

Fernand Léger, ca. 1950

André Masson, 1954

Vassily Kandinsky, 1912/13

Wassily Kandinski, 1912/1913

Wassily Kandinsky, 1922

Franz Marc, 1913

Paul Klee, 1921

Klee

Paul Klee, 1915

Paul Klee, 1929

Rolf Nesch, 1956

Rolf Nesch, 1952/53

Org Litho Ophelia   Gilles 1947   Ophelia

Werner Gilles, 1947

Werner Gilles, 1919

HAP Grieshaber, 1953

Zao Wu-Ki, 1953

Max Ernst, ca. 1951

Henri Laurens, 1950

Henry Moore, 1951

196

Lynn Chadwick, 1960

Graham Vivian Sutherland, 1953

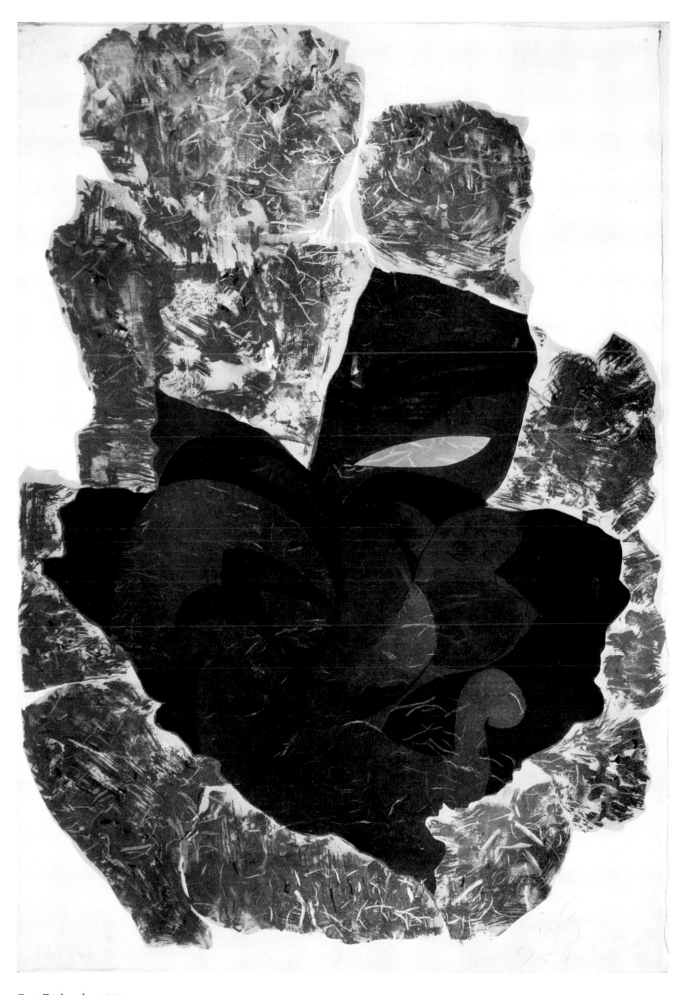

Ceri Richards, 1959

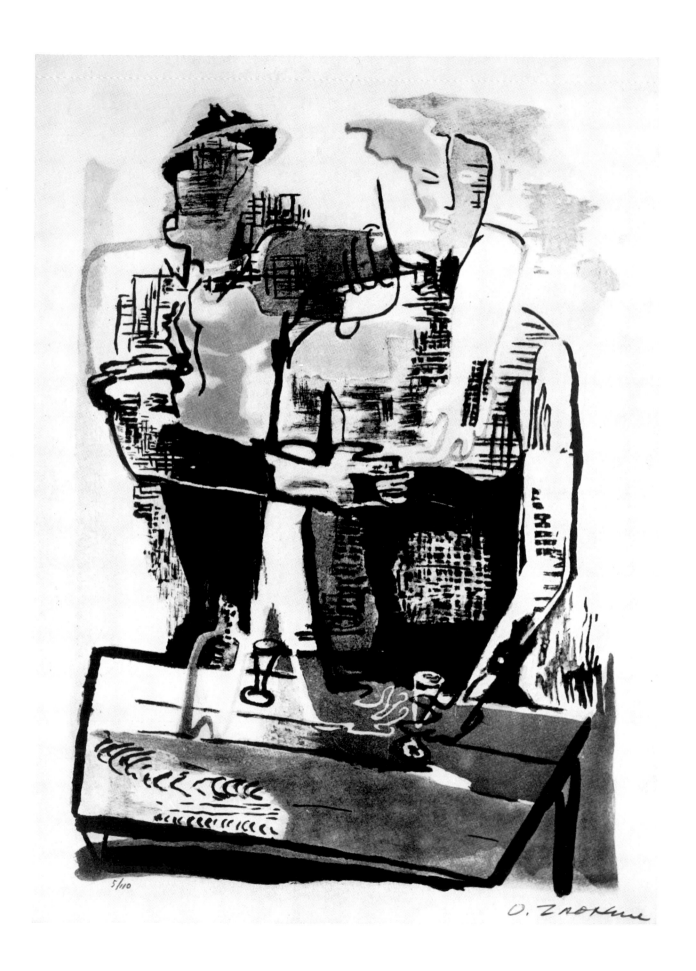

5/110

Ossip Zadkine, 1960

Marino Marini, ca. 1952

"CONCRETE" ART AND AUTONOMOUS GRAPHIC ART

It had become increasingly apparent that non-representational forms have powers of optical attraction, which, however, possess very different degrees of effectiveness, depending in each case on how the artist has treated the pure form and pure colour. A new criterion of artistic power appropriate to abstract creation obviously lay in the strength of the coerciveness with which an abstract work suggests to the eye that it is learning something significant, even though this significance evades logical definition. Not only artists readily accepted the "truth" of such effects after an initial moment of surprise (Kandinsky's approving amazement at the impact of his — still — representational picture turned upside down); even the reasonably tolerant beholder unpreoccupied with fixed aesthetic conceptions soon gave up denying them. He got used to no longer expecting only precise messages from the work of art and regarding it as a special kind of source of an information in which affective elements are certainly active, but whose content is in the last analysis determined cognitively and open to discursive judgment. He now observed that the communication between a picture and himself no longer has the character of informing, and that an abstract work has to be appraised not according to its capacity for making statements — there is nothing articulate in it — but according to its power of invocation. He found out that one could not get to understand such works via statements verifiable by reference to something or other directly given. So, in view of this new pictorial optics, there emerged quite logically from the thought on aesthetics determined by the form-content dualism the question: "Does form not directly depend on something that, for its part, is not form?"

Most answers given during the early days of abstract creation were in the affirmative. Even if they had ceased to regard as a characteristic feature of the work of art its property of being the figuration of a content both relatable to something real and definable in words, people still saw in art a world of expression confronting the real world. In fact, they viewed the work of art as a fashioned object expressing something spiritually significant, which means that they kept in principle to the form-content idea — basically, therefore, to the very trend of thought through which art had previously been "explained". Only now, as this idea was adapted in modern art, a "spirit-form" confronts the nature-form. If one called this spirit-form "abstract", it meant that one was still linking it too closely with the nature-form from which it had been abstracted. What seemed important was, on the contrary, to affirm the absolute polarity of spirit- and nature-form and to insist that the spirit-form wrongly called "abstract" is just as "real" as concrete form. This is why Theo van Doesburg's manifesto of 1930 contains, and it is an extremely pithy remark, the proposition: "... nothing is more concrete, more real than a line, a colour, a surface." Since "concrete" art was thus conceived as a human world of expression, it had a natural correlation with the foundations of human experience, and the question was therefore inevitably raised of whether fixed relations exist between specific pure form- and colour-elements and specific contents within the broad compass of what could be experienced. Psychological research endeavoured to establish "primary phenomena of vision", and finally concluded that a particular experiential content could not be clearly associated with particular "concrete" forms and colours, though, to be sure, the expressive scope of given "concrete" forms proved wholly circumscribed and did not get lost in vagueness. People were inclined to accept that dynamic processes in the sphere of contemplable forms could show a certain relationship to vitalistic ones in the human psyche. Conclusions of this kind have basic similarities with the conviction often voiced by non-figurative painters that the world of phenomena is incapable of undergoing any real transformation — one, that is to say, which changes its very nature and exposes its inner core. Intuitions of the forces hidden behind the phenomenal world or intimations of cosmological processes can, however, be paraphrased in giving form. With this, art becomes a means of widening experience, and it is understandable that the demand was made again and again that new forms be devised so as to accommodate new knowledge-like mental representations. For when abstract art no longer felt bound to portray what had already taken shape and thus to be content with surfaces, it boldly set about exploring the essence of things, which is in no respect identical with their fully developed external form. In so doing, it proceeded — to adopt a comparison much used at the time — in an "unspoilt" way like "primitive peoples", whose eye is not yet burdened by the rational assimilation of external data, and who seek to represent the "spirit of the fire", not the fire itself.

This conception of the nature and power of pure form also includes the expressive intent from which artistic creation now obtains its deeper meaning. Formal elements are no longer hung on the rack of nature-forms. Hence they no longer generate via an *a priori* content, from within a given motif therefore, that substance which constitutes the essential quality of the work of art. Colours, lines and forms are put together as an abstract organization in which these visual elements condense into an intellectual significance without giving rise to the notion of an object. This type of pictorial action is performed above all in order to master the phenomenon world. The task of art is now to interpret reality while avoiding the data of its appearance that distract one from what is "essential". Art arises out of contemplative behaviour and reflects, through this aesthetic contemplation, on forces and principles in the groundwork of existence.

Both the new employment of absolute forms and the ideas conceived for giving meaning to these completely changed pictorial figurations were prefaced by a deliverance from obstructive conventions, and, at the time, the joyous sense of release infiltrated thought and action alike. An impulse that frequently provokes artistic creation today was already then, at the beginning of non-representational art, quite often of contributive influence. As much more commonly now, one is bound to see here and there in the artistic activity of that period above all a positive reaction to the puppet-like behaviour prescribed for the individual in his every movement on the fully ordered stage of social life. Such activity is often a deliberate turning away from directed or trained action and an unmediated display of natural abilities developed from individual talent. This wish to decide without being bound by any rules, this desire for spontaneous expression, makes the constant search for new forms that marks the behaviour of many modern artists comprehensible from here as well.

Seen in relation to these drafts and proposals for pictorial activity, modern graphic art's richly facetted appearance, which comprises disparates, becomes clear. Everywhere graphic art was helping to realize very unusual, very bold desires, for whose embodiment often not even the bare outline of a formal conception was on hand. Further, graphic technique undertook repeated trials, and probed opportunities for achieving new surface qualities and structural states that lie beyond the range of painterly methods. Graphic art received wholly specific commissions, however, in consequence of an ever-growing tendency already noticeable at the time of the first experiments with abstract forms. It appears in the change of character undergone by the work of art as a material object. Canvas and paint layer, sheet and impressed mass of ink, had had no part until then in the intellectual intention of the work. It accorded with the picture's illusional quality (which perforce involved a denial of the picture surface, since it treated the frame of the picture as a window-frame through which one looked into an illusionistic space) to exclude support and paint — as also the materials pertaining to the graphic image: paper and ink — from the mental space in which forms become pictorial phenomena. In the attempt to exclude illusionistic references to reality, however, the nature of the material creation, whether painted or printed, changed. From the sphere to which it belonged as a mere precondition of results occurring in the mind, from its function of just being a component of the work of art that, though necessary for technical reasons, did not participate in the aesthetic outcome, this product struggled forth to become an integrant factor of the artistic effect itself. Hitherto a prerequisite to reproducing an artistic idea, the painting as a thing or the print as matter now took on the character of an artistic object. Just as art itself no longer wants to be a commentating interpreter of outward appearances and tries instead to provide from the autonomy of its own aspect equivalents for the invisible, so the material structure wishes to be released from its ancillary duty of being a vehicle of expression not itself present to the mind. At the same time there began a deliberate blurring of the artistic categories. Surface values turned into sculptural ones, printing-pigments into plasticine for spatial structures. Hans Arp has indicated such metamorphic tendencies with a cogent sentence: "I find a picture that has not had an object as its model just as concrete as a leaf and a stone." With ever-renewed attempts, graphic art plays its part in actualizing this new intention.

Their changed tasks have set the graphic methods astir. Already widened so as to be able to bestow on the planar print any timely expression, they now work up active components that go beyond two-dimensional effects, and in so doing develop instruments no longer serving strictly graphic purposes. It is correct that, in the radical experiments, the influence of the graphic means as such on the artist's decision continually grows, and that — here again following a latent bent of modern graphic creation — precisely in graphic activity a planned outcome is not always awaited; for the final appearance of the print often depends on the artist's *placet*, on his approval of a particular look among the many that succeed each other in a more or less influenceable process of change during the printing operations. It is also correct that, with the newly inaugurated use of the graphic technique, the printers frequently play a crucial part in determining how the end-result turns out (as has already happened once, at the time when graphic art began to be independent), and that co-operation between artist and printer is absolutely necessary for certain processes. Less inclined to violate the system of craft practices, the printers have none the less given a sympathetic reception to those aims of the artist that go beyond the bounds of customary techniques, and have helped to realize them by applying their great experience. Modern graphic art, especially that involving colour, would not hold so many vitally important posts in the association of modern art forms, but for the encouragement and support it has received in, say, the graphic studios of Lacourière, Mourlot and Visot in Paris.

Extending the graphic possibilities, already so rich, now furthers above all the transformation of the graphic structure from a pure bearer of an image into an independent artistic object. The application of ultra-"graphic" inks having always been widely varied through the alternate use of ductile and viscous colouring substances, of dry and damp paper, the graphic artist now gives his mind chiefly to building up a surface in relief with a depth made up of many layers. Certain questions arouse interest. Where does the line lie: in the sheet or on it? What is the surface like: smooth or rough? In which planes are the different colours operative, and how does one applied later stand in relation to that laid on before it? With an exceptionally fruitful systematics, Stanley William Hayter and his Atelier 17 have taken such considerations Pages 239, 241 as a basis in developing new technical treatments for etching and copper-engraving. Starting out from the idea that graphic technique, when it does not sink to the level of a mere means of reproduction, constitutes an integral part of graphic activity, and is indeed in a certain sense its very condition, as its pondered use wakens the artistic imagination, Hayter claims that, by getting thoroughly acquainted with his technical means, the artist can foresee and employ their effects as a composer puts together a score through knowing the character of the separate instruments. In particular, Hayter sets store by an exact spatial localization of the individual active elements within the depth of the ink layers covering the sheet. For this reason, he evolved in many experiments a method allowing several expanses of colour, varied planar bitings and engraved lines to be produced on one and the same plate. This he regards as important because the plate does not change its size, whereas a damp sheet of paper printed over in a number of operations from different plates stretches, and hence does not permit the accurate placing of graphic accents. The artist also attaches weight to deciding beforehand what effects are to appear as a result of laying on several colours in superimposed strata: whether one shall be allowed to hide another or whether, applied transparently, it shall let the one below co-operate in producing a third, new effect. To achieve such glaze effects, the viscosity of the colouring matter is determined with precision. So that ink layers applied later shall remain active in the print, even though modified, the earlier ones have to be less viscous, in fact more fluid, than those following them. All the inks must, again, be less gluey than the copper-engraving black that establishes the lineation. During 1947 at Atelier 17, Joan Miró worked several plates in such a way that, through biting, they obtained two printing surfaces at different levels. For each of them, different ink was used. Line-engraving ink was, say, applied at the lower level and the still unworked upper surface was spread with one or even several glazing colours by means of a roller that, being hard, did not press into the hollows already filled with black ink. Thus, on a plate prepared in this way, sundry colour strata lie one over another, and below them in the deepest hollows comes the line-engraving ink. It is the other way round with the print. On the paper, the engraved work forms a relief whose greatest heights are determined by the profound grooves of the burin, and whose minor prominences correspond to the more shallowly engraved or the etched textures. Then, below these, lie the succession of colour layers. The variableness of the lineation was likewise increased through an effective process involving a wax unable to resist the mordant in all circumstances; it gradually disappears under the action of the nitric acid. However, a slowly drawn line brings on to the plate enough of this substance to stop this action altogether. Such lines therefore appear white in the print. Quickly drawn lines, on the contrary, yield a smaller application of wax. The acid is consequently able to eat through the varyingly thick layer of wax at certain points, and so produce more or less scattered bitten patches. In a single movement, but one of varying speed, a line can thus be made to pass from black to white via grey, depending on the current swiftness of the gesture.

Among the many treatments, these have been cited as examples because they still issue from essentially graphic processes and, in the broadest sense, remain within the latter's compass. Other more "bold" and reckless procedures were eagerly adopted by other artists, some after they had been learnt from "mistakes". Like a sudden invasion of explosive foreign bodies, they burst the old, ensured methods of graphic action, leading the print-orientated projects to the furthest bounds, and then even beyond them into the realms of different artistic categories: biting through the plate to produce bold relief, for instance, or giving relief to the plate by laying on it such things as wire, punching steel, and variously shaped flat bits of metal — procedures that, with Nesch, demonstrate the permutability of the artistic kinds in the logical emergence of the material picture. Provided with colours, framed, and intended to make a direct impact, a printing plate of Nesch's consistently changes its artistic nature, whereas a line-engraving plate of Dürer's, gilded and framed in the seventeenth century, remains an image like the prints previously struck off from it. Printing from loose, movable pieces of metal laid over a flat support also has a different meaning today from that of a similar process used, for example, by Henri Guérard in Paris around 1895. He silhouetted masks in metal and placed them on engraving plates so that, under the strong pressure of the press, the damp paper swelled through the cut-out apertures of the eyes and mouths, arching up at these points in the print: the result was then a picture-like low relief. Page 189

A lithography endowed with stupendous ability, and the versatile techniques of intaglio and relief printing that are often combined, not only make it hard for the artist to control the final aesthetic result, but at times give rise in the beholder as well to fundamental reflections, which can in certain cases come to a head in the question as to whether he is still looking at an original at all. The concept "original" must indubitably be widened, if one is not to forego numerous expressive virtues of modern graphic art. As, however, many artists autograph prints whose plates have been made by someone else after original works that the signing artist has indeed produced, but by a different method and in only one example — as, then, such a signature really does no more than indicate the artist's approval of the reproduction's quality, doubts issuing from the love of many collectors for genuine graphic art have led to new definitions of what alone may be regarded as truly original graphic work. Very helpful and clear is the one formulated with forceful brevity in 1960 by the Print Council of America, an association founded in 1956 of print collectors, artists, art dealers and the directors and curators of leading American art galleries. According to this definition, a work of graphic art is an "original print" when the following conditions are satisfied:

1. The artist alone has made the image in or upon the plate, stone, wood-block or other material, for the purpose of creating a work of graphic art.
2. The impression has been made directly from that original material by the artist or pursuant to his directions.
3. The finished print is approved by the artist.

The rules that the Internationale Kongress für bildende Kunst laid down the same year at Vienna are slightly more precise. According to them, the artist alone is to decide how large the edition shall be, and also to record on each impression the size of the edition and the number of the print within it. Prints taken from blocks not made by the artist himself should not only be considered reproductions but also marked as such. This marking ought especially to be undertaken in the case of those reproductions whose quality is so high that, wishing to show his appreciation of the printer's work, the artist feels justified in signing them. It was generally agreed that, if an image drawn on transfer-paper is conveyed to the stone by a non-photographic process, then the artist must be deemed its author; and that proofs showing unfinished states are not to be regarded as part of an edition.

From very diverse notions of the meaning of artistic creation and with a reach of variation in the expressive forms that embraces extremes, graphic works are now being produced in abundance. The relationship between form and content is determined less than ever before by fixed associations, and a single formal canon in an artist's work is often expected to decode different ranges of content, just as, conversely, an attempt is made to depict a specific theme by means of various formal systems. If "real" contents formerly made it possible to verify the artist's intentions, this check, supposedly providing measurable data, in fact related at most to what the artist had in mind. Its findings referred solely to thematic factors; it was unable to make any pronouncement about the grade of the artistic figuration of the "real" content. The fact that such tests can no longer be undertaken in present-day art does not prevent us from having access to its artistic value. It is a question of a necessary consequence of the attempt to make statements by artistic figuration in a spiritual space that has meanwhile undergone a considerable extension of its limits, and thus makes finding one's way about by no means easy. The indication once given by a work's describable content of the formative aim's approximate direction is bound to be omitted with an art that wishes to present something articulable through its medium, and in no other way. For this reason, reflections on the essential starting-points and fundamental lines of sight in graphic creation lead further today than a series of separate studies of particular artists' œuvres could do, especially since — as has also occurred at times in the past — the personal decisions of many artists, harassed by inner contradictions, often show no uniform tendency. Besides, a study aiming at monographs on œuvres would in the present situation of the visual arts frequently result in a mere description of form.

STRUCTURALISM AND AUTOMATISM
NEW OBJECTIVE REFERENCES AND FIGURATION

In "abstract" art, classes of pictorial aims can of course still only be inferred from the appearance of the form itself, and only become "visible" in the particular character of this appearance. As in painting, the contrast in the graphic arts between form structures built with rectangular, geometric elements and form conglomerates of curving lines or amorphous creation is at present most clearly marked. Not only does one observe this polarity from a purely formal standpoint again and again, but for each of the formal groups there are also, in the mind of the artist committed to them, special interpretations, which shows how very deliberate is the use of a particular formal group on a particular occasion. All this naturally does not mean that pictorial activity is wholly confined by this dualism in the character of form. Now, as at every phase of the development we have studied, art is not tied down to principles, and it very frequently offers results fully valid in themselves that point to evident obscurings of the boundaries, inasmuch as they let themselves take shape anywhere within the field of force between these poles.

Behind a configuration that avails itself mostly of constructive forms and that aims to make manifest in the composition an immanent regularity, one can generally surmise the presence of rational operative factors. Time and again, the rigorously constructive artist claims to convert the inner structure of the universe into a viewable equivalent, and thereby demonstrates not his sharing in, but his sympathy with modern physics's ideas of structure. His pictorial formulations are thus intended as messages about a common intellectual experience. It is a question here of creative activity descending from those conceptions that have accompanied abstract art since the very beginning and seek possibilities of communication between non-representational forms and the inmost essentials of the cosmos. This principle of artistic creation parallel to nature appears more wide-ranging in attempts to suggest rhythms in cosmic happenings by means of rhythmic configurations, and so make "autonomous principles" of existence the *primum mobile* of formative action. Through submergence in the form-moulding primary forces that increasingly reveal themselves to natural science in, say, electric waves, diverse fields of force, or processes of crystallization, the artist would like to press forward to an experience of universal predicates that, while of a higher nature than things, constitute their foundations. For he tries to provide analogues of these primary forces by using formal events. As, therefore, dynamic occurrences or universal properties have now become the subject-matter of pictures, new images are nearly always given "abstract" titles: *Agitated, Fiery, Calming, Wintery, Rising, Extinguishing,* and so on. Moreover, there is a special variant among these pictorial analogues whose beginnings are already apparent in romantic subjects: analogues for the processes active behind all phenomena. At the start of the last century, they were, of course, still realized through objects interpreted symbolically. Then as now, the pictorial theme set its sights on polarities and phases in the activity of nature — aimed, that is, at presenting an aggregative event manifest in every happening of existence. Unlike the romantic, the artist of today does not convey with "hieroglyphs" his knowledge of the action of conflicting forces, his thoughts on tension and balance in the creative processes of the cosmos, but through a composition built of "concrete" formal elements, whose immaterial qualities such as slackness, tenseness, denseness and diffuseness are brought into play. The general look of the picture may then be determined by tension or equalization or even the combined effect of both states. Pictorial arrangements of formal contrasts are often based upon ideas of equilibrium in the universe, as, through neutralizing such formal contrasts by compositional means, the artist aims to catch a clear reflection of the cosmic balance of opposing forces.

Such pictorial paraphrases of "pre-material" states, situations and qualities, of equilibrium functions and creative tendencies, always issue from conscious principles of order. The artist adjusts the creative process in accordance with an organizational scheme that enables him to control his action. He moves towards a planned result. Usually a "purist", he regards the inclusion of anything emotional as downright sacrilege in relation to his art, which calls for asceticism, reflection and severe formal order. The artistic value of such projections is thus not measured by the expressive strength with which a feeling manifests itself in the picture, but fixed by the purity of the forms and the inner logic with which they show themselves to be variants of a formal type or pattern.

Decisive is the degree of the formal consistency, a consistency that now, however, can differ greatly in structure. But since colours cannot strictly speaking be given a structure — though attempts have already been made to establish for them a circle of equal values that would be a kind of psychological colour circle confronting the physical one of the spectrum — it is above all the pronouncedly graphic artists who incline to structural compositions. Yet the latest representatives of "structuralism" often no longer deem their constructions to be pictorial allusions to something that lies beyond the form. Structures are thus looked upon by many young artists as things of intrinsic value, and not as antitypes of imaginable basic models of universal constructings or processes. From this moment, form has given up its task of being a bearer of meaning. The work of art, become fully autonomous, draws its significance exclusively from the constructive impetus as such. Here the break with earlier views deriving from representational art has been finally completed. Out of "abstract" art, a "concrete" one has now come into being on the programmatic plane as well. A creative activity begins that, building on intelligible foundations, deliberately keeps aloof from those inducements to figuration that can only be referred to metaphorically, and for which names like "Inspiration" and appeals to mythological creators like the Muses or psychic controllers like the affective forces were formerly introduced. Such reasons for artistic action are now regarded as "collective illusions"; they are considered too vague and disposed of as animistic, prelogical or magical thinking. At most it is conceded that "feeling" is not to be separated from other human mental functions and that accordingly it is quite impossible to oppose the emotional to the intellectual — a conclusion whereby an art that is "just feeling" appears to be ruled out in its turn. Artistic creation is based rather on organized knowledge and concerns the arrangement of parts. Proceeding as it does mainly from contrasts and similarities of form, artistic pictorial organization means building structures of formal gradations or establishing relations between formal sequences, in the course of which a formal continuum — at times extremely lively in its rhythm — has to be achieved. It is a question, therefore, of a "canalized imagination" that deliberately sets itself tasks, and thereby at the same time fixes the limits needed to exclude from the very start a free-flowing phantasy with its immeasurable and only "believed" results. Task and limit thus form the actual preconditions of the emergence of artistic qualities, since it is only through them that the criteria for judging the pictorial value of what is to be created are given. This process presupposes an extensive knowledge of the principles of graphic construction, and hence shows a certain kinship with modern ideas in music, poetry, dancing and mathematics. Knowledge of this kind, so one often hears in artistic circles, is at present much less widespread than that concerning the representation of an object. Credent enthusiasm as an artistic ethos has had finally to give way to an ethos of rigorously planned construction. Art now appears just as "freed from mystery" as so many other activities of modern man.

Wholly self-referent, the world of forms now acquires meaning from itself. In interpretations of works like this, the forms are therefore often regarded as figures acting out a formal drama. It is understandable that picture contents whose message appears so very much tied to the form itself that it really and truly coincides with the forms, cannot put up much resistance, and in actual fact have often ceased to be considered the object of artistic creation. Accordingly, the products of *art informel* are indeed no longer tendent compositions. The configurating of such freely realized, ungeometric and amorphous forms does not take place in the wake of a visual experience or a pictorial idea, but constitutes the sum of the traces left behind by a spontaneous and often eruptive action. Not just the ordering of representational forms, not just their gradation and their arrangement determined by emphases are given up; the forms themselves have dissolved into a flowing and eddying of motional projections. In extreme cases, the opposition of form and colour as well as that of form and plane is abolished. All that remains in tachism is the *tache*, the patch in the most general sense of a trace. The word "painterly" comes forcibly to mind when one looks at such "cast" phenomena, although one knows that this quality certainly is not intended, but automatically suggests itself because one sees no construction, no counterpoint of forms, no arrangement of interlocking planes. Charles Estienne, the founder of the Nouvelle Ecole de Paris, also had a leading say in connection with these Page 223 "Significants de l'Informel". Undoubtedly, Wols (Wolfgang Schulze) has provided widely effective stimuli in his hair-thin lines that, nervous, tangled, crumpled, get driven hither and thither. But with all those artists who obey direct inner commands, a personal handwriting Page 235 is to be found, as, say, in Hans Hartung's differentiation of his *graphismes*, in Hann Trier's Page 243 overnetting of the form ground, or in Sonderborg's ebullient streams of energy, to mention highly Page 237 contrasting painters. One can understand that artists who, in their subjective gesturing with no matter what instruments, which record some motional impulse or other in some way or other — that these *informels* see in the planned creation of the structuralist merely a "cold" activity detached from the *élan vital* and hence without substance. For them, the process of making becomes the essential point of figuration and takes the place of content. "Painting is an event, an occurrence for experiencing the certainty of one's own existence." "If I start out from neither an idea nor an object," says Serge Poliakoff, "then the most essential thing, the expression of my self, remains in the non-representational composition."

Programmes, theories and artistic fact belong together, though this does not mean that they really correspond. The true value of the results of new concepts is seldom ascertained while they are in action. Inconsistencies among present-day artistic ideas have often been pointed out. How far they can provide a basis for genuine objections to the pictorial endeavours of our times remains in question. Doubts have been expressed as to whether it is not frequently a case of overdrawing artistic possibilities. Far from having always been raised unreflectingly and just dismissingly in a dogmatic spirit (although this has happened as well), such doubts have often resulted from genuine uneasiness and mental labour aware of its responsibilities. But disquiet about the art of one's own period is also found in the past, and then too it was not just expressed by those devoid of understanding through want of effort. Attention has been drawn to the inconsistency between the view that artistic action must be regarded as a verification of one's own existence — "I act, therefore, I am" (Appel) — and is therefore not directed towards a result, and the assertion that a work of art is an independent object of autonomous thingness. We have been made to reflect that, when Platschek postulated the "suspension of causal thought" in the creative process, he probably actually abolished with this demand the basic conditions of all creative activity, because doing is always working towards a result, even though this is by no means everywhere determinable in advance.

Even if not unswervingly, artistic effort proceeds without interruption: as a whole, accepting the element of uncertainty "be that as it may", and for the individual, according to more or less precise ideas — just as it always has. Today, at all events, it takes place between settings some of which have been sketched in outline here. It seems, though this remains a personal opinion, as if the feeling for the thingish significance of the graphic material as well is particularly operative in the work of etchers and engravers like Adam, Friedlaender, Hayter, Heyboer, Hartung, Peterdi, Soulages and Courtin, and as if, on the contrary, the significance of the pure plane is especially felt by artists like Arp and Meistermann, who for that very reason use lithography or planar etching. The Nouvelle Ecole de Paris — which is not really formative of style, since in it many varied forces meet and interact, without, however, losing their genuine qualities—is distinguished by the clean look and great refinement of its creations. Perhaps a contribution is made to this stirling perfection of its graphic works by the fact that the findings of abstract art reached Paris relatively late and only took effect when the clumsiness of its beginnings, but also the vehemence of its *Sturm und Drang* period, had long ago been overcome and subdued. Not until after the last war did the Paris School reveal its noble splendour, which, much and variously faceted, shines forth in the prints of Bissière, Bazaine, Estève, Le Moal, Manessier, Pignon, Poliakoff, Singier, Soulages, de Staël, Ubac, Vasarely and Vieira da Silva.

Pages 220, 226, 239, 250, 235, 238, 234, 224, 218, 219

Pages 233, 230, 236, 231, 245, 227, 229, 247, 226

Meanwhile, the view that, because of its pure formal character, art should have no "external relations" whatever has in many cases been given up. Yet the young advocates of a conception that again allows extra-formal elements to be included in the complex of artistic creation still attach great importance to emphasizing explicitly something basically obvious, namely that their fresh starts are in nowise a revival of the old "literary" contents. Thus strongly is the introduction of abstract forms felt even now to be a revolutionary act able, as it were, to lay bare what is artistic in art. With Schumacher and Dahmen, say, the formal structures focus on new, determinate factual situations, which can only be termed content in so far as these facts manifest themselves objectively. Related to earthly matter, "telluric" creations are intended as allusions to a primitive antiquity, which, of a geological character, is symbolized as something timeless and spaceless in the surface and its relief. To this "actual archaism", K. O. Götz, Sonderborg, Thieler and Platschek oppose a paraphrase of space that strives for a similar independence of the spaces presented at any given moment as we experience reality, and that hence contrives an antitype of spatiality, which can only be represented through handling "purely artistic" means. With these, it is not a question of using graphic instruments to produce any image of any space lighted upon, but of creating spatiality in general primarily through movements executed by implements as they draw. Also pointing beyond mere thing references to a new kind of "message", works like Willi Baumeister's or many by Ubac, Schumacher and Dahmen show textures that recall the weathering of masonry: object-tied surface appearances in which the history of the thing wall has found an indirect expression, just as has the history of the earth's surface in the scriptorial traces that, after being recorded in the ground by man and beast, wind and water, recast themselves in prints by Tapies as graphic signs. There is

Page 225

Page 219

Page 250 a connection here with the *objet trouvé* and its strange advices, a link with the suggestions that a "found" object in its phenomenic purity can give to the artist. It is a call that would be lost were its receiver to present the "found" object in natural association with other things, or in the logical frame of its intrinsic or practical significance. Mindful, as regards compo-Page 198 sition, of the material and spiritual isolation of the *objet trouvé*, an artist like Graham Sutherland is able in his graphic works to win new visual experiences from it. Sometimes, on these textures of mineral substances from a remote geological antiquity, on these beautiful grounds attacked by solvent processes, injured by traces, and covered in scars, hints of figurative shapes Pages 248, 249 become visible again and, recorded in a timorous script, help the prints of Jean Dubuffet to achieve via new "subjects" a visual poetry that no longer has any contact with the realm of literature.

The search for certainties numbers among the primary undertakings of the human spirit in its struggle for self-affirmation. Already early on, therefore, it formed supposedly convincing "theories of the fine arts", which the course followed by these arts has now wholly confuted. People have also tried time and again to define what graphic art really is, and, time and again, they have succeeded — in ever different ways. If one asks the excited and lively young artists of our days about the meaning of their creative activity, one will get answers sounding very certain and will probably be assured as well that "now at last we have arrived"... So long as genuine conviction supports these avowals, they contain truth: their truth. But how all these notions, conceptions and postulates, and the expressive forms and the figurations obtained from them, are to be ranged in the scale of artistic values depends entirely upon the demand our spirit makes on art. Here there are no binding instructions.

Gino Severini, ca. 1954

Hans Arp, 1960

rechts oben: Willi Baumeister, ca. 1944
rechts unten: Georg Meistermann, 1953

220

Henri-Georges Adam, 1952

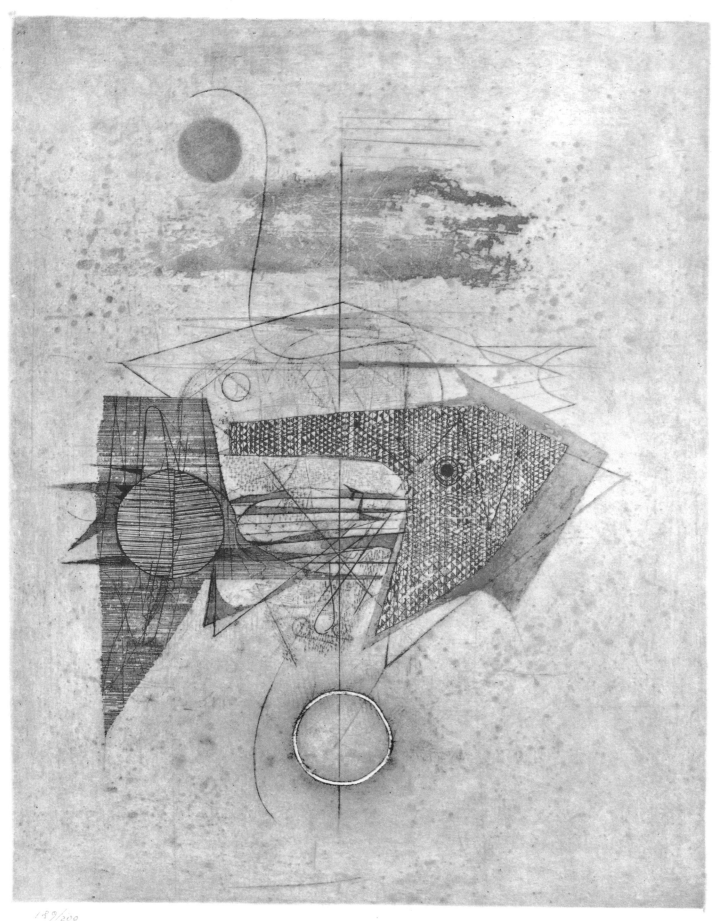

187/200

Johnny Friedlaender, 1955

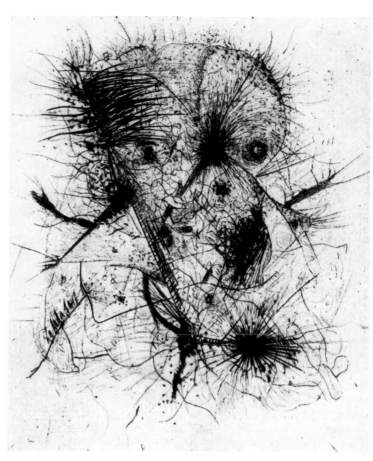

Wols, ca. 1945

Wols, ca. 1950

223

Pierre Courtin, 1959

Emil Schumacher, 1958

Victor Vasarely, 1961

Gustave Singier, 1957

Gustave Singier, 1951

Jean Bazaine, 1953

Alfred Manessier, ca. 1954

Roger Bissière, ca. 1956

Pierre Soulages, ca. 1957

Hans Hartung, 1954

Maurice Estève,
1956

Fritz Winter,
ca. 1952

K. R. H. Sonderborg, 1958

Joseph Faßbender, 1957

238

33/200

SWHayter 56

Stanley William Hayter, 1954

239

Gabor Peterdi, 1959

Stanley William Hayter, 1946

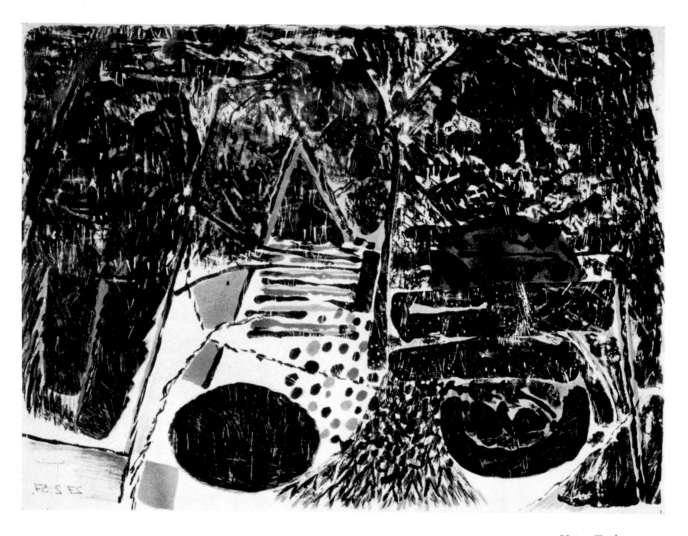

Heinz Trökes, 1957

Joan Vila-Casas, ca. 1959

Hann Trier, 1957

Hans Jaenisch, 1959

Serge Poliakoff, ca. 1955

Raoul Ubac, 1958

Jean Dubuffet, 1953

Jean Dubuffet, 1959

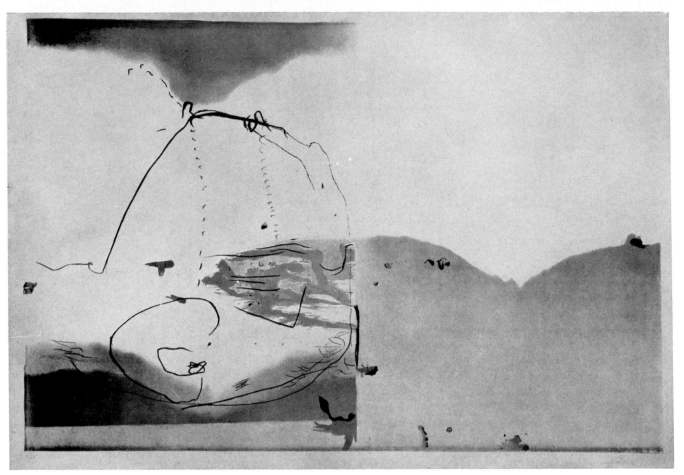

Antoni Tàpies, ca. 1959

Anton Heyboer, 1959

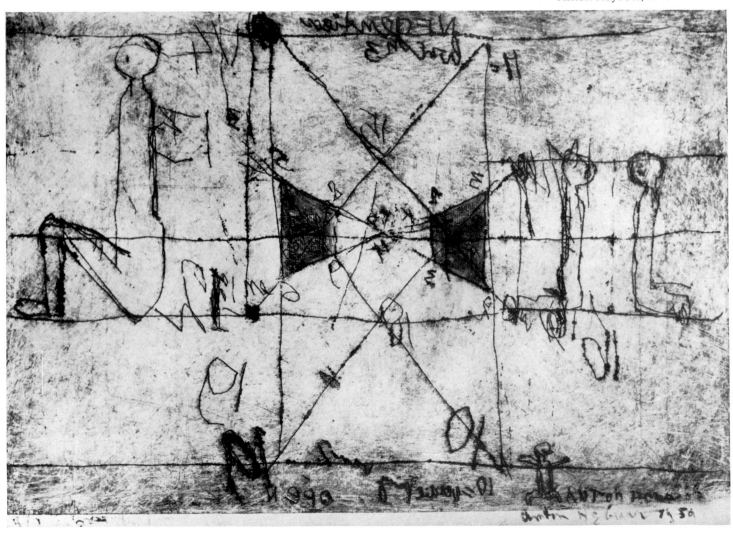

BIOGRAPHIES

COMPILED BY KURT STERNELLE

The literature mentioned comprises only a narrow selection. As a rule, the information is limited to an authoritative monograph or a dictionary article and to a complete catalogue, if one exists. Articles in periodicals are only cited now and then. For the younger artists, one is often dependent on exhibition catalogues. In the case of well-known artists, too, the catalogues of the big retrospective shows with their chronologies and bibliographies are very helpful.

ABBREVIATIONS

BENEZIT — Emmanuel Bénézit, Dictionnaire des peintres, sculpteurs, dessinateurs et graveurs, new ed., 8 vols, Paris 1948—55.

DELTEIL — Loys Delteil, Le Peintre-graveur illustré (XIXe et XXe siècles), 31 vols, Paris, 1906—26.

DORIVAL — Bernard Dorival, Les peintres du XXe siècle, 2 vols, Paris, 1957.

SERVOLINI — Luigi Servolini, Dizionario illustrato degli incisori italiani moderni e contemporanei, Milan, 1955.

THIEME-BECKER — Allgemeines Lexikon der Bildenden Künstler von den Anfängen bis zur Gegenwart, founded by Ulrich Thieme and Felix Becker, 37 vols, Leipzig, 1907—50.

VOLLMER — Allgemeines Lexikon der Bildenden Künstler des XX. Jahrhunderts, ed. by Hans Vollmer, 6 vols, Leipzig 1953-62.

ABRAMO, Livio — Lives at São Paulo, where he was born in 1903. A self-taught artist. First show in 1942. At the 2nd São Paulo biennial exhibition in 1953 won prize as "best national graphic artist". Since 1950 represented at the Venice Biennales and the big exhibitions of Brasilian artists in Europe and Tokyo.
Lit: Cat. of the exhibition of Brasilian art at Munich and Hamburg in 1959—60.

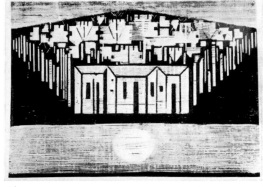
Abramo

ADAM, Henri-Georges — Born on 18 January 1904 in Paris into a family of goldsmiths. Began as a draughtsman and painter. Later a sculptor, graphic artist, and tapestry designer. First sculptural works during the Second World War, first abstract sculpture in 1947. From 1947—49 stayed with Picasso at Boisgeloup. The earliest tapestry cartoons belong to these years. Graphic works since 1934. First works with cut-out plates in 1952. International graphic art prizes: 1953 São Paulo, 1957 Ljubljana (Laibach) and Tokyo. Lives in Paris.
Lit: *Catalogue de l'œuvre gravée, 1939—57*, La Hune, Paris, 1957 (120 works listed)   *Ill. p. 220*

AFRO (Basaldella, Afro) — Born on 4 March 1912 at Udine, the younger brother of the abstract sculptor Mirco (Basaldella). Studied at Venice and Florence. To Paris in 1937, then went to Rome. From 1941—44 taught at the Venice Academy. In Rome since 1948. One of Italy's leading abstract painters.
Lit: L. Venturi, *Painting in Italy*, London, 1959; James Johnson Sweeney, *Afro*, Rome, 1962 (German ed., Hamburg, 1962).

Adam

APPEL, Karel — Born on 25 April 1921 at Amsterdam, where he attended the Academy from 1940—43 and in 1948 became a co-founder of the Dutch "Experimental Group". In 1949 and after represented in the COBRA exhibition (young painters from Copenhagen, Brussels and Amsterdam) and all major exhibitions of modern art. Living in Paris since 1950.
Lit: R. Nacenta, *School of Paris*, London, 1960.

ARMITAGE, Kenneth — Born in 1916 in Leeds, the artist studied at the Slade School, London. After the war, he taught sculpture from 1946—56 at the Bath Academy of Art, and from 1953—55 held the Gregory Fellowship in Sculpture at Leeds University. Exhibited at the 26th Venice Biennale in 1952 and since then in the big international shows. Won the prize at the 5th international exhibition of drawing and graphic art at Lugano in 1958.
Lit: R. Penrose, *Kenneth Armitage*, London, 1960; *A Dictionary of Modern Sculpture*, London, 1962.

Afro

ARP, Hans (Jean) — Born on 16 September 1887 in Strasbourg. Lives at Meudon near Paris. Studied in Weimar and Paris. Active in the crucial art movements of Germany and France: 1912 with the *Blaue Reiter* group at Munich, 1913 in connection with *Der Sturm* at Berlin, 1914 in Apollinaire's circle in Paris. Co-founder of "Dada" at Zurich in 1916 during the war; Cologne Dada in 1920 with Max Ernst. Moved to Meudon in 1926 with his wife, the painter Sophie Taeuber. From 1926 to 1930 a member of the surrealist group; then belonged to the Circle and Square and Abstraction-Creation groups (1930—31). Fled in 1940 to Grasse in southern France. Spent 1942—45 in Switzerland, where his wife died in 1943. Returned to Meudon in 1945. Arp is both a visual artist and a writer. With his sculptures, reliefs and *collages*, he has inspiringly enriched the formal vocabulary of abstract art. Literary works: poems and essays in German and French. Graphics: Arp prefers woodcut, it being the technique that suits him. Comparatively few lithographs and etchings.
Lit: Full bibliography in his *On My Way*, New York, 1948; C. Giedion Welcker, *Hans Arp*, London, 1957 (with cat. of the sculpture and bibl. by M. Hagenbach); J. T. Soby, cat. monogr. for an exhibition (with bibl.), Museum of Modern Art, New York, 1958; *Hans Arp Graphik 1912—1959*, Klipstein and Kornfeld cat., Bern, 1959.   *Ill. p. 218*

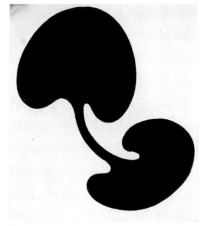
Arp

Armitage

Appel

Atlan

Bargheer

Bartolini

ATLAN, Jean — Born on 23 January 1913 at Constantine in Algeria, this artist of Judeo-Berber descent went to Paris in 1930, took a degree in philosophy at the Sorbonne, then wrote poems, and began to paint in 1941. During the war, he lived hidden away as a patient at St Anne's Hospital. His book of poems *Le Sang profond* appeared in 1944 at the time of the first exhibition of his pictures. In 1945 lithographs for Kafka's *Description of a Battle*. Died on 12 February 1960.
Lit: André Verdet, *Atlan*, London, 1957.

BARGHEER, Eduard — Born on 25 December 1901 on the Elbe island Finkenwärder, near Hamburg. After a brief period of instruction from the Hamburg painter Ahlers-Hestermann, self-taught on many visits to Italy, Holland, Paris and London. Till 1933 a member of the Hamburg *Sezession*. Has lived since 1938 mainly at Foro d'Ischia and, since the war, on Ischia and at Blankenese near Hamburg. Besides oil-paintings has done many water-colours and, as a graphic artist, etchings and lithographs.
Lit: Fritz Baumgart, *Der Maler Eduard Bargheer*, Stuttgart, 1955.

BARLACH, Ernst — Born 2 January 1870 at Wedel in Holstein. Died on 24 October 1938 at Rostock. After attending the Hamburg School of Arts and Crafts and the Dresden Academy, he went to the Académie Julian at Paris (1895—96). Again spent five months in Paris the following year. From 1899—1901 he lived at Berlin, from 1901—04 at Wedel, and he spent 1904—05 teaching at a school of ceramics at Göhr in the Westerwald. The experience of a journey to Russia in 1906 had a decisive effect on his life. Afterwards, he lived for another three years in Berlin, and in 1909 passed a few months at Florence, where he met Theodor Däubler, but where "the Etruscans merely confirmed what was already present". In 1910 he withdrew to Güstrow in Mecklenburg, where his work was only interrupted by a brief spell of military service during 1915—16. His later years were blighted by the proscription of his works after 1933. He was a sculptor, graphic artist and writer. His graphic *œuvre* of almost 300 woodcuts and lithographs was produced in the main between 1910 and 1930. It consists principally of illustrations to his own plays and to poetic works by Goethe and Schiller, and of independent sets with themes like *The Manifestations of God* and *The Outcasts*.
Lit: Carl D. Carls, *Ernst Barlach, Das plastische, graphische und dichterische Werk*, Berlin, 1931, 7th edit. 1958; Complete cat., vol. 1, *Das plastische Werk*, Hamburg, 1960; vol. 2, *Das graphische Werk*, Hamburg, 1958. Both vols compiled by Friedrich Schult, vol. 1 with full bibl.
Ill. p. 95

BARTOLINI, Luigi — Born on 8 February 1892 at Cupramontana di Ancona, the artist is a painter, print-maker, poet and prose-writer. After being trained at the Academies of Rome, Siena and Florence, he soon became a leading representative of the (expressionist) "School of Rome". Many changes of residence until he settled in Rome, where he now works as a professor at the Museo Artistico Industriale. His first etchings appeared in 1914 under Segonzac's influence. Today his graphic production comprises over 200 works, mostly printed in small editions.
Lit: C. A. Petrucci, *Le incisioni di Bartolini*, Rome, 1951; L. Bartolini, *Gli esemplari unici o rari*, Rome, 1952; SERVOLINI.

BASKIN, Leonard — Born on 15 August 1922 at New Brunswick, New Jersey. Trained as a sculptor and graphic artist at various schools in New York. After finishing his art studies as a B. A., he attended the Académie de la Grande Chaumière in Paris in 1950 and the Florence Academy in 1951. Became a teacher of print-making at the school of the Worcester Art Museum in 1952, and since 1953 has taught sculpture and graphic art at Smith College, Northampton (Mass.).
Lit: *American Prints Today*, 1959; List of his woodcuts, wood-engravings, and linocuts from 1948—56 (178 works) in a catalogue of the Worcester Art Museum (1956—57).   *Ill. p. 139*

BAUMEISTER, Willi — Born on 22 January 1889 at Stuttgart. Died there on 31 August 1955. In 1906 became a pupil of Adolf Hölzel without, however, subscribing to his teachings. From 1908 friendly with Meyer-Amden and Oskar Schlemmer. First visit to Paris in 1912 (Toulouse-Lautrec and Gauguin). In 1913 exhibited at the First German Autumn Salon at

Barlach

Baskin

Baumeister

Berlin. Second visit to Paris in 1914 (Cézanne), with Oskar Schlemmer. Military service from 1914–18. After the war active as a typographer, stage designer, and architectural painter from 1919 till 1921. Met Ozenfant, Le Corbusier and Léger in Paris in 1924. During 1928–33 taught commercial art at the Städel School. After his dismissal in 1933 followed some years of "work on the quiet" at Stuttgart. From 1939–44 employed in the paint industry at Wuppertal. From 1946 took a painting class at the Stuttgart Art Academy. As a graphic artist produced illustrated books and portfolio works in lithography, especially during 1943–47.
Lit: W. Grohmann, *Willi Baumeister*, Stuttgart, 1952 (also lists Baumeister's own writings on art). *Ill. p. 219*

Bazaine

BAZAINE, Jean — The artist lives in Paris, where he was born on 26 December 1904. Studied at the Ecole des Beaux-Arts. After début as a sculptor opted for painting and attended the Académie Julian. In 1932 began his connection with Bonnard and Gromaire. First commission for stained-glass windows in 1937. During the 'forties, church windows (Assy) and mosaic for church façade (Audincourt near Belfort). First show at the Galerie Maeght, Paris, in 1949. During the 'fifties, visits to America, Spain and Zeeland; further commissions for windows and mosaics.
Lit: A. M., *Jean Bazaine*, Paris, 1953 (pub. by the Galerie Maeght with full bibl.); Jean Bazaine, *Notes sur la peinture d'aujourd'hui*, Paris, 1953. *Ill. p. 230*

Beck

BECK, Gustav Kurt — Now living at Wolfsburg, the artist was born in 1902 at Vienna. Studied in Rotterdam and at the Vienna School of Arts and Crafts. Travelled to the Balkans, Italy and North Africa. During 1939–46 in Venice and Rome. Returned to Vienna in 1946. Visited America and Brazil during the 'fifties. Since 1952 has directed the "Art of the Present" Gallery at Salzburg.
Lit: *Knaurs Lexikon abstrakter Malerei*, Munich and Zurich, 1957.

BECKMANN, Max — Born on 12 February 1884 at Leipzig. Died on 27 December 1950 at New York. After studying at Weimar (1899–1903) first visit to Paris in 1903–04. From 1905–14 in Berlin with interruptions caused by journeys to Paris and Florence. Member of the Berlin *Sezession*. During 1914–15 a medical orderly in Belgium. From 1915–33 lived at Frankfurt am Main, as a teacher at the Städel School from 1925. After his dismissal in 1933, he remained at Berlin till 1937, when he went to Paris, and then lived in Amsterdam from 1938–47. From 1947 in America, first teaching at Washington University, St Louis, then, from 1949, at the art school of the Brooklyn Museum, New York. Graphics: His *œuvre* comprises 305 works, chiefly lithographs and etchings, only 16 woodcuts.
Lit: Curt Glaser (Meier-Graefe, Fraenger, Hausenstein,) *Max Beckmann*, Munich, 1924 (with full cat. of the prints up to 1923); full bibl. up to 1947 in the cat. of the Beckmann exhibition at the City Art Museum of St Louis in 1948; *Max Beckmann: Tagebücher* (1940–50), ed. by Erhart Göpel, Munich, 1955; Lothar-Günther Buchheim, *Max Beckmann*, Feldafing, 1959; Günter Busch, *Max Beckmann*, Munich, 1960; complete cat. of prints, *Die Druckgraphik*, Badischer Kunstverein Karlsruhe, 1962. *Ills. pp. 102, 103, 104*

Beckmann

BERGMANN, Anna-Eva — Norwegian but born at Stockholm in 1909, she has lived in Paris since 1952 as the wife of the painter Hans Hartung. Studied at the Art Academies of Oslo and Vienna, visited Paris and Dresden in 1929, and made journeys through Europe during 1935–39. Abstract paintings and etchings in a wholly personal style since 1947. Big exhibition at the Galerie de France in 1958.
Lit: M. Seuphor, *A Dictionary of Abstract Painting*, London, 1958.

BERKE, Hubert — Born on 22 January 1908 at Buer in Westphalia. Lives at Alfter near Bonn. Studied in Münster and Königsberg, first art history and philosophy, then painting. In 1932–33 a pupil of Paul Klee at Düsseldorf. After the war a member of the Zen 49 group. Cornelius prize in 1948.
Lit: VOLLMER I, 1953.

Bergman

Berke

Boussingault

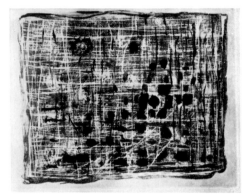
Bissière

Boccioni

BIROLLI, Renato — Born on 10 December 1906 at Verona. Died in 1959 at Milan, where he had lived since 1928. Co-founder there of the Corrente group in 1938 and the Fronte nuovo delle Arti in 1947. Abstract *(astratto-concreto)* paintings from 1952 on. Also active as a writer on art. Graphics: Illustrations for a translation by Quasimodo of the *Carmina Catulli* (1942) and for an edition of Rimbaud's works (1944) followed, from 1948, by original lithographs.
Lit: L. Venturi, *Birolli*, Rome, 1955 (with bibl.).

BISSIERE, Roger — Born on 22 September 1888 at Villeréal (Lot-et-Garonne). Went to Paris in 1910 after attending the art school at Bordeaux. First took part in an exhibition at the Salon d'Automne of 1919, together with André Lhote. Friendship with Braque began in 1921. From 1924–37 taught at the Académie Ranson. Lived during the war, from 1939, at the old family house in the Lot region in a "Franciscan landscape" near the Lascaux caves. After a break in work lasting five years produced "pictures without a title", which were exhibited successfully In 1952 honoured as the foremost painter through being awarded the "grand national art prize". In the graphic field has made colour woodcuts, colour etchings, and colour lithographs.
Lit: Max-Pol Foustet, *Bissière*, Paris, 1955 (Musée de Poche). *Ill. p. 233*

BOCCIONI, Umberto — Born on 19 October 1882 at Reggio di Calabria. Died on 16 August 1916 at Verona. Painter, graphic artist and sculptor. After being trained by Giacomo Balla in Rome (1898–1902), he became, thanks to meeting Marinetti at Milan (1907), one of the most consistent representatives of futurism, which he also publicized in manifestos and other writings. From his pre-futurist early period (1898–1909) date about twenty unusual and *recherché* etchings and drypoints.
Lit: G. C. Argan and M. Calvasi, *Boccioni*, Rome, 1953 (with bibl.); Cat. of prints and drawings from the Harry Lewis Winston collection, The Art Institute, Chicago, 1958.

BONNARD, Pierre — Born on October 1867 at Fontenay-aux-Roses (Seine). Died on 23 January 1947 at Le Cannet near Cannes. Studied law in Paris and from 1880 attended the Académie Julian, at the same time as Vuillard, Maurice Denis, Vallotton, and other young painters who broke with impressionism around 1888 under the impact of Gauguin's art and shortly came under the influence of the symbolists too. They called themselves "Nabis" (prophets or the enlightened) and soon became known as keen contributors to the *Revue Blanche*, founded in 1891, for which Toulouse-Lautrec also did lithographs during the same years. Bonnard was the group's "Nipponizing Nabi". He liked to live in the country as an "anchoret", and, having travelled about a lot in Europe and North Africa around 1910, he later withdrew increasingly to Le Cannet.
Graphics: After early posters in 1899 and the illustrations, covers and posters for the *Revue Blanche*, Bonnard created for the publisher Vollard round about 1900 his illustrational master-pieces: the 109 lithographs for Verlaine's *Parallèlement* (pub. 1900) and the 150 for a translation of Longus's *Daphnis and Chloë* (pub. 1902). During the 'twenties and 'thirties he also illustrated books with etchings and woodcuts. In 1946 appeared the 24 lithographs for *Le Crépuscule des nymphes* by Pierre Louys.
Lit: J. Rewald, *Pierre Bonnard*, New York, 1948, Mayflower Books (with bibl.); Claude Roger-Marx, *Bonnard Lithographe*, Monte Carlo, 1952 (The ninety-three numbers of the descriptive cat. include only the single prints and album sets. In the appendix are examples from the most important books illustrated with lithographs.) *Ill. p. 47*

BOUSSINGAULT, Jean-Louis — Born on 8 March 1883 in Paris. Died there in 1943. Belonged with his friend and contemporary Dunoyer de Segonzac, with La Fresnaye, Luc-Albert Moreau, and other painters, to the *Bande Noire*. Became noted above all for his drawings, etchings and lithographs with scenes of Paris life from the period after the First World War.
Lit: J. Laran, *L'Estampe*, Paris, 1959.

Bonnard

Birolli

Bozzolini

256

BOZZOLINI, Silvano — Born on 3 November 1911 at Fiesole near Florence, the artist has lived in Paris since 1947. Began studying at the Florence Academy in 1937, and has done abstract paintings since 1947. Has also produced murals, book illustrations, and, in the field of original graphics, lithographs and woodcuts.
Lit: *Témoignages pour l'art abstrait*, Paris, 1952.

Braque

BRAQUE, Georges — Born on 13 May 1882 at Argenteuil, the son of a painter and decorator. In 1890 the family moved to Le Havre. After being apprenticed briefly to his father, he attended the art school there. Went to Paris in 1900, terminating his studies at the Ecole des Beaux-Arts in 1904. Painted at Honfleur in 1904, at Antwerp with Othon Friesz in 1906, and from then till 1908 repeatedly at L'Estaque. In 1906 his first fauve pictures. With the landscapes of 1908—09 in Cézanne's style, he was on the road to cubism, which, jointly with Picasso, he developed through all its phases in the following years. The war interrupted work, which he only resumed in 1917 after being wounded. Though the still-life remained the principle theme of his painting, the severe cubist style was "softened" through new experiences of reality and much varied through a new art of drawing and colour.
Graphics: Following the ten etchings from the cubist years 1908—12 and the six etchings and lithographs from 1921—34, over 70 single prints have appeared since 1945. There have also been over 25 books with original prints since 1921.
Lit: Henry R. Hope, *Georges Braque*, New York, 1949, Mayflower Books (with bibl. by Hannah B. Muller); Maurice Gieure, *Georges Braque*, London, 1956; Nicole S. Mangin, *Catalogue de l'œuvre de Georges Braque*, Maeght, Paris, 1959 (in course of publication. So far: *Peintures 1948 bis 1957)*; *Cahier de Georges Braque*, Paris 1947 and 1956; *Catalogue de l'œuvre graphique originale*, Geneva, 1958; W. Hofmann, *Georges Braque, Das graphische Werk, Oeuvre-Katalog*, Stuttgart, 1961. *Ills. pp. 170, 171*

Brüning

BRAUND, Allin — Born on 25 May 1915 at Northam, the painter studied at the Bideford School of Art and at the Hornsey College of Art, where he now works as a teacher, after a break in his artistic activity due to his military service with the marines during 1940—46. Represented at the 1954 Venice Biennale, at São Paulo, and at the Cincinnati international exhibition of graphic art in 1960.
Lit: Cat. of the 4th international exhibition of graphic art at Ljubljana in 1961.

BRUNING, Peter — Born in 1929 at Düsseldorf. Lives at Ratingen near Düsseldorf. Studied from 1950—52 under Baumeister at Stuttgart. Abstract paintings since 1950. Has exhibited at group shows in Düsseldorf and Frankfurt.
Lit: *Knaurs Lexikon abstrakter Malerei*, Munich and Zurich, 1957; VOLLMER V (Suppl.), 1961.

Buffet

BRYEN, Camille — Born on 17 September 1907 at Nantes, this poet, draughtsman and painter now lives in Paris. Like Wols, he is considered one of the initiators of a lyrical trend in abstract art.
Lit: R. Nacenta, *School of Paris*, London, 1960.

BUFFET, Bernard — Born on 10 July 1928 in Paris. Studied art from 1943, first at evening classes, then at the Ecole des Beaux-Arts. First show in 1947. Prix de la Critique in 1948. Books he has illustrated include ones by Jean Cocteau. Graphics: Original etchings.
Lit: P. Berge, *Bernard Buffet*, Geneva, 1958 (with cat. of the prints and illustrated books). *Ill. p. 133*

CAMARO, Alexander — Born on 17 September 1901 in Breslau, the artist has taught at the Berlin College of Art since 1951. First tried his hand as a musician and artiste, then, from 1920—25, studied painting at Breslau under Otto Mueller, but became a dancer again from 1928 till 1930, partnering Mary Wigman. Berlin city art prize in 1950.
Lit: W. Haftmann, *Painting in the Twentieth Century*, 2 vols, London, 1961; Cat. Kunstverein Wolfsburg, 1961.

Camaro

Bryen

Braund

257

Campendonk

Campigli

Capogrossi

Carrà

CAMPENDONK, Heinrich — Born on 3 November 1889 at Krefeld. Died on 9 May 1957 at Amsterdam. Studied under Jan Thorn Prikker at the Krefeld School of Arts and Crafts, joined the *Blaue Reiter* in 1911 after visiting Italy, and lived at Seeshaupt by the Starnberger See from 1916. In 1926 appointed professor at the Düsseldorf Academy. Emigrated to Holland in 1933 and became a professor at the National Academy in Amsterdam. From 1926 on produced chiefly murals and stained-glass windows. His woodcuts date in the main from 1912–19.
Lit: P. Wember, *Heinrich Campendonk*, Krefeld, 1960 (with bibl.); M. T. Engels, *Campendonk, Werkverzeichnis der Holzschnitte*, Stuttgart, 1959 (77 woodcuts listed). *Ill. p. 146*

CAMPIGLI, Massimo — Born on 4 July 1895 in Florence, Campigli went at an early date to Paris, where he became a self-taught painter in the early 'twenties, referring to the art of Picasso, Léger and Ozenfant. Found his own archaically decorative figure style when he encountered Etruscan art on a visit to the Villa Giulia museum at Rome. From 1929–39 lived at Milan, going to Rome in 1951. Since 1953 again living at Paris.
Graphics: Lithographs, many book illustrations.
Lit: Own writings: *Scrupoli*, Venice, 1955 (also in French: Paris and Zürich, 1957); R. Carrieri, *Massimo Campigli*, Milan, 1941 (with bibl.). *Ill. p. 137*

CAPOGROSSI, Guerna Giuseppe — Born on 7 March 1900 at Rome and living there now, the artist first studied law, then became a painter. In Paris during 1927–33. Began to turn away from *pittura tonale* in 1932 under the influence of Carrà, Cézanne, Picasso and Modigliani. Started painting abstract works in 1950, from when date his first lithographs.
Lit: M. Seuphor, *Capogrossi*, Venice, 1956.

CARRA, Carlo — Born on 11 February 1881 at Quargnento di Alessandria, the artist now lives in Milan. After concluding his studies at the Brera Academy in Milan (1909), he played a leading rôle, as a writer on art as well, in the decisive revolutionary movements of Italian art: futurism (1910–15), metaphysical painting (1917–21), and the *Valori plastici* art of the 'twenties. Also has an important place in Italian art as a graphic artist. Etchings since 1922, but mostly during 1924 and only pulled in small editions of 25 prints. Lithographs and book illustrations in the 'forties.
Lit: His own writings include an autobiography: *La mia vita*, Milan, 1943 and 1945; C. A. Petrucci, *Le incisioni di Carra*, Rome, 1952. *Ill. p. 135*

CARZOU, Jean — Born on 1 January 1907 in Paris. Studied at a school of architecture. Further training as a painter in the studios of Montmartre. First one-man show in the autumn of 1930. Since then regularly represented at the Paris Salons and, since the war, at the big exhibitions abroad. During 1952–54 worked as a stage designer and did tapestry cartoons. Picture cycle *The Apocalypse* finished and exhibited 1957.
Graphics: Drypoints and colour lithographs. 21 lithographs of Venice (for Jacques Audiberti's *Lagune hérissée*) and ten colour lithographs (for *France*, with text by André Maurois) produced during 1957–58.
Lit: J. A. Cartier in *Art-Documents*, Geneva, 1959; Florent Fels, *Carzou*, Geneva, 1959 (with bibl.); A *cat. raisonné* of Carzou's engravings and lithographs, to be published by Pierre Cailler, Geneva, in preparation. *Ill. p. 132*

Casorati

Carzou

CASORATI, Felice — Born on 4 December 1886 at Novara, the artist is among the leading painters of the "School of Turin". After studying in Padua, Naples and Verona has lived at Turin since 1919, and, since the 'twenties, has championed a neo-classic art.
Graphics: Large output. Many works only printed in small editions.
Lit: A. Galvano, *Casorati*, Milan, 1940 and 1947 (with bibl.); VOLLMER I, 1953.

CASTELLANI, Leonardo — Born on 19 October 1896 at Faenza, the artist now lives in Urbino. Studied at the Florence Academy; gave up in 1925, after three years, a ceramics studio founded by him at Cesena, and since then has worked as a painter and etcher. In the graphic field noted above all for his landscape etchings.
Lit: C. A. Petrucci, *Le incisioni di Castellani*, Rome, 1951.

Castellani

CAVAEL, Rolf — Born on 27 February 1898 at Königsberg, the artist now lives in Munich. Studied at the Frankfurt School of Art, where he became teacher of commercial art and lettering. His first attempts at non-figurative painting led in 1931 to a meeting with Kandinsky. After the war, a member of the Zen 49 group. 1957, Munich art prize.
Lit: Susstellungs, Cat. of exhibition at Kleemann Galleries, New York, 1956; M. Seuphor, *A Dictionary of Abstract Painting*, London, 1958.

CHADWICK, Lynn — Born in 1914 in London, the artist now lives at Stroud in Gloucestershire. Having begun as an architect, he did not come to sculpture till 1945, first producing mobiles and stabiles in metal and eventually zoomorphic or anthropomorphic forms with a casing of sheet-iron. International prize for sculpture at the 28th Venice Biennale in 1956.
Lit: H. Read, *Lynn Chadwick*, London, 1958; *A Dictionary of Modern Sculpture*, London, 1962.
Ill. p. 197

Cavael

CHAGALL, Marc — Born on 7 July 1889 at Vitebsk, the artist now lives at Vence in France. First came to Paris, via St Petersburg, in 1910. "The earth that nourished the roots of my art was Vitebsk, but my art needed Paris as much as a tree needs water. I had no other reason for leaving my home, and I believe I have always been true to it in my painting." In Paris Chagall lived then in the Montparnasse *avant-gardiste* circle centering around Apollinaire. During 1914 Herwarth Walden arranged his first one-man show at the *Der Sturm* gallery in Berlin. That same year, the war caught the artist in Russia, where, after the Revolution, he founded an art school at Vitebsk in 1917 and did work for the Jewish State Theatre at Moscow in 1920. In 1922 he returned to Paris via Berlin. His residence in France has since only been interrupted by two trips to Israel and Poland, and by the years he spent in America, from 1941—47. On returning to France, he finally retired to Vence in 1950.
Graphics: First came the etchings that, commissioned by Paul Cassirer, he did in 1922 as illustrations to the autobiography he had begun. From 1923 on, thanks to his association with the Paris publisher Ambroise Vollard, he produced the sets illustrations to Gogol, La Fontaine and the Bible, comprising about 400 prints. During 1946 appeared the colour lithographs for *The Arabian Nights,* in the United States, and, since 1950, many lithographs have issued from the studio of the Mourlot brothers at Paris.
Lit: *My Early Life,* London, n. d.; Full biographical data and bibliographies in both cats of the big Chagall exhibitions of 1959 at Hamburg, Munich, and Paris; *Catalogue de l'œuvre gravée de Marc Chagall*, Bibl. nat., Paris, 1957; Franz Meyer, *Marc Chagall, Das graphische Werk*, Stuttgart, 1957; *Chagall Lithographe*, Monte Carlo, 1960; Chagall's portfolios and the books illustrated by him listed in the cats. of the 1959 Chagall exhibitions; Franz Meyer, *Marc Chagall, Leben und Werk*, Cologne, 1961 (with bibl.), Eng. ed. in preparation.
Ills. pp. 119, 120, 121

Chagall

CHESNEY, Lee — Born in 1920 at Washington, the artist has taught print-making at the University of Illinois in Urbana since 1950. Previously, he had taught drawing from 1946—50 at the University of Iowa, after gaining his B. A. there in the post-war Lasansky group. Journeys for study took him to Mexico and, in 1956—57, to Japan, among other countries. Since 1948 has been represented by his etchings and drypoints at many international exhibitions in America, Europe and Japan.
Lit: *American Prints Today*, 1959.

Chesney

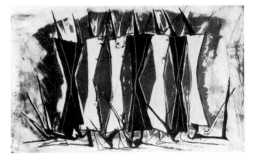
Chadwick

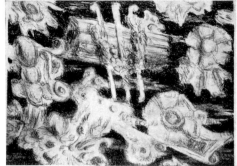
Chirico

CHIRICO, Giorgio de — Born on 10 June 1888 at Volo in Greece, the son of an Italian railway engineer. Now lives in Rome. Earliest artistic training at the Athens Polytechnic. Went to Munich in 1906 for further study. In 1910 in Florence appeared his first "metaphysical" pictures, inspired by impressions of Greece, by the paintings and prints of Böcklin, Klinger and Kubin, and by his readings from Nietzsche. In 1911 went to Paris, where he met Apollinaire. During 1915–16 at Ferrara with the painter Carrà. Framed a theory of *pittura metafisica*. Studying the old masters, he began in the 'twenties at Florence and Rome to turn away from "metaphysical" painting. But his surrealist dream-novel *Hebdomeros* (which is not his only piece of writing) appeared as late as 1929.
Graphics: Of the hundred or so etchings and lithographs, the works with surrealist motifs from 1927–30 are especially in demand. Illustrated books, some with original graphic works, produced from 1928–51.
Lit: G. Lo Duca, *Dipinti di Giorgio de Chirico*, Milan, 1945 (with bibl.); J. T. Soby, *Giorgio de Chirico*, New York, 1955 (only the early works), Mayflower Books; SERVOLINI, p. 225.

Ill. p. 134

CLARKE, Geoffrey — Born on 28 November 1924 at Darley Dale, Derbyshire, and trained at the Royal College of Art in London, this sculptor has also become well-known as a printmaker and stained-glass artist. His windows for Coventry Cathedral have made him one of the revivers of this art in Britain. Won a prize for his graphic work at the 1st international graphic art biennal at Tokyo in 1957.
Lit: *A Dictionary of Modern Sculpture*, London, 1962.

CLAVE, Antoni — Born on 5 April 1913 at Barcelona. Living in Paris since 1939. Artistic training at the Barcelona Academy of Art. In Paris and London has also worked as a stage designer. Sets for the Andersen film at Hollywood during 1952. Various art awards. In 1954 prize for graphic art at the Venice Biennale.
Graphics: Along with many single prints, illustrations for *Carmen* and Mérimée's *Lettres d'Espagne*, and 60 colour lithographs for *Pantagruel*.
Lit: W. Haftmann, *Painting in the Twentieth Century*, 2 vols, London, 1961; BENEZIT II; VOLLMER, 1953.

CLERICI, Fabrizio — Born on 15 May 1913 at Milan. Living in Rome. Architect, painter and stage designer. As a painter, a "veristic surrealist".
Lit: SERVOLINI, p. 208; VOLLMER I, 1953.

CLIFFE, Henry — Born on 14 December 1919 at Scarborough in Yorkshire. Studied at the Bath Academy of Art, where he teaches painting and print-making. Represented at the big international exhibitions in Venice, at documenta II in Cassel, and at the graphic art exhibitions in Lugano and Ljubljana (most recently in 1961).
Lit: Cat. of the 4th international exhibition of graphic art at Ljubljana in 1961.

CONSTANT (C. Nieuwenhuys) — Lives at Amsterdam, where he was born on 21 July 1920. Belonged with Appel and Corneille to the Dutch Experimental Group and was a co-founder of COBRA in 1948, but later withdrew from these groups and went his own way. Exhibitor at documenta II in Cassel.
Lit: documenta II, cat. of the prints, 1959.

CORINTH, Lovis — Born on 21 July 1858 at Tapiau in East Prussia. Died on 17 July 1925 when visiting Zandvoort in Holland. Studied at the Art Academies of Königsberg (1876–80) and Munich (1880–84), and attended the Académie Bouguereau and Académie Julian in Paris (1884–87). Then lived for a few months at Königsberg, ten months at Munich, and, in 1900, went to Berlin. There, as a member of the *Sezession* and later its president, he represented, beside Liebermann, the lightened-up *plein air* painting of the German impressionists. Through his expressive late period, which was initiated around 1911 by a serious illness, he belongs to twentieth-century art history.

Clarke

Clavé

Clerici

Cliffe

Constant

Graphics: First etching experiments at Munich in 1891, first lithographs in 1895. New promptings at Berlin from Hermann Struck. Increased graphic output during the war years and in the last creative phase. The 918 items of his graphic *œuvre* are mostly etchings and lithographs. Many portfolios and illustrated books.
Lit: His own numerous writings include an autobiography; complete cat. of the paintings, by Charlotte Berend-Corinth, Munich, 1958 (with bibl.); the graphic works catalogued by Karl Schwarz, Berlin, 1917, and (extended to 1920) Berlin, 1922; and by Heinrich Müller in his *Die späte Graphik von Lovis Corinth,* Hamburg, 1960 (continuation of Schwarz with addenda).

Ill. p. 94

Corinth

CORNEILLE (Cornelius van Beverloo) — Born on 4 July 1922 at Liège, of Dutch parentage. Living since 1950 in Paris. Studied from 1940—43 at the Amsterdam Academy. Co-founder of the COBRA group in 1948, with Appel and Constant. Journeys to Africa and South America. Ceramics and book illustrations. Guggenheim award for the Netherlands in 1956. Represented at documenta II in Cassel and at the Ljubljana exhibitions of graphic art.
Lit: R. Nacenta, *School of Paris,* London, 1960.

COURTIN, Pierre — Born in 1921 at Rebrechien (Loiret), the artist now lives in Paris. Exhibitor at documenta II in Cassel. His etchings, printed from zinc and limited to about five examples, are published by Berggruen: a catalogue appeared in 1959.
Lit: Cimaise 7/50, 1960.

Ill. p. 224

Corneille

CRAWFORD, Ralston — Born on 25 September 1906 at St Catherine's, Ontario, but of American parentage. Lives in New York. Studied at American art schools and in Paris (1932—33). Teacher at various art schools since 1940 and, from 1952, at the New School for Social Research. Tiffany scholarship in 1931.
Lit: VOLLMER I, 1953; *American Prints Today,* 1959.

CRIPPA, Roberto — Born 1921 at Milan, where he now lives as a painter and sculptor. In 1948 joined Fontana's *Movimento spaziale.* Sculpture since 1956. From 1948 on a regular exhibitor at the Venice Biennale.
Lit: *A Dictionary of Modern Sculpture,* London, 1962.

CRODEL, Carl (Charles) — Born on 16 September 1894 in Marseilles, of German parentage. Went to Germany at fifteen. After being an apprentice lithographer, he studied art history and archaeology at Jena. A self-taught painter influenced by Munch and Kirchner. During 1927—33 and 1946—51 taught at the Giebichenstein Art School near Halle. Professor at the College in Munich from 1951. Murals at Jena and Halle. Designs for stained-glass, mosaics and textiles. Early graphics: woodcuts. Later: colour lithographs.
Lit: VOLLMER I, 1953.

Crawford

DAHMEN, Karl Fred. — Born on 4 November 1917 at Stolberg near Aachen and lives there now. Studied in Aachen under Wendling. Visits to Paris and Athens.
Lit: VOLLMER I, 1953; K. Goerres, "Karl Fred Dahmen" in *Junge Künstler 60/61,* Cologne, 1960.

Crodel

Dahmen

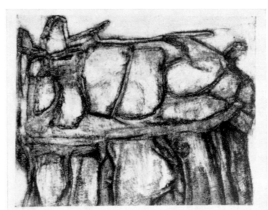

Courtin

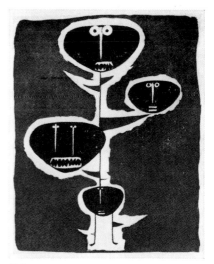

Crippa

Dali

Davis

Delaunay

DALI, Salvador — Born on 11 May 1904 at Figueras near Barcelona. Living since 1940 in the United States. Began to attend the Madrid Art Academy in 1921, and concerned himself with Freud and studying philosophy. From catalogues and periodicals learnt about futurism and *pittura metafisica*, and later also about cubism. During 1928 met Picasso and the surrealists at Paris. In 1928 and 1931 helped to make two surrealists films: *Un chien Andalou* and *l'Age d'or*. Artistic creation was for him at that time "une activité paranoique-critique". On a visit to Italy in 1937 changed to a neo-classicism, later to baroque compositions.
Graphics: A few etchings and lithographs. Some illustrated books.
Lit: His own writings include a *Secret Life of Salvador Dali*, 3rd ed., London, 1949; J. T. Soby, *Salvador Dali,* London, 1946 (with bibl.).

DAUBIGNY, Charles-François — Born on 15 February 1817 in Paris, the son of a landscape painter. Died on 19 February 1878 at Auvers. Belonged from 1840, as an exponent of the *paysage intime,* to the Barbizon School and liked painting the banks of the Oise, which he navigated in a house-boat.
Graphics: Chiefly etchings. In 1851 and 1852 there appeared two series as *Cahiers d'eaux fortes* and in 1862 about twenty glass etchings. The graphic *œuvre* comprises 150 works.
Lit: DELTEIL XIII, 1921.   *Ill. p. 9*

DAVIS, Stuart — Born on 7 December 1894 at Philadelphia. Pupil of Robert Henry in New York from 1910. Exhibited water-colours in 1913 at the Armory Show, where he first met works by Gauguin, Van Gogh and Matisse. During 1928—29 saw pictures by Toulouse-Lautrec, Seurat, Léger, Picasso and Beardsley in Paris. In 1931 became a teacher at the Art Students League, during 1934—39 worked for the Artistic Congress, and from 1940 taught at the New School for Social Research, New York. Developed from cubism to abstraction in 1938.
Lit: Cat. of an exhibition at the Walker Art Center, Minneapolis, in 1957 (with bibl.).

DAY, Worden — Born in 1916 at Columbus, Ohio. Lives in New York. Artistic training at the Art Students League, where S. W. Hayter was among her teachers. Has taught at various schools. Helped forward by scholarships and art prizes. Her art shaped by the American East.
Lit: *American Prints Today,* 1959.

DEBENJAC, Riko — Born on 8 February 1908 at Kanal on the Soca in Yugoslavia. Studied at Belgrade during 1930—37. Takes part in all the major graphic art exhibitions, even abroad. Has been awarded many prizes, most recently at São Paulo (1959) and Ljubljana (1960).
Lit: Cat. of the 4th international exhibition of graphic art at Ljubljana in 1961.

DELAUNAY, Robert — Born on 12 April 1884 at Paris. Died on 25 October 1941 at Montpellier. His beginnings as a painter influenced by the Pont-Aven School and in 1905 by Seurat's neo-impressionism. The *Saint-Séverin* picture series of 1909 belongs to the first phase of cubism, but with the *Windows* series of 1912 Orphic cubism began. The *Discs* and *Cosmic Circular Forms* were already purely abstract colour compositions. During the First World War Delaunay lived in Spain and Portugal. Returned to Paris in 1921. In 1937 carried out the big murals for the palaces of the Paris World Fair. Took refuge in Auvergne and at Mougins in 1940. Crucially important for German art was his association with the *Blaue Reiter* group, arranged by Kandinsky (1911), and the Delaunay exhibition held at the *Der Sturm* gallery, Berlin, in 1913, with the introductory speech by Apollinaire.
Example of the rather few graphic works: the series of 20 lithographs *Allo: Paris!* from 1926.
Lit: Robert Delaunay, *Du cubisme à l'art abstrait,* Ed. Pierre Francastel, Paris, 1957 (with complete cat. and bibl.).   *Ill. p. 123*

Debenjac

Daubigny

Day

DENIS, Maurice — Born on 25 December 1870 at Granville (Manche). Died on 3 November 1943 at Paris. As early as 1888 Sérusier converted him, along with Bonnard, Vuillard and other pupils of the Académie Julian, to Gauguin's art doctrine, and he soon became the real theorist of the symbolist art of the Nabis. Later painted chiefly religious scenes, and with his murals for churches became the successor of Puvis de Chavannes.
Graphics: woodcuts and colour lithographs.
Lit: Own writings: *Théories (1890–1910)*, 2nd ed., Paris, 1920; *Nouvelles théories*, Paris, 1922; S. Barazetti, *Maurice Denis*, Paris, 1945 (with bibl.).

Derain

DERAIN, André — Born on 17 June 1880 at Chatou near Paris. Died on 8 September 1954 at Garches near Paris. Attended the Académie Carrière at Paris in 1898–99 and the Académie Julian in 1904. Belonged with Matisse and Vlaminck to the fauves, came under the influence of Cézanne and the cubists around 1908, and in his figure pictures of about 1912–14 followed the "gothic" realism of fifteenth-century painting. After the First World War, he was the only important French artist to represent a new classicizing realism. Also worked as a stage designer. His sculptures were produced mainly during the later years of his creative activity, from 1939, under the influence of archaic and primitive art.
Graphics: Early work in the fauve style. With Dufy, one of the originators of a new art of woodcut for book illustrations.
Lit: VOLLMER I, 1953; Georges Hilaire, *André Derain*, Geneva, 1959; Cat. of the graphic art exhibition at the Bibl. nat., Paris, in 1955 (132 works listed). *Ill. p. 129*

DIX, Otto — Born on 2 December 1891 at Untermhausen near Gera, the son of a moulder. After four years as an apprentice painter and decorator began attending the Dresden School of Arts and Crafts on a scholarship in 1909. Soldier during 1914–18. After the war studied at the Art Academies of Dresden and, under Nauen, of Düsseldorf. Lived till 1925 at Düsseldorf, during 1925–27 at Berlin, and in 1927 became a professor at the Dresden Art Academy. Following his dismissal, lived during 1933–36 at Randegg near Singen and from 1936, except for military service and imprisonment (1945–46), at Hemmenhofen near Radolfzell by Lake Constance. Dix found his own style in the aggressive verism of the 'twenties. The portfolio *The War* also appeared at that time.
Lit: Fritz Löffler, *Otto Dix*, Dresden, 1960 (with bibl.); Cat. of the Dix exhibition at the Galerie Meta Nierendorf, Berlin, in 1961 (list of all graphic works from 1913 to 1960). *Ill. p. 98*

DOMINGUEZ, Oskar — Born on 7 January 1906 at Tenerife, the son of a planter. Took his own life on 31 December 1957 at Paris. A self-taught painter from 1924, he went to Paris in 1927 and attended the art schools of Montparnasse and Montmartre. Turned to Surrealism during the 'thirties, giving it up in 1945.
Lit: R. Nacenta, *School of Paris*, London, 1960.

Dix

DRENKHAHN, Reinhard — Born on 9 February 1926 at Hamburg. Took his own life there on 26 March 1959. After three years as an apprentice decorator attended the State Art School at Hamburg, studying interior decoration till 1947 (with a break for military service in 1944–45), then painting. A painting student at the Baukreis during 1948–50. First study trip to Paris in 1951. Destroyed all his early works in 1953. During the following years many visits to the seaside, to Italy and Spain, and time after time to Paris. City of Hamburg Licht-wark award in 1958.
Graphics: Etchings, including colour ones.
Lit: Cat. of the exhibition at the Hamburg Art Club in 1960; VOLLMER V (Suppl.), 1961.

Drenkhahn

DUBUFFET, Jean — Born in 1901 at Le Havre. Lives at Vence. A few months at the Académie Julian in Paris during 1918. After years of private study in various fields of art and literature went to Buenos Aires as an industrial designer in 1924. Returned to Paris in 1930, living there first as a wine-merchant, then as an artist. Since 1944 exhibitions of his paintings, lithographs and *collages*, which provoke great public interest.
Lit: VOLLMER I, 1953; BENEZIT III, 1950; *A Dictionary of Modern Sculpture*, London, 1962. Lithographs: Berggruen, 1960. *Ills pp. 248, 249*

Dominguez

Denis

Dubuffet

Dufy

Dunoyer de Segonzac

Edmondson

DUFY, Raoul — Born on 3 June 1877 at Le Havre. Died on 23 March 1953 at Forcalquier (Basses-Alpes). In 1900 went to Paris to study painting. His models: 1901 Van Gogh and the impressionists, 1905–06 Matisse and the fauves, 1907–08 Cézanne and Braque. From 1911 on, designs for printed fabrics. In the 'twenties after the war painted racecourses, landscapes and orchestras. Murals in 1937 for the Palais de l'Electricité at the Paris World Fair. Lived during 1940–49 at Perpignan.
Graphics: First woodcuts in 1910–11. From 1918 on chiefly lithographs and etchings.
Lit: P. Courthion, *Paintings (Dufy)*, London, 1955; G. Besson, *Raoul Dufy*, London, 1953; Cat. of the exhibition at Geneva in 1953. *Ill. p. 128*

DUNOYER DE SEGONZAC, André — Born on 6 July 1884 at Boussy-Saint-Antoine (Seine-et-Oise). Lives in Paris. Began attending a private art school in Paris in 1903. In 1907 studio partnership with the painter and graphic artist Boussingault. Loose temporary connection with cubism. Then as a soldier during the First World War evolved his independent drawing style, which also characterizes his prints. His imposing output, since 1919–20, of sets of etchings and book illustrations comprises about 2,000 items, generally done straight on the copperplate without preliminary drawings. Among the principle works are the *Georgics*, published in 1947, and the illustrations to Colette's writings.
Lit: Aimée Lioré and Pierre Cailler, *Catalogue de l'œuvre gravée de Dunoyer de Segonzac*, Paris and Geneva, 1958 f. (six vols planned); D. de Segonzac, *Oeuvre gravée*, Expos. Bibl. nat., Paris, 1958. *Ill. p. 130*

EDMONDSON, Leonard — Born in 1916 at Sacramento, California. Lives in Pasadena. Studied art at the University of California. Taught at Pasadena City College during 1947–54, then became head of the design department at the Los Angeles Country Art Institute. Prefers drypoint.
Lit: *American Prints Today*, 1959.

EGLAU, Otto — Born on 20 April 1917 at Berlin. Studied during 1947–53 at the Berlin College of Art under Max Kaus. Prize for graphic art at the Tokyo biennial in 1957.
Graphics: Etchings: including colour ones.
Lit: Cat. of the 3rd international exhibition of graphic art at Ljubljana in 1960; H. Th. Flemming in *Die Kunst und das schöne Heim*, Jg. 56, 1957.

ELENBAAS, Valdemar Hansen — Born on 21 April 1912 at Rotterdam. Began to study painting in 1932 and took up lithography as well in 1947. Won the prize with his lithographs at the Venice Biennale in 1952.
Lit: Cat. of the 4th international exhibition of graphic art at Ljubljana in 1961; VOLLMER V (Suppl.), 1961.

ENSOR, James — Born at Ostend on 13 April 1860, the son of an English father and a Flemish mother. Died on 19 November 1949 at Ostend. Attended the Brussels Academy of Art, but on returning home in 1879 hardly ever left Ostend again. Famous above all through his mask pictures as the painter of a grotesque and ludicrous world.
Graphics: 129 etchings during 1886–1904, three drypoints in 1933, and one soft-ground etching in 1934.
Lit: DELTEIL XIX, 1925; A. Croquez, *L'Oeuvre gravée de James Ensor*, Geneva and Brussels, 1947; P. Haesaerts, *James Ensor*, London, 1959. *Ill. p. 51*

Elenbaas

Eglau

Ensor

EPPLE, Bernhard — Born on 11 October 1912 at Eutingen, the artist now lives at Heidelberg. Studied at the art schools in Pforzheim and Karlsruhe. Now does abstract pictures.
Lit: VOLLMER II, 1955.

Epple

ERNI, Hans — Born on 21 February 1909 at Entlebuch near Lucerne. Living at Lucerne since 1935. Attended the Lucerne School of Arts and Crafts and the Académie Julian in Paris. Works as painter and graphic artist, illustrator and poster designer. From Picasso via surrealism and abstract art has arrived at a decorative classicism.
Lit: VOLLMER II, 1955; C. Roy, *Hans Erni*, Geneva, 1957.

ERNST, Max — Born on 2 April 1890 at Brühl near Cologne. Studied philosophy in Bonn from 1909 and taught himself to paint. Saw the *Sonderbund* exhibition at Cologne in 1912 and took part in the First German Autumn Salon of 1913. Military service during 1914–18. In 1919 founded the Cologne Dada group jointly with Arp and Baargeld. To France in 1922. Co-founder of surrealism in 1924. Interned in southern France during 1939–40. Lived in America from 1941–53, when he returned to France.
Ernst is a painter, sculptor and writer. As a surrealist he likes to use new art techniques for his surprise effects, working with *collage, frottage* and *montage,* which he also employs to illustrate his books.
Lit: His autobiography *Beyond Painting and Other Writings,* New York, 1948, Mayflower Books; P. Waldberg, *Max Ernst*, Paris, 1958; Cat of Ernst exhibition at the Museum of Modern Art, New York, in 1961 (with bibl.); Cat of Ernst exhibition in Cologne and Zürich, 1963; Cat. of Ernst exhibition at the Tate Gallery, 1961. *Ill. p. 194*

Erni

ESTEVE, Maurice — Born on 2 May 1904 at Culan (Cher). Lives in Paris. In 1923 designer at a Barcelona textile factory. Then attended the Académie Colarossi, Paris, till 1927. Under surrealist influence in 1928. Abstract paintings since 1945.
Lit: BENEZIT III, 1954–55; VOLLMER II, 1955. *Ill. p. 236*

EVANS, Merlyn — Born on 13 March 1910 at Cardiff. Teaches drawing and print-making at the Central School of Arts and Crafts in London. After attending art schools in Glasgow and London (1927–33), and making various journeys, lived during 1937–40 in South Africa. In 1957 did the aquatints of the *Suite Verticale* after African masks and figures.
Lit: VOLLMER II, 1955; Cat. of the 4th international exhibition of graphic art at Ljubljana in 1961.

Ernst

FASSBENDER, Joseph — Born on 14 April 1903 at Cologne. During 1926–29 studied at the Cologne Werkschulen under Richard Seewald. Villa Romana prize of the German Artists Association in 1929. Proscribed as an artist in 1936. 1953, guest-teacher in Hamburg. In 1955 became head of the graphics department of the Krefeld Werkkunstschule and in 1955 professor at the Düsseldorf Art Academy. Murals, tapestries, and commercial art.
Independent graphics: Monotypes, woodcuts and lithographs.
Lit: W. Holzhausen, "Joseph Fassbender" in *Junge Künstler 58/59*, Cologne, 1958; Cat. of the exhibition at the Kestner-Gesellschaft, Hanover, in 1961. *Ill. p. 237*

Fassbender

Evans

Estève

FAZZINI, Pericle — Born on 4 May 1913 at Grottamare in the Marche. Studied sculpture under Arturo Martini. Temporarily a member of the Fronte nuovo delle Arti in 1947. A few lithographs.
Lit: VOLLMER II, 1955; *A Dictionary of Modern Sculpture,* London, 1962.

FEININGER, Lyonel — Born on 17 July 1871 in New York of German parents. Died there on 13 January 1956. In 1887 went to Europe to study art. Studied at Hamburg, Berlin and Paris, then worked at Berlin and Paris till 1908, doing drawings for the press. Met Delaunay and came in contact with cubism in 1911. Association with the *Blaue Reiter* in 1913. During 1919—33 at the Bauhaus. Lived from 1933 in Berlin, from 1937 in New York.
Graphics: Etchings and lithographs during 1910—17, but from 1918 mainly woodcuts.
Lit: Hans Hess, *Lyonel Feininger,* London, 1961; The hitherto most extensive list of the graphic works in the cat. of the Hamburg Feininger exhibition in 1961 (80 works recorded); E. Ruhmer, *Lyonel Feininger, Zeichnungen, Aquarelle, Graphik,* Munich, 1961.
Ills pp. 148, 149

Feininger

FELIXMULLER, Conrad — Born on 21 May 1897 at Dresden. Lives at Tautenhain in Saxony. Studied at the Dresden Art Academy, living as an independent painter in Dresden from 1915 and in Berlin during 1934—40. Spent 1940—44 at Darnsdorf in the Mark. One of the *Brücke* followers. His graphic work almost entirely in woodcut.
Lit: VOLLMER II, 1955.

FIEBIGER, Helmut — Born on 12 May 1928 at Haan in the Rhineland. Lives at Solingen-Ohligs. Studied at the Wuppertal Werkkunstschule and Düsseldorf Academy.
Lit: VOLLMER II, 1955.

FIETZ, Gerhard — Born on 25 July 1910 at Breslau. Studied at the Breslau Academy under Kanoldt and Schlemmer in 1930—32, at Düsseldorf under Nauen in 1932—33, and at Berlin in 1937—38. A co-founder of the Zen group after the war and today a professor at the Berlin College of Fine Arts.
Lit: VOLLMER II, 1955.

FINK, Herbert — Born in 1921 in Rhode Island. Attended Yale University and the art school in Rhode Island, where he now teaches drawing and print-making.
Lit: IGAS (Internat. Graphic Arts Soc., New York) 41 / Nov. 1960.

FISCHER, Hans (fis) — Born on 6 January 1909 at Bern. Died on 19 April 1958 at Interlaken. During 1927—30 attended art schools at Geneva and Zurich. Spent 1931—32 in Paris as an advertising artist and at Fernand Léger's art school. Worked in Bern and Zurich as a graphic artist and stage designer from 1932. Besides twenty-six murals produced twenty-three illustrated books and several hundred prints and drawings.
Lit: Bibl. in *Art-Documents 5,* Geneva; Cat. of the exhibition at Bern in 1960.

FLOCON, Albert (Albert Mentzel) — Born on 24 May 1909 at Köpenick in Brandenburg. Living since 1933 in Paris. Previously studied in Germany at the Bauhaus under Oskar Schlemmer. During 1949—52 ran a school of graphic art in Paris with Johnny Friedlaender. Teacher at a school of print-making since 1954. As a graphic artist prefers line-engraving, and has written two treatises on the nature of this technique: *Traité du burin* in 1952, *Topographies* in 1960.
Lit: BENEZIT III, 1950.

FRASCONI, Antonio — Born on 28 April 1919 at Montevideo in Uruguay. Lives at South Norwalk, Connecticut. After attending an art school in Montevideo, he went early on to the New School for Social Research, New York, where he has been teaching in the art faculty for years. Various scholarships and prizes. For twenty years he has done mainly woodcuts.
Lit: *American Prints Today,* 1959.
Ill. p. 142

FREUNDLICH, Otto — Born on 10 July 1878 at Stolp in Pomerania. Died in 1943 at a concentration camp in Poland. Painter and sculptor. First studied art history. Attended a Berlin art school during 1907—08. Met Picasso and came in contract with cubism in Paris. Spent 1914—24 in Germany. Earliest abstract pictures in 1919. From 1924 back in Paris, where he created his monumental sculptures during 1929—33. Deported to Poland in 1943.
Graphics: Woodcuts and prints from zinc.
Lit: Günter Aust, *Otto Freundlich,* Cologne, 1960 (with bibl.).

Fazzini

Felixmüller

Fiebiger

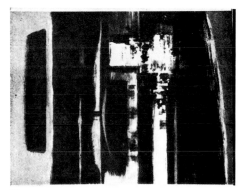

Fietz

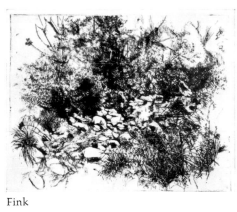

Fink

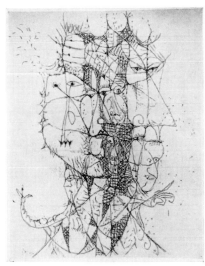

Fischer

Frasconi

Flocon

Freundlich

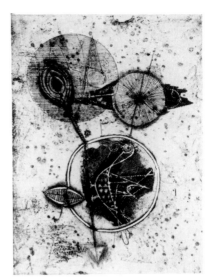
Friedlaender

FRIEDLAENDER, Johnny — Born on 21 June 1912 at Pless in Upper Silesia. Spent 1922—28 at Breslau Grammar School and Art Academy (under Otto Mueller and Karl Mense), 1930—34 as a draughtsman and graphic artist at Dresden. Migrated to Czechoslovakia in 1935, to Paris in 1937. During 1939—43 at French internment camps, then in the resistance movement. Returned to Paris in 1945. Ran the Ermitage Studio with the engraver Albert Flocon during 1949—52. An influential graphic art teacher afterwards too. Since 1930 has produced almost exclusively water-colours and etchings — above all colour ones.
Lit: Cat. by Rolf Schmücking of the graphics from the years 1949—60 publ. on the occasion of an exhibition at Brunswick in 1960 (includes 74 works). *Ill. p. 221*

FUHR, Xaver — Born on 23 September 1898 at Neckarau near Mannheim. Living since 1951 at Rymsburg. A self-taught painter. After various trips abroad worked at Mannheim till 1937. Spent 1943—50 at Nabburg in the Upper Palatinate. Since 1946 a professor at the Munich Academy.
Lit: VOLLMER II, 1955.

GAUGUIN, Paul — Born on 7 August 1848 in Paris. Died on 8 May 1903 in the Marquesas. From 1874 painted as well as working for a stockbroker, but gave up his job in 1883. Left his Danish wife in 1885.
Pissarro, Van Gogh, Pont-Aven on the Breton coast, and the South Sea mark the stages of his artistic journey from impressionism to "synthetic" and "symbolic" painting, which he made during the brief period 1886—1903.
Lit: J. de Routonchamp, *Paul Gauguin,* Paris, 1925; M. Guérin, *l'Oeuvre gravée de Paul Gauguin,* Paris, 1927 (2 vols); R. Goldwater, *Gauguin,* New York and London, 1957; R. Huyghe, *Paintings (Gauguin),* London, 1959. *Ill. p. 34*

GEIGER, Rupprecht — Born on 26 June 1908 at Munich. Studied at the Munich Technical College. Worked as an architect up to the war and after it as a painter. Member of the Zen group at Munich.
Lit: Cat. of the Zen group exhibition at Munich and Hamburg in 1955; Graphic cat. of documenta II, Cassel, 1959.

GENIN, Robert — Born on 11 August 1884 at Vysokoye near Smolensk, the artist became well-known principally as a graphic artist through portfolio works from the 'twenties. In 1902 went via Vilna and Odessa to Munich, then lived in Paris and Berlin, and since 1930 has dwelt wholly at Paris.
Lit: THIEME-BECKER XIII, 1920; VOLLMER II, 1955.

GENTILINI, Franco — Born on 4 August 1909 at Faenza. After serving a brief apprenticeship as a potter at Faenza and studying painting at Bologna, went in 1929 to Rome, where he joined the "Scuola romana".
Lit: VOLLMER II, 1955; SERVOLINI, p. 376.

Fuhr

Gauguin

Geiger

Genin

Gentilini

GIACOMETTI, Alberto — Born on 10 October 1901 at Stampa in the Bregaglia, Switzerland, a son of the painter Giovanni Giacometti. Lives in France and works mainly as a sculptor. After briefly attending the Geneva School of Arts and Crafts and passing a year in Italy, went in 1922 to Paris, which he exchanged during the war years (1940–45) for Geneva. Spent 1922–25 studying under Bourdelle at the Académie de la Grande Chaumière. Went through the school of cubism and of surrealism, from which he withdrew in 1935. New endeavours in the sphere of the figure and portrait. Has evolved in his sculpture and drawings, with his delicate elongated figures, a highly personal style. Many etchings and lithographs, especially since 1953.
Lit: Cat. of the exhibition at Klipstein and Kornfeld, Bern, in 1959; *A Dictionary of Modern Sculpture*, London, 1962.   *Ill. p. 131*

Giacometti

GILLES, Werner — Born on 29 August 1894 at Rheydt in the Rhineland. Died on 23 June 1961 at Munich. Study of art at Cassel interrupted in 1914 by the First World War. Went in 1919 to Weimar, first attending the Academy, then from September the Bauhaus (Feininger's class). During 1921–22 paid first of many visits to Italy: Ischia became his second home. In Germany varied his residence between Düsseldorf, Berlin and the Baltic. From 1949 in Munich.
Points of departure for his art: Klee, Chagall, Picasso, and occasionally Munch. Besides oil-paintings many water-colours. Woodcuts only in the early days, etchings at the start of the 'twenties, lithographs from 1947 on.
Lit: Alfred Hentzen, *Werner Gilles*, Cologne, 1960.   *Ills pp. 191, 192*

GILLET, Roger Edgar — Born on 10 July 1924 in Paris. Learnt cabinet-making at the Ecole Boulle and studied at the Ecole des Arts décoratifs. Taught at the Académie Julian during 1946–48. Paints abstracts.
Lit: R. Nacenta, *School of Paris*, London, 1960; DORIVAL II.

Gilles

GISCHIA, Léon — Born on 8 June 1903 at Dax (Landes). Studied art history and archaeology, and from 1923 painting as a pupil of Othon Friesz and Fernand Léger. Spent 1927–30 in the United States. Organized travelling exhibitions of contemporary art in America during 1927–37. His own art "abstract-figurative" since 1948.
Lit: DORIVAL II.

GOLLER, Oskar — Born in 1914 at Aachen, this abstract painter and graphic artist studied at the School of Arts and Crafts in his native city and now lives at Frankfurt.
Lit: VOLLMER II, 1955.

GOTSCH, Friedrich Karl — Born on 3 February 1900 at Pries in the Danish Wohld. Studied during 1920–23 at Dresden under Kokoschka, then for two years in the United States. Attended the Académie Colarossi at Paris in 1926–27 and after various travels lived at Berlin during 1933–40. Military service 1940–45. Residing at the North Sea resort of St Peter in Holstein since 1950.
Lit: Cat. of the exhibition at Hamburg in 1960 for his sixtieth birthday; VOLLMER II, 1955; H. Th. Flemming, *Friedrich Karl Gotsch*, Hamburg, 1963 (with bibl.).

Gillet

Goller

Gotsch

Gischia

Gramaté

Gresko

Grieshaber

GRAMATE, Walter — Born on 8 January 1897 at Berlin. Died on 9 February 1929 at Hamburg. Badly wounded as a soldier during the First World War. Moved to Barcelona in 1924, back to Berlin in 1926, and lived lastly at Hamburg. His *œuvre* is that of a *Brücke* follower.
Lit: F. Eckardt, *Das graphische Werk von Walter Gramaté*, Vienna 1932.

GRESKO, Georg — Born on 7 February 1920 at Berlin. Skilled glass-painter. Soldier from 1940—46. After the war, first in Berlin but since 1959 a teacher at the Hamburg College of Fine Arts. Died on 28 July 1962.
Lit: VOLLMER II, 1955; Cat. of exhibition at Galerie Brockstedt, Hamburg, 1960.

GRIESHABER, HAP — Born on 15 February 1909 at Rot an der Rot, Upper Swabia. During 1926—27 apprentice compositor at Reutlingen. At the same time star pupil of Ernst Schneidler in Stuttgart till 1928. Study trips in 1928—33: London, Paris, Egypt, Arabia and Greece. First woodcut in 1932. Spent 1933—40 at Reutlingen as an additional worker. Soldier during 1940—45. Made his home on the Achalm near Reutlingen and has been a professor at the Karlsruhe Academy since 1955.
Lit: W. Boeck, *HAP Grieshaber, Holzschnitte*, Pfullingen, 1958; (The complete cat. lists 314 works from the years 1932—58); *HAP Grieshaber*, Exhibition cat., Munich, 1963.   *Ill. p. 193*

GRIMM, Willem — Born on 2 May 1904 at Eberstadt in Hessia. Studied at Offenburg and Hamburg, belonged to the circle of the Hamburg *Sezession*, and since 1946 has taught at the Hamburg College of Fine Arts.
Lit: VOLLMER II, 1955; Cat. of exhibition, Kunsthalle, Darmstadt, 1962.

GRIS, Juan (really José Victoriano González) — Born on 23 March 1887 at Madrid. Died on 11 May 1927 at Boulogne-sur-Seine. First tuition in drawing and painting at Madrid. To Paris in 1906. From 1911 an exponent of "analytical cubism" and from 1913 one of the leading representatives of "synthetic cubism", which he also championed in lectures and discussions.
Graphics: Solely from the late period (1921—26) and besides his book illustrations only six individual prints.
Lit: D. H. Kahnweiler, *Juan Gris*, Bradford, 1947; J. T. Soby, *Juan Gris*, The Museum of Modern Art, New York, 1958, Mayflower Books (with bibl.).   *Ill. p. 169*

GROCHOWIAK, Thomas — Born in 1919 at Recklinghausen, where he now works as an abstract painter.
Lit: VOLLMER II, 1955; Cat. of exhibition at Galerie Günar, Düsseldorf, 1959.

GROMAIRE, Marcel — Born on 24 July 1892 at Noyelles-sur-Sambre. Living since 1910 at Paris. Until the start of the First World War under the influence of the Matisse school and Cézanne's art. After the war encountered the art of Léger. Through his expressive and monumental style became in 1939, with Lurçat, a reviver of the art of tapestry at Aubusson. Also works as a graphic artist and illustrator: woodcuts and etchings.
Lit: BENEZIT IV, 1951; VOLLMER II, 1955.

GROSS, Anthony — Born on 19 March 1905 in London, where he now teaches graphic art at the Slade School of Fine Arts. Studied in London and at the Académie Julian in Paris. Worked as a war artist during 1941—45. Awards for graphics in 1955 at Lugano and Ljubljana.
Lit: Cat. of the 4th international exhibition of graphic art at Ljubljana in 1961.

GROSSMANN, Rudolf — Born on 25 January 1882 at Freiburg im Breisgau, the artist died there in December 1941. Lived at Paris during 1905—14 and belonged there to the Café du Dôme circle. Then went to Munich and in 1926 became a teacher at the State Art School in Berlin. Grossmann was chiefly a draughtsman and graphic artist producing portraits, caricatures
Lit: VOLLMER II, 1955; *Rudolf Grossmann, Drawings and Graphic Work*, cat., Karlsruhe, 1963.

GROSZ, George — Born on 26 July 1893 in Berlin. Died there on 5 July 1959. Studied from 1909 in Dresden and from 1911 under Emil Orlik in Berlin. In Paris in 1913. A soldier during the First World War. Connection at Berlin in 1918 with the dadaists, around 1925 with the *Neue Sachlichkeit*. Became well-known through his aggressive caricatures from the 'twenties. Went in 1932 to America, where he became a professor at the Art Students League.
Lit: "Self-portrait" entitled *Ein kleines Ja und ein großes Nein*, Hamburg, 1955; H. Bittner, *George Grosz*, New York and Cologne, 1960—61.   *Ill. p. 99*

GULINO, Nunzio — Born on 16 June 1920 at Comiso (Ragusa), the artist now works at the Istituto del Libro, Urbino.
Lit: C. A. Petrucci, *Le incisioni di Gulino*, Rome, Calcografia Naz., 1954; SERVOLINI, p. 412.

Grimm

Gris

Grochowiak

Gromaire

Gross

Grossmann

Gulino

Grosz

271

Guttoso

Haage

GUTTUSO, Renato — Born on 2 January 1912 at Bagheria (Palermo). Studied painting in Rome from 1931. During 1940—42 belonged to the Corrente expressionist group and was a co-founder of the Fronte nuovo delle Arti. Today one of the best-known representatives of Italian neo-realism.
Lit: VOLLMER II, 1955.

HAAGE, Sixten — The artist lives at Stockholm, where he was born in 1926. Belongs to a partnership of Swedish graphic artists who at Grödinge near Stockholm have formed the Grödinge Group, for the craftsmanlike production of colour graphics.
Lit: Cat. of the Grödinge Group exhibition at Gelsenkirchen in 1960.

HAASE, Volkmar — Lives as an independent metal sculpture and graphic artist at Berlin, where he was born in 1930. Star pupil in Max Kaus's painting class at the College of Fine Arts in 1956. Was already making iron sculptures in 1955; colour etchings since 1957. In 1960 awarded scholarship by the *Kulturkreis* of the Federal Association of German Industry.
Lit: Cat. of the exhibition at the Märkisches Museum, Witten (Ruhr), in 1959; VOLLMER VI (Suppl.), 1962.

HAASS, Terry — Born on 15 November 1923 at Olomuc in Czechoslovakia. In 1939 studied art and art history in Paris, in 1941 on a scholarship at New York. Worked in 1947 at Hayter's Atelier 17, where she taught print-making in 1949—50. As an archaeologist took part in an expedition to the Near East.
Lit: Cat. of the 4th international exhibition of graphic art at Ljubljana in 1961 ("Ecole de Paris").

HAJEK, Otto Herbert — German Bohemian sculptor, born on 27 June 1927 at Kaltenbach in Czechoslovakia. Studied at the Stuttgart Academy during 1947—54. Visit to Paris for study in 1952.
Since 1955 has taken part in many exhibitions, most recently the 1958 Biennale at Venice and documenta II at Cassel.
Lit: VOLLMER II, 1955; *Otto Herbert Hajek*, publ. by the Galerie Anne Abels, Cologne, 1960.

HAMAGUCHI, Yozo — Born on 5 April 1909 at Watayama (Japan). Spent 1928—30 studying sculpture at the Academy in Tokyo, 1930—39 being trained as a painter and graphic artist in Paris, where he has lived since 1953. First international graphic arts prize at São Paulo in 1957.
Lit: Hamaguchi, *Manière noire*, Berggruen, Paris, 1958.

HANSEN, Karl Heinz (Hansen-Bahia) — Born in 1915 at Hamburg. Made his name with the woodcuts he did in Brazil, to which he emigrated in 1950, settling in Bahia in 1955. For the last few years has been living in Germany again (Tittmoning, Upper Bavaria).
Lit: Hansen-Bahia, *Stationen und Wegmarken eines Holzschneiders*, Hamburg, 1960 (with bibl.).

Haase

Haass

Hamaguchi

Hajek

Hansen

HARTUNG, Hans — Born on 21 September 1904 in Leipzig. From 1924 studied at Leipzig and Dresden. In 1925 came to terms with the early art of Kandinsky. From 1927 on, journeys and many stays in Paris. Minorca during 1932–34. In 1935 migrated to Paris, where he lives now. Foreign Legion during the war. Badly wounded in Alsace in 1944.
Lit: Domnik, *Hans Hartung*, Stuttgart, 1950; R. V. Gindertael, *Hans Hartung*, Paris, 1960, Berlin 1962. *Ill. p. 235*

HARTUNG, Karl — Sculptor and graphic artist, born on 2 May 1908 at Hamburg. Spent 1929–32 in Paris, 1932–33 in Florence. Back in Hamburg in 1933–36. From 1936 at Berlin, since 1951 as a professor at the College of Fine Arts.
Lit: Carl Linfert, "Karl Hartung" in *Junge Künstler 59/60,* Cologne, 1959.

HAYTER, Stanley William — Born on 27 December 1901 in London, the son of a painter. Lives in Paris. During 1921–22 graduate chemist in the oil industry in Persia. From 1922–25 studied painting at his father's studio. Went to Paris in 1926. Encountered surrealism. In Atelier 17, founded at Paris in 1927 for investigating new graphic techniques, he created one of the most influential graphic teaching studios. Spent 1940–50 in New York, where his training studio gave powerful impetus to American action painting.
Lit: His own *New Ways of Gravure*, New York and London, 1949; VOLLMER II, 1955.
Ills pp. 239, 241

Hartung, Hans

HECK, Erich — Born on 24 May 1897 at Frankfurt am Main, where he lives as a painter and wood-cutter. Studied there at the School of Arts and Crafts and the Städel Art School. A pupil of Max Beckmann.
Lit: VOLLMER II, 1955.

HECKEL, Erich — Born on 31 July 1883 at Döbeln in Saxony. Living since 1944 at Hemmenhofen by Lake Constance. Self-taught as a painter. In 1904 studied architecture at the Dresden Technical College. In 1905 founded the *Brücke* group jointly with Kirchner, Schmidt-Rottluff and Bleyl. Visited Italy in 1909. Moved to Berlin in 1911. During 1914–18 a medical orderly in Flanders, where he visited Ensor. After the war he again settled at Berlin, where bombs destroyed his studio and home in 1944 during the Second World War.
Graphics: His very extensive production so far includes about 370 lithographs, 360 woodcuts and 180 etchings. Heckel was among the first of the *Brücke* circle to take hand impressions of his lithographs.
Lit: THIEME-BECKER XVI, 1923; VOLLMER II, 1955; L. G. Buchheim, *Die Künstlergemeinschaft Brücke*, Feldafing, 1956 (with bibl.); L. G. Buchheim, *Erich Heckel, Holzschnitte 1905–1956*, Feldafing, 1957. *Ills pp. 75, 77, 85*

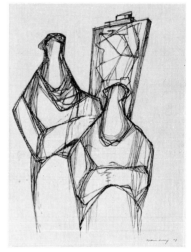

Hartung, Karl

HEGENBARTH, Josef — Born on 15 June 1884 in Kamnitz, Bohemia. At the Dresden Academy in 1900–15, star pupil under Gotthart Kühl. During the First World War, in Prague. From 1919 at Dresden. His work hindered after 1933. In 1945 loss of his works in Czechoslovakia. Professor at the Dresden Academy during 1947–49. Until his death on 27 July 1962, lived in Dresden as an independent artist. Book illustration his main field of activity.
Lit: VOLLMER II, 1955; W. Grohmann, *Josef Hegenbarth*, Berlin, 1959.

Hayter

Hegenbarth

Heck

Heckel

Heiliger

Heldt

Herkenrath

HEILIGER, Bernhard — Born on 11 November 1915 at Stettin. Became an apprentice stone-mason and attended Stettin's art school. During 1935—37 star pupil of Scheibe in Berlin. In Paris in 1938—39. Only came into notice after 1945. Since 1949 a professor at the Berlin College of Fine Arts.
Lit: VOLLMER II, 1955; H. Th. Flemming, *Bernhard Heiliger*, Berlin, 1962 (with bibl.).

HELDT, Werner — Born on 17 November 1904 at Berlin. Died on 3 October 1954 at Sant' Angelo on Ischia. Studied at Berlin. Visited Paris in 1930. During 1933—35 on Majorca, 1935—40 in Berlin. Berlin again from 1946.
Lit: VOLLMER II, 1955; Cat. of the exhibition at the Kestner-Gesellschaft, Hanover, in 1957.

HERKENRATH, Peter — Lives at Cologne, where he was born in 1900. A self-taught artist. First group show at Cologne in 1932. Many exhibitions since the war (in 1952 at the Galerie Der Spiegel, Cologne). In 1958 awarded the city of Hagen Karl Ernst Osthaus prize and the Villa Romana prize.
Lit: Günter Aust, "Peter Herkenrath" in *Junge Künstler 59/60*, Cologne, 1959.

HEYBOER, Anton — He was born on 9 February 1924 at Sabang in Indonesia and grew up in Curaçao. Now living at Amsterdam as a graphic artist. Pulls all his prints himself in limited editions of nine examples.
Lit: *Anton Heyboer*, Galerie Der Spiegel, Cologne, 1960 (the 62 works of the last two years catalogued with illustrations). *Ill. p. 250*

HINTSCHICH, Gerhard — Born on 26 June 1926 at Hof in Moravia. Lives at Frankfurt am Main. In 1949 studied under Willi Baumeister, during 1949—56 at the Frankfurt College of Fine Arts. In Paris in 1951—52 on a scholarship. Prize for colour graphics at Grenchen in 1958.
Lit: Cat. of the 4th international exhibition of graphic art at Ljubljana in 1961.

HOEHME, Gerhard — Born in 1920 at Greppin near Dessau. Lives at Düsseldorf-Kaisers-werth. Freed from captivity in 1946, he went to Halle. 1949 saw the beginnings of his abstract painting — inspired by early works of Kandinsky and the art of Paul Klee.
Lit: *Knaurs Lexikon abstrakter Malerei*, Munich and Zurich, 1957; VOLLMER VI (Suppl.), 1962.

HOFER, Karl — Born on 11 October 1878 at Karlsruhe. Died on 3 April 1955 at Berlin. After studying in Karlsruhe under Hans Thoma and L. von Kalckreuth, spent many years between 1903 and 1913 at Rome and at Paris, where he studied Cézanne's pictures. Journeys to India in 1909 and 1911. At Berlin in 1913. Interned in France in 1914. To Zurich during 1917 on an exchange. Taught at the Berlin Academy during 1918—33. After an abstract inter-lude, returned in 1932 to his old style. In 1945 became head of the Berlin College of Fine Arts. The bulk of his earlier works lost through seizure and bombing.
Lit: His own autobiographical *Aus Leben und Kunst*, Berlin, 1952; VOLLMER II, 1955. *Ill. p. 96*

IHLE, John Livingston — Born in 1925 in Chicago. Lives at Mill Valley, California. Pupil of Maurice Lasansky in Iowa during 1949. Gained his M. A. in 1951 at Bradley University. Instructor in art at the San Francisco State College in 1955 and assistant professor of art in 1959. The formal world of his etchings is suggested by his work as a draughtsman at the Natural History Museum in Chicago, by Mesopotamian clay tablets, and by examples of ancient Mexican art.
Lit: *American Prints Today*, 1959.

ITEM, Georges — Born in 1925 at Biel, Switzerland. Living since 1948 at Saint-Rémy-de-Provence. The main theme of his pictures is the scenery of the Camargue.
Lit: IGAS (Internat. Graphic Arts Soc., New York) 11/Nov. 1954.

JAENISCH, Hans — Born on 19 May 1907 at Eilenstedt near Halberstadt. Bauhaus student at Weimar. In 1927 showed his first abstract pictures at *Der Sturm*. After his release from captivity, back at Berlin since 1946. Berlin city art prize in 1950. Since 1953 professor at the College of Fine Arts.
Lit: VOLLMER II, 1955; *Knaurs Lexikon abstrakter Malerei*, Munich and Zurich, 1957. *Ill. p. 244*

JANSSEN, Horst — Born on 14 November 1929 at Hamburg. Trained at the State Art School under Alfred Mahlau. Lives in Hamburg as an independent artist.
Lit: H. Th. Flemming in *Quadrum 14*, Brussels, 1957; and *Die Kunst und das schöne Heim*; Jg. 57, 1958.

JANSSON, Vide — Born in 1924 at Stockholm, he now lives at Grödinge (south-west of Stockholm) and, like Sixten Haage, is one of the graphic artists of the Grödinge Group.
Lit: Cat. of the Grödinge Group exhibition at Gelsenkirchen in 1960.

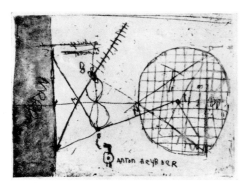

Heyboer

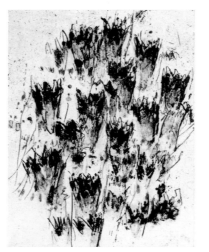

Hoehme

Hintschich

Ihle

Jaenisch

Hofer

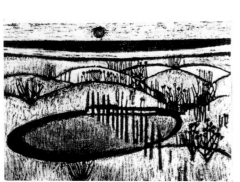

Item

Janssen

Jansson

Jongkind

Jawlensky

Jorn

JAWLENSKY, Alexei von — Born on 26 March 1864 near Torscholk, Province of Tver. Died on 15 March 1941 at Wiesbaden. After attending the Moscow Military Academy studied painting at the Academy in St Petersburg under Ilya Repin. Went with Marianne Werefkin in 1896 to Munich, meeting Kandinsky there at Anton Azbé's art school. In Brittany and Provence during 1915: Cézanne, Van Gogh, Matisse. Co-founder of the Munich New Artists' Federation. In Switzerland during the First World War. From 1921 at Wiesbaden. The Blue Four in 1924: Kandinsky, Klee, Feininger, Jawlensky.
Graphics: A few lithographs and one etching.
Lit: C. Weiler, *Alexei von Jawlensky*, London, 1960 (with bibl.).

JONGKIND, Johan Barthold — Born on 3 June 1819 at Lattrop (Overijssel, Holland). Died on 9 February 1891 at La Côte-Saint-André near Grenoble. Studied at The Hague. In 1846 met Isabey, Corot and the Barbizon painters in Paris. Lived on the Channel coast during the 'fifties. To Rotterdam in 1855, to Paris in 1860, at Le Havre in 1863. From 1878 at La Côte-Saint-André. This very sensitive and unbalanced painter is considered one of the precursors of impressionism.
Graphics: Etchings from 1862 on.
Lit: THIEME-BECKER XIX, 1926; DELTEIL I, 1906 (twenty prints listed); P. Signac, *J. B. Jongkind*, Paris, 1927 (with complete cat. of the etchings). *Ill. p. 9*

JORN, Asger — Danish painter and writer on art, born on 3 March 1914 at Vejrun in Jutland. Worked during 1936–37 in Paris with Léger and Le Corbusier. Graphics award at Ljubljana in 1959.
Lit: Cat. of the 4th international exhibition of graphic art at Ljubljana in 1961; Ph. Wellbach, Dansk Kunstnerleks II, 1947–52; VOLLMER VI (Suppl.), 1962.

JUKITA, Fumiaki — Born in 1926 at Tokushima (Japan). Lives at Ota-ku, Tokyo. Prize at the 1st international triennial for colour graphics at Grenchen (Switzerland).
Lit: Cat. of the exhibition of graphic art at Grenchen in 1958.

KANDINSKY, Wassily — Born on 5 December 1866 at Moscow. Died on 13 December 1944 at Neuilly-sur-Seine. After beginning as a law-student, went in 1896 to Munich to attend Anton Azbé's art school. There he met Jawlensky, with whom he founded the Munich New Artists' Federation in 1909. Exhibited at the *Blaue Reiter* exhibition in Munich in 1911 with works by Marc, Macke, Kandinsky and Klee. In Russia during 1914–21. Taught at the Bauhaus in Weimar and Dessau from 1922 to 1939. The Blue Four in 1924: Kandinsky, Klee, Feininger, Jawlensky.
Graphics: First woodcuts in 1902, 56 for *Klänge* in 1913; *Kleine Welten* in 1922 (12 prints: lithographs, woodcuts, etchings).
Own writings: *Concerning the Spiritual in Art*, Mayflower Books and Vision Press, 1947; *Der Blaue Reiter*, Munich, 1912 (jointly with Franz Marc).
Lit: W. Grohmann, *Wassily Kandinsky*, London, 1959; *Wassily Kandinsky*, special number of the periodical *Sélection*, Antwerp, 1933 (with cat. of the graphics from 1903 to 1932); W. Grohmann, *Kandinsky, œuvre gravée*, Berggruen, Paris, 1954 (all 12 prints of *Kleine Welten* album reproduced); P. A. Riedl, W. Kandinsky, *Kleine Welten*, Stuttgart 1962. *Ills pp. 179, 180, 181*

KAUS, Max — Born on 11 March 1891 at Berlin, where he attended the School of Arts and Crafts during 1909–13 and worked as a decorator till 1914. From 1919–33 taught at the Vereinigten Staatsschulen für Bildende Kunst in Berlin, where he has been a professor at the College of Fine Arts since 1945. As a pupil of Heckel, Kaus belongs to the circle of the German expressionists.
Lit: VOLLMER III, 1956; L. G. Buchheim, *Graphik des deutschen Expressionismus*, Feldafing, 1959.

Kaus

Kandinsky

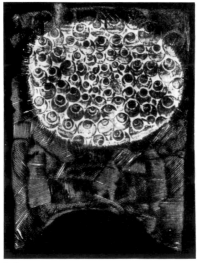
Jukita

276

KINERT, Albert — Born on 6 April 1919 at Vinkovci in Yugoslavia. Attended the Zagreb Academy. Study trips to Italy, France and Holland. Various art awards, most recently at Ljubljana in 1959 and Zagreb in 1960.
Lit: Cat. of the 4th international exhibition of graphic art at Ljubljana in 1961.

Kinert

KIRCHNER, Ernst Ludwig — Born on 6 May 1880 at Aschaffenburg. Took his own life on 15 June 1938 at Davos. Spent 1901–05 studying architecture and painting at Dresden and Munich. Co-founder in 1905 of the *Brücke* at Dresden. In 1905 to Berlin, where *Der Sturm* obtained the German expressionists as contributors as well. A soldier during 1914–15. To Königstein im Taunus in 1915, gravely ill. From 1917 lived permanently in Switzerland. Kirchner made the most important contribution to the graphic art of German expressionism.
Lit: W. Grohmann, *E. L. Kirchner*, London, 1962; Gustav Schiefler, *Die Graphik E. L. Kirchners*, vol. 1, Berlin, 1926 (cat. of the works to 1916); vol. 2, Berlin, 1931 (cat. from 1917 till 1927 with additions to vol. 1); A. Dube-Heyning, *Ernst Ludwig Kirchner, Graphik*, Munich, 1961; Cat. of the exhibition at the Düsseldorf Art Club in 1960 (with full biograph. data, list of exhibitions, and bibl.). *Ills pp. 67, 69, 71, 73, 86*

Kirchner

KLEE, Paul — Born on 18 December 1879 at Münchenbuchsee near Bern, the son of a German father and a Swiss mother of southern French descent. Died on 29 June 1940 at Muralto near Locarno. In 1898 studied painting at Munich, and moved there from Bern in 1906 after his marriage. In 1911 association with the *Blaue Reiter* artists, above all Kandinsky; in 1912 in Paris meeting with Apollinaire, Picasso and Delaunay, and with the art of Cézanne, Van Gogh and Matisse. Travelled to Tunis and Cairo in 1914. Spent 1916–18 as a soldier. Taught at the Bauhaus in Weimar and Dessau during 1922–31, at the Düsseldorf Academy in 1931–33. Moved to Bern in 1933, after his dismissal.
Drawing has a special importance in Klee's *œuvre*. He held his first exhibition of graphics at Zurich in 1910 and until the trip to Tunis of 1914 remained primarily a draughtsman. His prints comprise about 100 to 120 works from the years 1901–32.
Lit: W. Grohmann, *Paul Klee*, London, 2nd ed., 1958; F. Klee, *Paul Klee, Leben und Werk in Dokumenten*, Zürich, 1959; J. T. Soby, *The Prints of Paul Klee*, 2nd ed., New York, 1947, Mayflower Books; *Paul Klee: The thinking Eye. The Notebooks of Paul Klee*, ed. Jürgen Spiller. London, 1961. *Ills pp. 185, 186, 187*

Klee

KLEINSCHMIDT, Paul — Born on 31 July 1883 at Bublitz, Pomerania. Died in 1949 at Bensheim an der Bergstrasse. Studied at Berlin and Munich, then lived at Berlin. Emigrated to Holland and France in 1935. At Bensheim from 1943.
Lit: VOLLMER III, 1956.

KLIEMANN, Carl-Heinz — Born on 8 June 1924 at Berlin, where he lives now. Studied from 1945 till 1950 at the Berlin College of Fine Arts, first under Max Kaus, later as star pupil of Schmidt-Rottluff. Berlin city graphics award in 1950, Ljubljana graphics prize in 1955, Villa Romana prize in 1958.
Lit: Cat. of the 4th international exhibition of graphic art at Ljubljana in 1961; H. Platte, "Carl-Heinz Kliemann" in *Junge Künstler 60/61*, Cologne, 1960.

KLINGER, Max — Born on 18 February 1857 at Leipzig. Died on 5 July 1920 at Grossjena near Naumburg. Painter, sculptor and graphic artist. After finishing his studies lived at Karlsruhe and Berlin. From 1885 on spent many years in Paris, Berlin and Rome, then settled at his native city, Leipzig, in 1893.
Graphics: Large *œuvre* of about 400 prints. Principle works are fourteen sets of etchings from the years 1881–1916, among them *The Glove* of 1881 (opus VI) and the *Brahms Fantasia* (opus XII).
Lit: THIEME-BECKER XX, 1927; Graphic works up to 1909 cat. in H. W. Singer, *Max Klingers Radierungen, Stiche und Steindrucke*, Berlin, 1909. *Ill. p. 10*

Kleinschmidt

Kliemann

Klinger

Kogan

KOGAN, Moissey — Born on 24 May 1879 at Orgeyev in Bessarabia. Died in 1942 in a German concentration camp. Mostly self-taught. Went to Munich in 1903. Worked as a lapidary, medallist, potter and designer of textiles and embroidery. Foundation member of the New Artists' Federation, the forerunner of the *Blaue Reiter*. Through K. E. Osthaus went to the Folkwang School at Hagen, through Van de Velde in 1912 to Weimar. Later lived mostly in Paris, Germany and Holland. Besides his applied art and many drawings, produced etchings, woodcuts and linocuts.
Lit: *Moissey Kogan*, pub. by the Clemens-Sels-Museum, Neuss, on the occasion of the Kogan exhibition in 1960; VOLLMER III and IV (Suppl.), 1962.

KOHLER, Max Ernst — Born on 6 October 1919 at Solothurn in Switzerland. Lives in Paris, where he studied under Severini and Friedlaender.
Lit: Cat. of the 3rd international exhibition of graphic art at Ljubljana in 1959.

KOHN, Misch — Born on 26 March 1916 at Kokomo, Indiana, Since 1950 a teacher at the Institute of Design, Chicago. After concluding his studies (B. A., 1939) lived in Chicago, Mexico (1943—44) and Paris. Has taken part in many exhibitions in the States, Latin America and Europe. Numerous awards. Lithographs since 1939.
Lit: *American Prints Today*, 1959; V. Zigrosser, *Misch Kohn*, New York, 1961, (Pub. by the American Federation of Arts. Lists 161 prints from the years 1939—60.) *Ill. p. 140*

KOKOSCHKA, Oskar — Born on 1 March 1886 at Pöchlarn on the Danube. During 1904—08 attended the Vienna School of Arts and Crafts and worked for the Wiener Werkstätten. Lived till 1914 alternately in Vienna, Switzerland and Berlin — here as a *Der Sturm* contributor. Wounded during the First World War, went in 1917 to Dresden. Taught during 1920—24 at the Dresden Academy. Journeys through Europe and the Mediterranean lands. To Vienna in 1931, teaching at the Prague Academy in 1934, migration to London in 1938. After the war more long visits to Italy, America and Germany. Living since 1953 at Villeneuve on the Lake of Geneva. In the summer directs a "School of Seeing" at Salzburg.
Early on, Kokoschka also made a name as an author and illustrator, and, besides his paintings, he has produced many graphic works.
Own writings: *Oskar Kokoschka, Schriften 1907—1955*, ed. by H. M. Wingler, Munich, 1956.
Lit: Edith Hoffmann, *Kokoschka, Life and Work*, London, 1947. (Appendix contains a cat. of the lithographs and drawings for illustrations from 1908—1945); H. M. Wingler, *Oskar Kokoschka, The Work of the Painter*, London, 1958 (with complete cat. of the paintings, list of Kokoschka's own writings, and bibl.); Cat. of the Munich Kokoschka exhibition of 1950 (with list of the graphic works to 1950, giving 163 numbers, by W. F. Arntz; *Kokoschka, A retrospective exhibition*, cat. of Arts Council, 1962. *Ills pp. 100, 101*

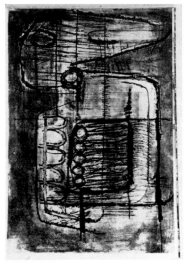

Kohler

KOLLWITZ, Käthe — Born on 8 July 1867 at Königsberg. Died on 22 April 1945 at Moritzburg near Dresden. Studied in 1885—86 under Karl Stauffer-Bern at Berlin and in 1888—89 under Ludwig Herterich at Munich. As the wife of a slum doctor, Karl Kollwitz, she lived from 1891 in north Berlin, and out of this milieu and the times created her extensive graphic *œuvre* with its strong social bias. Till 1919 chiefly etchings and lithographs, from then on woodcuts too.
Lit: K. Kollwitz, *Tagebuchblätter und Briefe*, Berlin, 1948; K. Kollwitz, *Aus meinem Leben*, Munich, 1957; A. Klipstein, *Käthe Kollwitz, Verzeichnis des graphischen Werkes*, Bern, 1955.
Ill. p. 97

Kollwitz

Kohn

Kokoschka

KONOW, Jürgen von — Born in 1915 at Ostersund, Sweden, the artist ultimately taught the graphics class at the Academy of Art in Stockholm. Died on 10 June 1959. Came late to print-making and found his graphic style at Paris under S. W. Hayter's influence. One-man show at the 3rd international graphic art exhibition at Ljubljana in 1959.
Lit: Cat. of the 3rd international exhibition of graphic art at Ljubljana in 1959.

Konow

KOROMPAY, Giovanni — Born on 26 April 1904 in Venice. Painter, sculptor and graphic artist. Represented at Venice in 1960 by a special exhibition of his etchings.
Lit: Cat. of the 4th international exhibition of graphic art at Ljubljana in 1961.

KRUCK, Christian — Born in 1925 at Hamburg, since 1953 the artist has been head of the printing-office and lithographic studio at the Städel Academy in Frankfurt am Main. After apprenticeship as a lithographer, attended the art schools at Nuremberg and Freiburg im Breis-gau. His colour lithographs printed from a single stone and as a rule only in fifteen examples.
Lit: Cat. of exhibition at the Frankfurt Art Club in 1960.

KUBIN, Alfred — Born on 10 April 1877 at Leitmeritz in Bohemia. Died on 20 August 1959 at Zwickledt.
After his early years at Salzburg, studied in 1898 at the Munich Academy. Visits to Paris and Italy in 1905. Lived from 1906 on his estate at Zwickledt near Wernstein am Inn. In 1910 association with the *Blaue Reiter* group.
Also a noted writer, the artist left, besides his prints, a mass of pen drawings and book illustrations as his main achievement.
Lit: P. Raabe, *Alfred Kubin*, Hamburg, 1957 (with bibl.). *Ill. p. 98*

Korompay

KUGLER, Rudolf — Born on 27 September 1921 in Berlin. From 1948 studied under Max Kaus at the Berlin College of Fine Arts, where for several years he has been a professor with an enamel-painting class.
Graphics: Colour etchings.
Lit: VOLLMER II, 1955; Cat. of exhibition in Egypt, arranged by the German art council, 1962.

LABOUREUR, Jean-Emile — Born on 16 August 1877 at Nantes. Died on 16 June 1943 at Kerfalher-en-Pénestin. Lived from 1909 in his native city as a graphic artist. His works done during the First World War stem from cubism and are important in the development of graphic art as a reanimation of line-engraving, which from 1916 on Laboureur used almost exclusively, it being the technique that suited him.
Lit: VOLLMER III, 1956; L. Godefroy, *l'Oeuvre gravée de J. E. Laboureur*, vol. 1, Paris, 1929; Cat. of the Laboureur exhibition at the Bibl. nat., Paris, in 1954.

Kubin

Kügler

Laboureur

Kruck

La Fresnaye

Lardera

Lasansky

LA FRESNAYE, Roger de — Born on 11 July 1885 at Le Mans. Died on 27 November 1925 at Grasse. During 1903—08 studied at the Académie Julian and the Académie Ranson, here under the nabis Maurice Denis and Sérusier. Their influence replaced by that of Cézanne, the cubists, and the *Séction d'or* (1911—13). Military service during 1914—17. His late works in a *Neue Sachlichkeit* style.
Lit: R. Coignat and W. George, *L'Oeuvre complète de Roger de La Fresnaye*, Paris, 1950.

LARDERA, Berto — Born on 18 December 1911 at La Spezia. Noted Italian metal sculptor who has lived at Paris since 1947 and evolved his own abstract style since 1944. His few lithographs are closely connected with his sculpture.
Lit: M. Seuphor, *Berto Lardera*, London, 1960.

LASANSKY, Mauricio — Born in 1914 at Buenos Aires, where he studied at the Academy of Art. Then became director of the Free Fine Arts School and the Taller Manualidades at Córdoba, Argentina. Since 1952 teaching print-making at the State University in Iowa City.
Lit: *American Prints Today*, 1959; C. Zigrosser, *M. Lasansky*, New York, 1960 (The American Federation of Arts). Lists 96 graphics from the years 1933—59.   *Ill. p. 141*

LAURENCIN, Marie — Born on 31 October 1885 in Paris, the artist died there on 8 June 1956. She was only temporarily influenced by her friendship with writers and artists of cubism in the style of her calm paintings with their fragile figures.
Graphics: About 200 etchings and lithographs.
Lit: VOLLMER III, 1956; J.-E. Laboureur, *Marie Laurencin, Catalogue de l'œuvre gravée*, MS., 1928 (one ex. in the Cabinet des estampes, Paris).

LAURENS, Henri — Born on 18 February 1885 in Paris, where he died on 5 May 1954. This skilled stone-mason came to cubism through Braque in 1911, and sought to solve his formal problems in the domains of sculpture, though also in his *collages* and graphic works. The severe cubism followed about 1925 by a short classicist phase and lastly by the period of his expressive, bulky, much deformed figures.
Graphics: Eight illustrated books from the years 1917—51 along with separate prints.
Lit: VOLLMER III, 1956; *Henri Laurens*, pub. by the Galerie Claude Bernard, Paris, 1960 (with bibl.); *H. Laurens, œuvre gravée*, cat. of the Galerie Ziegler, Zurich, 1960.   *Ill. p. 195*

LEGER, Fernand — Born on 4 February 1881, the son of Norman peasants at Argentan (Orne). Died on 17 August 1955 at Gif-sur-Yvette. Since 1897 he was at Caen; in 1900—02, Paris, as an architectural draughtsman. Art student from 1903. Through Cézanne and Matisse arrived at cubism in 1910. A soldier during 1914—16. In 1920 met Le Corbusier. Visits in 1931 to Greece and the United States, where he lived during 1940—45.
In 1917 Léger began to paint his "machinery pictures" and develop a monumental style of his own. First murals, for an exhibition pavilion by Le Corbusier, in 1925. One in 1937 for the Paris World Fair. In 1953 decoration for the great hall of the UNO headquarters, New York. Also mosaics and stained-glass windows for churches, and tapestry cartoons.
Lit: D. Cooper, *Fernand Léger et le Nouvel Espace*, London, 1949 (with bibl.); Cat. of the Léger exhibition at Paris and Munich in 1956 and 1957 (with bibl.).   *Ill. p. 173*

Léger

Laurencin

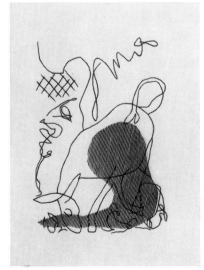
Laurens

280

LEHMBRUCK, Wilhelm — Born on 4 January 1881 at Duisburg-Meiderich, the son of a miner. Took his own life on 25 March 1919 at Berlin.
After attending the Düsseldorf School of Arts and Crafts (1895–99), an assistant in sculpture studios for a while. During 1901–06 at the Düsseldorf Academy, 1910–14 in Paris, 1914–19 in Berlin and (1917–18) Zurich.
Graphics: About 130 works, chiefly etchings on zinc. 15 lithographs.
Lit: August Hoff, *Wilhelm Lehmbruck*, Berlin, 1936 and 1961; Cat. of the exhibition at Mannheim in 1949 (with bibl.); E. Trier, *Wilhelm Lehmbruck, Zeichnungen und Radierungen,* Munich, 1955 (introduction), a cat. of the etchings of Lehmbruck is in preparation.

LEMCKE, Dietmar — Born on 13 January 1930 at Goldap in East Prussia, the artist now lives at Berlin, where he studied during 1948–54 at the College of Fine Arts as a pupil of Ernst Schumacher.
Lit: VOLLMER III, 1956.

LE MOAL, Jean — Born on 30 October 1909 at Authon-du-Perche (Eure-et-Loire). Lives in Paris. First studied architecture in Lyon; from 1929 in Paris. Friendly with Manessier and like him strongly influenced by the earlier work of Roger Bissière, who was then teaching at the Académie Ranson. During 1940–42 also active as a stage designer. Stained-glass windows for churches since 1956.
Lit: Cat. of the exhibition at Lübeck in 1961 (with bibl.); R. Nacenta, *School of Paris*, London, 1960.

LETICIA, Anna — Born in the state of Rio de Janeiro, Brazil, she attended courses at the Museum of Modern Art in Rio and was then for a while a pupil of André Lhote. Exhibitions since 1953. Leirner prize for graphics in 1959.
Lit: Cat. of the exhibition of Brasilian art at Munich and Hamburg in 1959–60.

LHOTE, André — Born on 5 July 1885 at Bordeaux. Died in January 1962 in Paris. After studying sculpture at Bordeaux, went to Paris in 1908. As a painter, self-taught. In 1911 encounter with cubism and the *Section d'or* artists. Founded his own art school in 1922. Lhote became well-known above all as a writer on art.
Lit: J. Cocteau and P. Courthion, *André Lhote*, Paris, 1959.

LICATA, Riccardo — Born on 20 December 1929 in Turin, this painter and graphic artist lives today in Venice and Paris. Formerly a teacher at the Venice Academy of Art, he now teaches at the Italian Art School in Paris.
Represented in 1955 at the Venice exhibition of Italian graphic art and at the graphics exhibition in São Paulo. Various prizes, including ones for his prints.
Lit: *Quadrum V*, p. 150, 1958; SERVOLINI, p. 438.

LIMA, José — Born in 1934 at Pernambuco, the artist studied at the School of Arts and Crafts and the Museum of Modern Art in Rio de Janeiro. Exhibitions since 1958.
Lit: Cat. of the exhibition of Brasilian art at Munich and Hamburg in 1959–60.

Lehmbruck

Lemcke

Lhote

Leticia

Licata

Le Moal

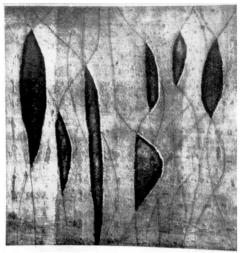

Lima

Lipman-Wulf

Lucebert

Lurçat

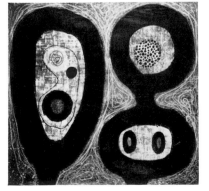

Maki

LIPMAN-WULF, Peter — Born in 1906 at Berlin, where he studied sculpture at the Academy. Lived as an appreciated sculptor in Berlin until he had to leave Germany in 1933. During 1933—47 taught sculpture and woodcut at the Académie Colarossi, Paris. Today lives in the United States, occupied of late chiefly with — sometimes big — colour woodcuts of biblical subjects.
Lit: Various exhibition cats. Most recently, exhibition at the Silvermine Guild of Artists in 1961 (Silvermine, New Canaan, Conn.); VOLLMER III, 1956.

LUCEBERT — Born in 1924 at Amsterdam, the artist now lives at Bergen (Holland). An exhibition of his works held in 1958 at the Galerie Der Spiegel, Cologne. Represented in 1959 at documenta II, Cassel.
Lit: *Geh durch den Spiegel*, pub. by the Galerie Der Spiegel, Cologne, 1958.

LURCAT, Jean — Born on 1 July 1892 at Bruyères (Vosges). Lives at Paris. After brief studies at Nancy, went in 1912 to Paris. Passed through the school of cubism during 1920—23. Later developed a "surreal expressionism", particularly in his tapestries, through the manufacture of which he gave the French factories new stimuli. Illustrations to his own and other people's poems in 1948—50.
Lit: P. Soupault, *Jean Lurçat*, Paris, n. d.; VOLLMER III, 1956.

MACCARI, Mino — Born on 24 November 1898 at Siena and a product of the "Scuola romana", the artist is one of Italy's most inventive illustrators and caricaturists. As a printmaker, he is at home with all techniques and has achieved an extensive graphic production alongside his drawings for the magazine *Il Selvaggio*.
Lit: L. Magagnato, *Maccari*, Verona, 1957.

MAGNELLI, Alberto — Born on 1 July 1888 at Florence, the artist has lived since 1931 at Paris and is today one of the leading Italian abstract painters. His final switch to a geometrical abstract style in 1933 was already briefly preluded at Florence back in 1915. Joint exhibition at the Venice Biennale of 1950.
Lit: Jean Arp, *Magnelli*, Paris, 1947; Cat. of the 1950 Venice Biennale; VOLLMER III, 1956.

MAILLOL, Aristide — Born on 8 December 1861 at Banyuls-sur-Mer in Roussillon, the artist died there on 28 September 1944. After beginning as a painter at the Ecole des Beaux-Arts in Paris (1882—86), and under the influence of Gauguin and the nabis, Maillol turned wholly to sculpture round about 1900. As a graphic artist, he created principally woodcut illustrations to works by Virgil, Ovid and Longus.
Lit: J. Rewald, *Maillol*, Paris, 1939 (with bibl.); M. Guérin, *L'Oeuvre gravée de Maillol*, Paris, 1948; J. Rewald, *The Woodcuts of Aristide Maillol*, New York, 1951 (lists all the woodcuts).

MAKI, Haku — Japanese artist. Born 1924. Represented in an exhibition of modern Japanese prints at the Art Institute, Chicago, in 1960.
Lit: Cat. of the "Japan's Modern Prints" exhibition at Chicago in 1960.

MANESSIER, Alfred — Born on 5 December 1911 at Saint-Ouen (Somme), the artist now lives at Paris. First studied at Amiens, then from 1931 in Paris at the Ecole des Beaux-Arts. Of decisive importance for his art was his meeting with Bissière in 1935 at the Académie Ranson. Oil-paintings, stained-glass, and colour lithographs.
Lit: VOLLMER III, 1956; DORIVAL II.   *Ill. p. 231*

Maccari

Magnelli

MANET, Edouard — Born on 25 January 1832 at Paris. Died there on 30 April 1883. Sea voyage as a cadet in 1848. Till 1856 a pupil of Thomas Couture. Studied at the Louvre: Frans Hals and the Spaniards Velázquez, El Greco and Goya. Visit to Spain in 1865. Time after time misunderstood by the public at his exhibitions. Supported by the younger impressionists, who then influenced his later works.
Manet's highly varied graphic *œuvre* from the years 1860—62 includes 86 etchings and lithographs besides a few woodcuts after his drawings.
Lit: Paul Jamot, G. Wildenstein, and M.-L. Bataille, *Manet*, 2 vols, Paris, 1932; Marcel Guérin, *L'Oeuvre gravée de Manet*, Paris, 1944.   *Ills pp. 12, 21*

Manessier

MANZU, Giacomo — Born on 22 December 1908 at Bergamo, into a hard-up family. After early apprenticeships as a wood-carver and stucco-worker, he began in 1928 to develop himself into a practically self-taught sculptor. Encountered the art of Rodin at Paris in 1936. This visit apart, has lived since 1930 at Milan and Bergamo, and from 1941 to 1954 was professor of sculpture at the Brera Academy, Milan. Through his bronze doors for St Peter's, Rome, and Salzburg Cathedral, Manzù is one the most important representatives of modern sacred art. Also well-known for his effigies of cardinals.
Many drawings, illustrated books, and a number of etchings and lithographs.
Lit: Carlo L. Ragghianti, *Giacomo Manzù*, 2nd ed., Milan, 1957; *Giacomo Manzù, Acquaforti e litografie, ed.* by H. Trentin, Venice, 1958 (cat. with list of the prints).

MARC, Franz — Born on 8 February 1880 at Munich. Fell at Verdun on 4 March 1916. After studying at Munich, visited Italy, Paris and Brittany. Settled at Sindelsdorf in 1910. Met Kandinsky and Klee and joined the New Artists' Federation at Munich. In 1911 a co-founder of the *Blaue Reiter*. To Paris in 1912, meeting Delaunay there. During the same year, futurist exhibition at Munich. He moved to Ried in 1914.
Graphics: 21 woodcuts, 23 lithographs.
Own writings: *Franz Marc, Briefe und Aufzeichnungen*, 2 vols, Berlin, 1920.
Lit: Alois J. Schardt, *Franz Marc*, Berlin, 1936 (with complete cat. and bibl.); L. G. Buchheim, *Graphik des Deutschen Expressionismus*, Feldafing, 1959; K. Lankheit, *Franz Marc, Water-colours, Drawings, Writings*, London, 1960.   *Ills pp. 147, 183*

Manet

MARCKS, Gerhard — Born on 18 February 1889 at Berlin, the sculptor has lived since 1950 at Cologne. Developed as a sculptor in Berlin, mainly self-trained. His activity interrupted by the First World War. During 1919—25 taught at the Bauhaus as head of the Dornburg ceramics studio. Instructor in pottery and sculpture at the School of Arts and Crafts at Burg Giebichen-stein near Halle during 1925—33. Visited Greece in 1928, thanks to the Villa Romana prize. From 1933 at Niehagen and Berlin. Spent 1947—50 teaching at the Hamburg State Art School.
Besides his sculptures has produced since 1920 a large body of woodcuts, so far only published in part.
Lit: THIEME-BECKER XXIV, 1930; VOLLMER III, 1956; Woodcuts from recent years listed in two cats. of the Galerie R. Hoffmann, Hamburg: *Africana* (1956) and *Holzschnitte aus den Jahren 1955—1960* (1961).   *Ill. p. 110*

Marc

Marcks

Manzu

Maillol

Marcoussis

Marini

Masereel

MARCOUSSIS, Louis — Born on 14 November 1883 at Warsaw (Louis Markus). Died on 22 October 1941 at Cusset (Allier). Having briefly attended the Warsaw Academy, went in 1903 to Paris. In 1910 joined the cubists, exhibiting with the *Section d'or* in 1912. French soldier during 1914–18. After the war gave up pure cubism. His later pictures show abstract tendency.

His rich graphic *œuvre* includes illustrations to books by Gérard de Nerval and Tristan Tzara.
Lit: THIEME-BECKER XXIV, 1930; VOLLMER III, 1956; A cat. of his works by A. Guichard in preparation.

MARINI, Marino — Born on 27 February 1901 at Pistoia. Studied at the Florence Academy. Until 1928 mainly a painter and graphic artist. Taught at the art school in Monzana near Milan during 1929–40. From 1928 on many study visits to Paris and numerous trips abroad in Europe and to the United States. Since 1940 instructor in sculpture at the Brera Academy, Milan.
Lit: H. Apollonio, *Marino Marini*, London, 1958 (with bibl.); *Marino Marini, Malerei und Graphik*, intro. by W. Hofmann, Stuttgart, 1960; 15 colour lithos from the years 1951–55 pub. by Berggruen, Paris, 1955.   *Ill. p. 201*

MASCHERINI, Marcello — Born on 14 September 1906 at Udine, the artist studied at Trieste, where he has lived ever since, apart from a brief sojourn in the Abruzzi during the First World War.
Lit: A. Pica, *Mascherini*, Milan, 1945; Cat. of the 27th Venice Biennale in 1954.

MASEREEL, Frans — Born on 31 July 1889 at Blankenberghe in Flanders, the artist lives today at Nice. Studied at Ghent and went in 1909 to England, in 1910 to Paris and Tunis. Spent 1914–21 in Switzerland. Illustrations to writings by Barbusse and Romain Rolland. In Germany during the 'twenties known above all through his woodcut books: *Passion eines Menschen, Stundenbuch* and *Geschichten ohne Worte*. After the Second World War, spent a few years teaching at the art school in Saarbrücken.
Lit: VOLLMER III, 1956; Gerhard Ziller, *Frans Masereel*, Dresden, 1949 (with cat. and bibl.); *Frans Masereel 1917–57*, Deutsche Akademie der Künste, East Berlin, 1957.   *Ill. p. 90*

MASSON, André — Born on 4 January 1896 at Balagny (Oise), the artist joined up in 1914. After the end of the war, he went in 1919 to Paris. Having briefly attended the Academies at Brussels and Paris, followed his own course as a painter, and in 1925–29 supported the aims of the surrealists.
Friendship with Miró: joint exhibition at New York in 1933. Lived in Catalonia during 1934–36. Back in Paris from 1937. Spent 1941–45 in the States. Paris in 1946, Aix-en-Provence in 1947.
Lit: Cat. of the "Graphic work of André Masson" exhibition at Bremen in 1954 (with provisional cat. of the graphics and illustrated books).   *Ill. p. 175*

MATARE, Ewald — Born on 25 February 1887 at Aachen, the artist first studied painting, in 1907–14 at the Berlin College of Fine Arts, in 1914 as a pupil of Lovis Corinth. Since 1920 active as a sculptor. In 1932 appointment at the Düsseldorf Academy. Dismissed in 1933. Reappointed at Düsseldorf in 1945. Lives at Büderich near Neuss.
Produced since 1920, his large corpus of graphics consists with few exceptions of woodcuts, and includes over 320 works up to 1958.
Lit: H. Th. Flemming, *Ewald Mataré*, Munich, 1955 (with bibl.); Heinz Peters, *Ewald Mataré, Das graphische Werk*, 2 vols, Cologne, 1957–58.   *Ill. p. 109*

Mataré

Mascherini

Masson

MATISSE, Henri — Born on 31 December 1869 at Le Cateau-Cambrésis. Died on 3 November 1954 at Nice.

Began to paint in 1890, studying in 1891–92 at the Académie Julian and from 1893 in Gustave Moreau's studio. After impressionist beginnings, Cézanne's work and that of the pointillists Signac and Cross was decisive for Matisse, who, with his colourful planar art, became one of the leading fauves during 1905–07. His production of prints, mainly etchings and lithographs, began around 1900. As yet unpublished, the complete catalogue of the graphics, compiled by the artist's daughter Mme Duthuit, lists about 400 works and about twenty monotypes from the years 1915–17.

Lit: A. H. Barr, *Matisse, His Art and his Public*, New York, 1951, Mayflower Books; W. S. Liebermann, *Matisse, Fifty Years of his Graphic Art*, New York, 1956; *Henri Matisse, Das illustrierte Werk, Zeichnungen und Druckgraphic*, Klipstein and Kornfeld cat., Bern, 1961; G. Cramer, *Le Livre illustré par Henri Matisse*, Geneva, 1959 (43 works listed).

Ills pp. 125, 126, 127

Matisse

MATTA (Roberto Sebastian Matta Echaurren) — Born in 1912 at Santiago de Chile, the son of a diplomat. Came to Europe in 1932, studying architecture under Le Corbusier during 1934–35. Self-taught as a painter. A surrealist from 1938–47. Went in 1939 to New York, in 1941 to Mexico. Lived during 1950–53 at Rome. Since then at Paris.
Murals for the UNESCO Building at Paris in 1958.
Lit: VOLLMER III, 1956; Cat. of the "Neue Malerei" exhibition at the Städtische Galerie, Munich, in 1960.

MEEKER, Dean Jackson — Born on 18 May 1921 at Orchard, Colorado. Studied in Chicago and Wisconsin. Since 1946 teaching aesthetic education at the University of Wisconsin.
Lit: *American Prints Today*, 1959.

MEIDNER, Ludwig — Born on 18 April 1884 at Bernstadt, Silesia. Studied during 1903–05 in Breslau, 1906–07 in Paris at the Académie Julian. Then lived at Berlin, where he exhibited for the first time in 1912 at *Der Sturm*. Military service during 1916–18. To Cologne in 1933. Emigrated to England in 1939, returning to Germany in 1953. Since 1955 living at Hofheim am Taunus. During 1925–32 chiefly literary works.
Graphics: Zinc engravings, drypoints and etchings.
Lit: THIEME-BECKER XXIV, 1930; VOLLMER III, 1956; L. G. Buchheim, *Graphik des Deutschen Expressionismus*, Feldafing, 1959.

Matta

MEISTERMANN, Georg — Born on 16 June 1911 at Solingen. During 1932–33 studied at Düsseldorf under Heuser, Nauen and Mataré. Stained-glass windows for churches since 1937. After the war, exponent of an "abstracting" art. From 1953 taught at the Städel Art School, Frankfurt am Main, from 1956 at the Düsseldorf Academy as instructor in painting and stained-glass. Since 1960 a professor at the Karlsruhe Art Academy.
Graphics: About 30 prints (pub. Galerie Der Spiegel, Cologne).
Lit: VOLLMER III, 1956; Cat. of the exhibition at the Kunsthaus Lempertz, Cologne, in 1961 (with full list of works and bibl.).

Ill. p. 219

Meidner

Meistermann

Meeker

Menzel

MENZEL, Adolf von — Born on 8 December 1815 in Breslau. Died on February 1905 in Berlin, where he had lived since 1830. Took over his father's lithographic studio in 1832 and, as a graphic artist, draughtsman and painter, became the depicter of the age of Frederick the Great. At the same time one of the earliest exponents of realism in Germany.
In 1834—36 appeared the crayon lithographs showing the history of Brandenburg-Prussia, in 1840—42 the 400 pen drawings reproduced in woodcut for Kugler's *Leben Friedrichs des Grossen*, and in 1887 the woodcuts for Kleist's *Der zerbrochene Krug*.
Lit: THIEME-BECKER XXIV, 1930; A recent bibl. in the cat. of the memorial exhibition at the Museum Berlin-Dahlem in 1955; Elfried Bock, *Adolf Menzel, Verzeichnis seines graphischen Werkes*, Berlin, 1923. *Ill. p. 8*

MEYBODEN, Hans — Born on 20 February 1901 at Verden an der Aller. Lives at Fischerhude near Bremen. During 1919—23 studied at the Dresden Academy as a pupil of Oskar Kokoschka. In the United States during 1923—24, especially New York. Spent 1929—33 at Berlin. His work hindered from 1933. In 1942 forbidden to exhibit. Professor at the Academy of Fine Arts, Freiburg im Breisgau, since 1956.
Lit: VOLLMER III, 1956.

Meyboden

MILLET, Jean-François — Born a peasant's son on 4 October 1814 at Gruchy near Gréville. Died on 20 January 1875 at Barbizon. Went to Paris in 1837, to Barbizon after 1848, and became through his open-air painting one of the forerunners of impressionism. Besides his oil-paintings, produced many drawings and pastels. His prints limited to twenty etchings, six lithographs, and two glass etchings.
Lit: E. Moreau-Nélaton, *Millet raconté par lui-même*, 3 vols, Paris, 1921; THIEME-BECKER XXIV, 1930; DELTEIL I, 1906. *Ill. p. 12*

MIRO, Joan — Born on 20 April 1893 at Montroig near Barcelona. Studied painting at Barcelona till 1915. To Paris in 1920. Friendship with Picasso, encountering of the art of Kandinsky, Arp and Paul Klee. Beginnings of surrealism: André Breton's manifesto in 1924, first surrealist exhibition at Paris in 1925. Participants included Miró, who soon won international recognition. In 1928 first one-man show in the States, in 1933 in London. Returned to Spain in 1940 and since 1944 has lived partly in Paris, partly in Spain at Montroig or at Palma de Mallorca.
Like Picasso, Miró has produced a large body of graphics, equal in rank to his paintings.
Lit: J. Prévot and G. Ribemont-Dessaignes, *Joan Miró*, Paris, 1956; M. Leiris, *The Prints of Miró*, New York, 1947; *Joan Miró, Das graphische Werk*, ed. by Paul Wember, Krefeld, 1957; *Joan Miró, His Graphic Work*, intro. by Sam Hunter, New York, 1958 (with list of the illustrated books), Mayflower Books; J. T. Soby, *Joan Miró*, New York, 1959, pub. by the Museum of Modern Art (with bibl.); Jacques Dupin, *Joan Miró*, London, 1962. *Ill. p. 177*

MODERSOHN-BECKER, Paula — Born on 8 February 1876 at Dresden. Died on 30 November 1907 at Worpswede near Bremen.
First attempts at drawing and painting in 1892. Spent 1896—97 at private art schools in Berlin. A pupil of Mackensen at Worpswede in 1898—99. During 1900 in Paris at the Académie Colarossi and the Ecole des Beaux-Arts. Married the Worpswede painter Otto Modersohn in 1901. On her many visits to Paris encountered the art of Cézanne and Gauguin.
Graphics: Only ten etchings.
Own writings: *Briefe und Tagebuchblätter*, Munich, 1921.
Lit: G. Pauli, *Paula Modersohn-Becker*, Munich, 1924; Otto Stelzer, *Paula Modersohn-Becker*, Berlin, 1958; Cat. of the exhibition at the Behnhaus, Lübeck, in 1959—60 (with bibl). *Ill. p. 93*

Millet

Modersohn-Becker

Mirò

MOORE, Henry — Born on 30 July 1898 at Castleford, Yorkshire. Military service in 1917—18. Spent 1919—25 studying sculpture at Leeds School of Art and the Royal College of Art, London. Taught during 1926—39 at the Royal College and the Chelsea School of Art. Visited France and Italy in 1926. In 1936 journey to the Pyrenean cave paintings and Spain. War Artist in 1940—42. Since 1949 big retrospective exhibitions at the European capitals, the last in 1960 with works from the years 1927—60. Art prizes and many honours, abroad as well.
Lit: W. Grohmann, *Henry Moore*, London, 1960 (with bibl.); H. Read, *Henry Moore, Sculpture and drawings*, vol. I, 4th ed., London and New York, 1957; vol. II, 1955 (with bibl.); Sets of new lithographs in Gerald Cramer's stock-catalogne, 1963. *Ill. p. 196*

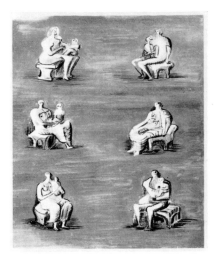
Moore

MORANDI, Giorgio — Born on 20 July 1890 at Bologna, where he studied and since 1930 has taught at the Academy. With futurist art, *pittura metafisica*, and the *Valori plastici* circle, Morandi maintained only loose, temporary links (1912, 1918—19, 1922). Since 1916 has been painting in an old-masterly way his successions of still-lifes. Grand prize for painting at the Venice Biennale of 1948.
Graphics: 117 etchings from the years 1912—56.
Lit: SERVOLINI, p. 544; Lamberto Vitali, *L'opera grafica di G. Morandi*, Turin, 1957; A. Beccaria, *Morandi*, Milan, 1939 (with bibl.); C. Brandi, *Morandi*, 2nd ed., Florence, 1952. *Ill. p. 136*

MORTENSEN, Richard — Born on 23 October 1910 at Copenhagen. Studied at the Copenhagen Academy. In 1932 his first abstract work. Went to Paris in 1937 to organize an "Ecole de Paris" exhibition at Copenhagen, and now belongs at Paris to this group, in which he represents, in Mondrian's footsteps, the geometric trend of abstract art. Lissone prize in 1955.
Lit: Th. Weilbach, *Dansk Kunstnerleks* II, 1947—52; VOLLMER III, 1956.

Morandi

MUELLER, Otto — Born on 16 October 1874 at Liebau in Silesia. Died on 24 September 1930 at Breslau. A trained lithographer, he attended the Dresden Academy during 1896—98, then lived as an adopted son with the Hauptmann family in the Riesengebirge, and went in 1908 to Berlin, where in 1910 he made the acquaintance of Kirchner and Heckel. During 1915—18 he served in the army, and from 1919—30 taught at the Breslau Academy. He developed an exotic, arcadian variety of German expressionism.
Graphics: Almost exclusively lithographs, only four woodcuts being known.
Lit: L. G. Buchheim, *Die Künstler-Gemeinschaft Brücke*, Feldafing, 1956 (with bibl.); H. Th. Flemming, *Otto Mueller, Farbige Zeichnungen und Lithographien*, Feldafing, 1957; *Otto Mueller, Das graphische Werk*, cat. of Galerie Meta Nierendorf, Berlin, 1960 (about 152 works). *Ills pp. 106, 107*

MUMPRECHT, Rudolf — Born in 1919 at Bern. During 1949—55 studied the graphic techniques at Paris, especially aquatint. Since 1959 has printed monotypes on his own press.
Lit: Mumprecht, *Monotypes 1960*, Berggruen, Paris.

MUNCH, Edvard — Born on 12 December 1863 at Løyten near Hamar. Died on 23 January 1944 at Ekely near Oslo.
Studied during 1881—84 at Oslo under Heyerdahl and Christian Krogh. From 1889, Munch lived for two decades in France and Germany, and at times also in Italy. He found in Paris in Van Gogh, Gauguin, and Toulouse-Lautrec, and in Berlin in the *Pan* circle the pictorial and spiritual starting points for the directive expressionism of this period — ending about 1908 — of his activity. From 1909 on in the isolation of his country-seat, after his return to Norway from the Copenhagen sanatorium, there appeared his late painted works.
The graphics of his first period — etchings but above all lithographs and woodcuts, colour

Munch

Mueller

Mumprecht

Mortensen

Munakata

Music

Nauen

as well as black-and-white — have a special importance in his *œuvre* and for German expressionism. In 1894 he treated his pictorial themes in etching. During 1896—97 he developed in Paris his technique for colour lithographs and colour woodcuts.

Lit: THIEME-BECKER XXV, 1931 (art. by Curt Glaser with bibl.); Jens Thiis, *Edvard Munch og hans samtid*, Oslo, 1933 (also in French and in 1934 an abridged German edit.); *Edvard Munch. Fra år til år (A Year by Year Account of Edvard Munch's Life)*, Oslo, 1961 (useful list of the dates otherwise scattered about in the voluminous Munch literature); Gustav Schiefler, *Verzeichnis des graphischen Werks Edvard Munchs bis 1906*, Berlin, 1907; Gustav Schiefler, *Edvard Munch, Das graphische Werk, 1906—26*, Berlin, 1928; Sigurd Willoch, *Edvard Munchs raderinger*, Oslo, 1950; *Edvard Munch Tresnitt* (woodcuts), cat. of the exhibition at Oslo in 1946 (55 additions to Schiefler's cat.). *Ills pp. 10, 39, 53, 55, 57*

MUNAKATA, Shiko — Born on 5 September 1903 at Aomori-shi (north Japan), the artist went in 1924 to Tokyo. At first he painted in a late-impressionist style. Gave up painting in 1928 as un-Japanese. Since then has worked as a woodcutter, usually straight on the block without preliminary drawing. Prefers subjects from the ancient Buddhist woodcuts. International graphic-arts prize at São Paulo in 1955. Grand prize at the 1956 Venice Biennale.

Lit: Cat. of the exhibition at Brunswick in 1960.

MUSIC, Zoran Antonio — Born on 12 November 1909 at Görz (then Austrian, now Italian Gorizia). Studied in Zagreb and later Madrid (1933), Paris and Italy. Frescoes for Venice churches in 1940. At Dachau concentration camp in 1943. To Venice in 1945. Living since 1953 at Paris and intermittently at Venice. Murals, tapestries, oil-paintings.

Lit: VOLLMER III, 1956; R. De Solier, *Music*, Rome, 1955; *Music, Das graphische Werk 1947—62*, Galerie Schmücking, Braunschweig, 1962 (about 84 works).

NAUEN, Heinrich — Born on 1 June 1880, the artist was one of the Rhenish expressionists. He died on 26 November 1941 at Kalkar. Studied at Düsseldorf and Munich, became star pupil of Leopold von Kalckreuth at Stuttgart, and lived till 1905 on the Lower Rhine and in Flanders. Spent 1905—11 at Berlin, then back in the Rhineland, where in 1912—14 he painted his murals for Burg Drove. A soldier in 1914—18, a teacher at Düsseldorf during 1921—36. Lived at Neuss till 1938, at Kalkar in 1938—40.

Lit: Cat. of the exhibition at Krefeld in 1950 (26 etchings, six lithographs listed); L. G. Buchheim, *Graphik des Deutschen Expressionismus*, Feldafing, 1959.

NAY, Ernst Wilhelm — Born on 11 June 1902 in Berlin, the artist became in Germany after the war one of the leading exponents of abstract art. During 1925—28 studied at the Berlin Academy under Karl Hofer, and in 1930 won the Rome prize. To Norway in 1936 and 1937 at Edvard Munch's invitation. Army during 1940—45. Since 1951 living at Cologne. Many journeys and won many art prizes, including abroad, since 1953.

Lit: W. Haftmann, *E. W. Nay*, Cologne, 1960.

NELE, Eva Renée — Born on 17 March 1932 at Berlin, a painter's daughter. Studied in London, Berlin and Paris. Represented at documenta II, Cassel, and at the Ljubljana and Grenchen international exhibitions of graphic art in 1961.

Lit: Cat. of the 4th international exhibition of graphic art at Ljubljana in 1961.

NESCH, Rolf — Born on 7 January 1893 at Oberesslingen (Württemberg). In Dresden in 1920—23 completed his studies interrupted by the war and captivity. In 1924 received decisive promptings for his art through a visit to E. L. Kirchner at Davos. Lived during 1926 at Berlin, 1927—30 at Esslingen, 1930—33 at Hamburg in the sphere of the Munch-influenced art of the Hamburg *Sezession*. Went in 1933 to Norway, where he now lives at Aal as a Norwegian citizen.

Graphics: He developed in his Hamburg years new methods of printing from metal that finally led beyond the now autonomous printing plate to the material picture.

Lit: A. Hentzen, *Rolf Nesch, Graphik, Materialbilder, Plastik*, Stuttgart, 1960 *Ills pp. 188, 189*

Nesch

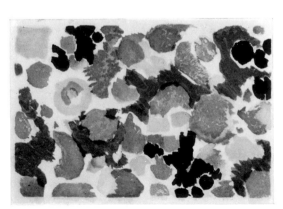
Nay

Nele

NIELSEN, Palle — Lives at Copenhagen, where he was born on 8 August 1920 and also studied. Graphic works since the late 'forties, in the last few years chiefly linocuts. Themes: Orpheus and Eurydice, Lamentations of Jeremiah. Art critics' grand prize at the 1958 Venice Biennale.
Lit: Cat. of the 4th international exhibition of graphic art at Ljubljana in 1961; *Palle Nielsen, Linocuts and Woodcuts*, Copenhagen, 1961.

NOLDE, Emil (Emil Hansen) — Born on 7 August 1867 at Nolde (Schleswig). Died on 13 April 1956 at Seebüll. After attending a woodcarving school at Flensburg (1884—88) and a year's study at Karlsruhe, Nolde spent 1892—98 teaching drawing at a trade school in St Gallen, then studied painting again in Munich and Dachau (under Adolf Hölzel), and in Paris (1899—1900). Lived from 1902 mainly in Berlin, occasionally in Dresden, where he was a *Brücke* member during 1906—07. Meeting with Edvard Munch in 1907. In 1910 stayed at Hamburg, 1911 in Holland, where he met Ensor. During 1913—14 took part in an expedition to New Guinea. Built a house at Seebüll in 1927. After 1933 his art proscribed; forbidden to paint. His Berlin home, with his print collection, destroyed in 1943.
Nolde came late to graphic art: in 1904 the first etchings, 1906 the first woodcuts, inspired by the *Brücke* artists, 1907 the first lithographs.
Lit: Max Sauerlandt, *Emil Nolde*, Munich, 1921; THIEME-BECKER XXV, 1931; VOLLMER III, 1956; Annals of the Seebüll Foundation, 1958—59 and 1959—60 (with bibl.); Gustav Schiefler, *Das graphische Werk Emil Noldes bis 1910*, Berlin, 1911; Gustav Schiefler, *Das graphische Werk Emil Noldes 1910—25*, Berlin, 1927; W. Haftmann, *Emil Nolde*, London, 1960.
Ills pp. 35, 60, 79, 81, 88

OBER, Hermann — The artist lives at Freilassing, Upper Bavaria, where he was born on 10 July 1920. Studied at Munich and, during 1948—51, at Salzburg under Slavi Souček. In his graphics Ober combines aquatint with relief printing.
Lit: VOLLMER III, 1956.

O'HARA, Frederik — Born in 1904 in Canada, this graphic artist has taken part in an exhibition of contemporary American prints at IGAS, and in the 5th international biennial of contemporary colour lithography at Cincinnati in 1958.
Lit: Cat. of the international biennial of contemporary colour lithography at Cincinnati in 1958.

OHMAE, Hiroshi — Born in 1926 in Japan, the artist learnt woodcut at the Japanese Art Print Society and now teaches art at the Komatengawa elementary school in Tokyo. Exhibitions in Japan and abroad — in America at the Art Institute of Chicago.
Lit: Cat. of the "Japan's Modern Prints" exhibition at Chicago in 1960.

ORLOWSKI, Hans — Born on 1 March 1894 at Insterburg, East Prussia. Lives at Berlin-Wilmersdorf. Attended in 1911—14 the School of Arts and Crafts at Berlin-Charlottenburg, in 1919 the Berlin State Art School. Took charge of a mural and glass-painting class at the Berlin College of Fine Arts in 1945.
Lit: VOLLMER III, 1956.

OROZCO, José Clemente — Born on 23 November 1883 at Zapotlán (Jalisco). Died in September 1949 at Mexico City. With Diego Rivera and David Alfaro Siqueiros, one of the founders of modern Mexican art, which as a result of the Revolution deliberately turned to the mural and print in order to influence the masses. Studied at the Academy in Mexico City during 1908—15. First frescoes in 1922—27. Returned to Mexico in 1934 after a longish stay in the United States and a visit to Europe.
Graphics: Lithographs.
Lit: José Clemente Orozco, *Autobiografia*, Mexico, 1945; VOLLMER III, 1956.

Nolde

O'Hara

Ober

Ohmae

Orozco

Orlowski

Nielsen

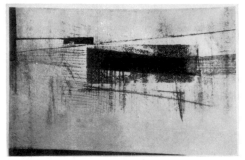

Ostrower

Pankok

Pascin

OSTROWER, Fayga — Born on 14 September 1920 at Lodz in Poland. The artist's home was in Germany till 1933, since when she has lived at Rio de Janeiro, where she studied drawing and print-making. Teacher of composition and criticism at the Museum of Modern Art in Rio. Won the international grand prize for graphics at the 29th Venice Biennale in 1958.
Lit: Cat. of the 4th international exhibition of graphic art at Ljubljana in 1961.

PANKOK, Otto — Born on 6 June 1893 at Mülheim an der Ruhr. Studied at Düsseldorf and Weimar, and after various sojourns and visits settled at Düsseldorf in 1920. Since 1947 a professor at the Academy there. Original prints and book illustrations, still in an expressive realist style after the war.
Lit: THIEME-BECKER XXVI, 1932; VOLLMER III, 1956; L. G. Buchheim, *Graphik des Deutschen Expressionismus*, Feldafing, 1959. *Ill. p. 110*

PASCIN, Jules (Julius Pincas) — Born on 31 March 1885 at Vidin, Bulgaria. Took his own life on 5 June 1930 in Paris. Studied in Vienna and Munich, where he early on became a contributor to *Simplicissimus*. Went to Paris in 1905. In America during the First World War, but from 1921 back in Europe, chiefly Paris.
Lit: G. Charensol, *Jules Pascin*, Paris, 1929; THIEME-BECKER XXVI, 1932.

PECHSTEIN, Max — Born on 31 December 1881 at Zwickau in Saxony. Died on 20 June 1955 in Berlin. Learnt trade painting before he attended the Dresden Academy. Became a member of the *Brücke* in 1906 and in Berlin in 1910 founded the *Neue Sezession*, which drew the other *Brücke* artists to Berlin as well. Voyage to the South Sea in 1914. Member of the Prussian Academy of Arts in 1922, expelled in 1933. In 1945 appointed instructor at the Berlin College of Fine Arts. His graphic production up to 1920 comprises at least 100 etchings, about 220 lithographs, and about 160 woodcuts. Few prints after 1920.
Lit: THIEME-BECKER XXVI, 1932; Paul Fechter, *Das graphische Werk Max Pechsteins*, Berlin, 1920; L. G. Buchheim, *Die Künstlergemeinschaft "Brücke"*, Feldafing, 1956; L. G. Buchheim, *Die Graphik des Deutschen Expressionismus*, Feldafing, 1959; Max Pechstein, *Erinnerungen*, ed. by L. Reidemeister, Wiesbaden, 1960. *Ill. p. 84*

PEDROSO D'HORTA, Arnaldo — Born in 1914 at São Paulo, this Brasilian artist won in 1953 the first prize for drawing at the 2nd biennial of São Paulo, and in 1954 a prize as the best foreign draughtsman and graphic artist at the 27th Venice Biennale.
Lit: Cat. of the exhibition of Brasilian art at Munich and Hamburg in 1959–60.

PEREZ, Rossine — Born in 1932 in Rio Grande do Norte. Took part in the 2nd and 4th São Paulo biennials, and awarded the second prize for Brasilian graphic artists.
Lit: Cat. of the exhibition of Brasilian art at Munich and Hamburg in 1959–60.

PERRIN, Brian — Born in 1932 at Streatham, England. Studied at the Croydon Art School and at the Royal College of Art in London. Won the Rome prize for graphics in 1954.
Lit: *Quadrum VII*, 1959.

Pechstein

Pedroso d'Horta

Perez

PETERDI, Gabor — Born on 17 September 1915 in Budapest, son of the noted Hungarian poet Andor Peterdi. Living since 1939 in the United States, now at Rowayton, Connecticut. The precocious artist studied at the Budapest Academy in 1929. Visited Italy during 1930 thanks to the Rome prize. In 1931 went to the Académie Julian, Paris, in 1933 to S. W. Hayter's Atelier 17. To the United States in 1939. Military service in the American army. From 1946 active as a graphic artist in New York. Taught at the art school in Brooklyn from 1949, later at Yale University and Hunter College.

His graphic production today includes more than 160 works, over 100 of them from the years 1951—59.

Own publications: G. Peterdi, *Printmaking Methods, Old and New,* New York, 1959.

Lit: *Gabor Peterdi, Twenty-five Years of his Prints 1934—59* (pub. by the Brooklyn Museum, prep. by Una E. Johnson), 1959; *American Prints Today,* 1959.   *Ill. p. 241*

Perrin

PIAUBERT, Jean — Born on 27 January 1900 at Feydieu (Gironde). Lives in Paris. In 1918 studied at the Bordeaux College of Art. To Paris in 1922. Designed fabric patterns and theatrical costumes for Paul Poiret. Studied at the Académie de la Grande Chaumière. First exhibition of non-representational works in 1946 at Paris. In 1950 appeared thirty-three big lithographs for Jean Cassou's *Trente-trois sonnets.*

Lit: J. Cassou, *Piaubert,* Paris, 1951; Jean Piaubert, *Les Cahiers d'art-documents,* No. 77, Geneva, 1958.

PICASSO, Pablo — Born on 25 October 1881 at Malaga of a Basque father, José Ruiz Blasco, and an Andalusian mother, Maria Picasso. Studied at Barcelona. First went in 1900 to Paris, where he finally settled in 1904 and soon won recognition through his ever changing, self-renewing art. After the early blue and rose periods a new painting came into being, under the influence of negro sculpture, in analytical cubism. *Collages* and synthetic cubism during 1912. Braque and Gris were Picasso's travelling companions then. The further stages as well — neo-classicism (beginning about 1920), the coming-to-grips with surrealism about 1925, *Guernica* of 1937, and the pictures from the war years — have become known all over the world thanks to the big exhibitions of the last decade.

Picasso's graphic production as catalogued by Geiser up to 1933 already comprises over 250 works. During 1930—37 appeared the 100 etchings of the *Vollard Suite.* Since November 1945 the lithographs produced in the workshop of the Mourlot brothers: 270 works to 1956. 1958—63: 99 linocuts. 1959: 26 aquatints for Pepe Illo's *Tauromaquia.*

Lit: T. Sabartez and H. Boeck, *Picasso: His Life and Work,* London, 1955; B. Geiser, *Picasso peintre-graveur, Catalogue illustré de l'œuvre gravée et lithographiée 1899—1931,* Bern, 1933; F. Mourlot, *Picasso lithographe 1919—1956,* 3 vols, Monte Carlo, 1949—56; B. Geiser, *Das graphische Werk von Picasso, Auswahl und Einführung von Bernhard Geiser* (with bibl. for the graphic works), Stuttgart, 1955 (in French: Lausanne, 1955); *Pablo Picasso, Drei graphische Folgen,* cat. of an exhibition at the Düsseldorf Art Club, 1961 *(Vollard Suite, Tauromaquia,* linocuts); Jean Cassou, *The Sources of Modern Art,* London, 1962.   *Ills pp. 111, 112, 113, 115*

Peterdi

PIGNON, Edouard — Born on 12 February 1905 at Bully near Marles-les-Mines (Pas-de-Calais), the artist went in 1927 to Paris, where he studied painting and sculpture at evening classes. Active since 1936 as an independent painter, first inspired by Matisse, later by Picasso. During 1953—54 worked with Picasso at the Vallauris ceramics studio.

Lit: *Catalogue des estampes contemporains,* Gutekunst and Klipstein, Bern, 1955; DORIVAL II.

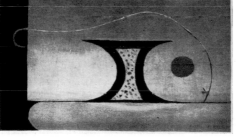

PIOTROWICZ, Edmund — Born on 9 August 1915 at Kherson in Russia, the artist studied at Warsaw, where he now lives. Has taken part in many exhibitions in Poland and abroad.

Lit: Cat. of the 4th international exhibition of graphic art at Ljubljana in 1961.

Piaubert

Picasso

Pignon

Piotrowicz

Pisis

Pissarro

Platiel

Poliakoff

PISIS, Filippo de (Luigi Tibertelli) — Born on 11 May 1896 at Ferrara. Died in 1956 at Venice. Spent many years in Paris and represented in Italy a late impressionism prompted by Bonnard, Vuillard and Dunoyer de Segonzac but of a cast modified by Venetian art.
De Pisis also made a name as a writer.
Graphics: About twenty works, among them some lithographs finished in watercolour, mostly done at Venice during 1944—45.
Lit: G. Raimondi, *De Pisis*, Florence, 1952.

PISSARRO, Camille — Born on 10 July 1830 on the then Danish island of St Thomas in the West Indies, the son of a Frenchman. Died on 13 November 1903 in Paris. First went to Paris in 1855. Earliest instruction in painting from Corot. Then association with Monet, later with Manet. In 1870 to London, where he studied Turner and Constable. With Cézanne at Pontoise during 1872—74. From 1874 on Pissarro organized the independent impressionist exhibitions in opposition to the official Salons. His graphic *œuvre* from the years 1863—1901 comprises 194 items.
Lit: L. Pissarro and L. Venturi, *Camille Pissarro*, 2 vols, Paris, 1939; *Camille Pissarro, Letters to his Son*, ed. J. Rewald and L. Pissarro, London, 1944; DELTEIL XVII, 1923.   *Ill. p. 11*

PLATIEL, Roger — Born on 2 January 1934 in Paris. After being trained at a printing office and a block-makers, studied at the Cassel Werkakademie in the commercial art class and for three years in Paris in Atelier 17 under S. W. Hayter. Has travelled to the Mediterranean, England, Mexico, the United States and Canada.
Lit: Cat. of the exhibition at Cassel in 1961.

POLIAKOFF, Serge — Born on 8 January 1906 at Moscow, the artist went in 1923 to Paris, where from 1930 he studied painting at the Académie Frochot and Académie de la Grande Chaumière. During 1935—37 in London at the Slade School. At Paris in 1937: meeting with Picasso, Otto Freundlich and Robert Delaunay. Abstract paintings since 1938.
Many exhibitions in France and abroad.
Lit: Dora Vallier, *Serge Poliakoff*, Paris, 1959 (with bibl.).   *Ill. p. 245*

POZZATI, Rudy — Born on 14 January 1925 at Telluride, Colorado, of Italian parents. Lives at Bloomington, Indiana. M. A. in 1950 at the University of Colorado. His teachers: Emilio Amero, Max Beckmann and Ben Shahn. During 1950—56 assistant at the University of Nebraska, since 1956 teacher in the art department at the University of Indiana. Through scholarships, study visits to Italy (1952—53) and Mexico (1959). Many exhibitions and awards.
Lit: Cat. of the exhibition at the Cleveland Museum of Art in 1956 (lists the prints from the years 1949—55); *American Prints Today*, 1959.

PRAMPOLINI, Enrico — Born on 20 April 1894 at Modena. Died on 17 June 1956 in Rome. Also a sculptor, stage designer and writer on art, this very active artist joined the futurists as early as 1912, after his training in Rome. In 1919 became a member of the Berlin November Group, in 1929 signed the *aeropittura* manifesto as co-author. His art later became "dynamic abstract". During 1925—37 he lived in Paris. Afterwards in Rome.
Lit: F. Pfister, *Enrico Prampolini*, Milan, 1940 (with bibl.).

Pozzati   Prampolini

PRASSINOS, Mario — Born on 30 July 1916 at Istanbul of a Greek father and an Italian mother. In 1922 came at the early age of six to Paris, where he lives today. After surrealist beginnings in the 'thirties, went over to abstract art. Came to notice also through his tapestry designs and book illustrations.
Lit: BENEZIT VII; VOLLMER III, 1956.

Prassinos

PRUDENZIATO, Angelo — Born on 24 October 1907 at Borsea di Rovigo, this graphic artist lives now at Rovigo. For three years he studied painting at Venice, then print-making at Bologna as a pupil of Giorgio Morandi. Since 1932 has been represented at many exhibitions, in 1958 by aquatints at the Venice Biennale.
Lit: SERVOLINI, p. 674.

PURRMANN, Hans — Born on 10 April 1880 at Speyer, the painter now lives at Montagnola in Switzerland. After being an apprentice decorator and attending the Stuttgart School of Arts and Crafts, studied from 1900–05 in Munich under Franz von Stuck. Went in 1906 to Paris, where in 1908, with Rudolf Levy and the Silesian Oskar Moll, he founded the Matisse school, which he led till 1914. At Berlin during 1916–29. From 1935 director of the Villa Romana at Florence. In 1943 to Lugano in Switzerland.
Lit: Edmund Hausen, *Hans Purrmann*, Berlin, 1950; VOLLMER III, 1956; Cat. of the exhibition at the Hamburg Art Club in 1960; B. and E. Göpel, *Leben und Meinungen des Malers Purrmann*, Wiesbaden, 1961.

Prudenziato

REDON, Odilon — Born on 22 April 1840 at Bordeaux. Died on 6 July 1916 at Paris. Studied at the art school in Bordeaux, and during 1863–65 in J. L. Gérôme's painting class at the Ecole des Beaux-Arts, Paris. At the same time acquaintance with the etcher Rodolphe Bresdin. Redon's first etchings in 1863. Moved to Paris in 1871. Attracted to lithography by Fantin-Latour. During 1877–99 appeared the big sets of prints, ending with the *Apokalypse*, which Vollard commissioned. To the late period, from 1900 on, belong almost nothing but oil-paintings and watercolours.
This exact contemporary of Monet created his graphic works as a follower of Bosch and Bruegel, Rembrandt and Goya. He interpreted the writings of Poe, Baudelaire and Flaubert in the spirit of the Belgian and French symbolists, thereby becoming the precursor of surrealism.
Lit: *A soi-même, Journal 1867–1915*, Paris, 1922; *L'Oeuvre graphique complet d'Odilon Redon*, pub. by Artz and De Bois, The Hague, n. d. (1913); A. Mellerio, *Odilon Redon*, 2nd ed., Paris, 1923 (with cat. of the graphic œuvre and bibl.); Cat. of the Redon exhibition at the Orangerie, Paris, in 1956–57 (with bibl. to 1956).   *Ill. p. 59*

REINER, Imre — Born on 18 August 1900 at Werschetz (Vršac) in Banat. After his training in Budapest, Frankfurt am Main and Stuttgart (under E. Schneidler), worked in America, London and Paris. Living since 1931 at Lugano-Ruvigliana in Switzerland. Principally a graphic artist for books and periodicals. Along with woodcut, favours the wood-engraving technique.
Lit: VOLLMER IV, 1958; *Imprimatur VI*, 1955.

RESTEK, Josip — Born on 7 March 1915 at Volavje in Yugoslavia. Concluded his study of art and art history at the Zagreb Academy and University in 1940–41. During 1948–50 a restorer at the Yugoslavian Academy of Sciences and Arts. Began teaching at the Zagreb School of Arts and Crafts in 1950. Studied print-making in Paris in 1955–56.
Lit: Cat. of the 4th international exhibition of graphic art at Ljubljana in 1961.

Redon

Restek

Reiner

Purrmann

Richards

Richier

Rödel

RICHARDS, Ceri — Born on 6 June 1903 at Swansea, he studied at the Swansea School of Art in London, where he now lives. The subjects of his colour lithographs are often suggested by musical themes: *The Pianist, The Piano* and various works after Debussy preludes.
Lit: VOLLMER IV, 1958; Cat. of the 4th international exhibition of graphic art at Ljubljana in 1961 (special show of his colour lithographs). *Ill. p. 199*

RICHIER, Germaine — Born on 16 September 1904 at Grans near Arles. Died on 31 July 1959 at Montpellier.
Studied during 1922—25 at the Montpellier School of Art under an assistant of Rodin. From 1925—29 continued her studies in Paris at Bourdelle's studio. Working as an independent sculptor from 1929. Blumenthal prize for sculpture in 1936. Spent 1939—45 in Switzerland and southern France. Returned to Paris in 1945. Developed her own style during the 'forties in her bronze sculpture.
Lit: VOLLMER IV, 1958; *A Dictionary of Modern Sculpture*, London, 1962. *Ill. p. 199*

RODEL, Karl — Born on 15 November 1907 at Neu-Isenburg near Frankfurt am Main. Studied in 1928—33 at the Halle-Giebichenstein studios (under Crodel and Gerhard Marcks among others) and in 1933—34 at the Leipzig Art Academy. During 1946—51 took a class on the Giebichenstein. Has lived in Mannheim since 1952.
Lit: VOLLMER IV, 1958; Cat. of the 4th international exhibition of graphic art at Ljubljana in 1961.

ROSSING, Karl — Born on 25 September 1897 at Gmunden, Upper Austria, of parents from Lower Saxony. Studied during 1913—17 at the Munich School of Arts and Crafts under F. H. Ehmke. From 1922 taught at the Essen School of Arts and Crafts, in 1926—31 professor at the Folkwang School. Spent 1934—44 teaching at the State College of Education in Art, Berlin. Since 1947 has taken the free graphics and illustration class at the Stuttgart Academy.
Worked from 1917 at reviving wood-engraving. Books with wood-engraved illustrations since 1920, independent sets of prints since 1952. In the last few years has done big chiaroscuro cuts.
Lit: VOLLMER IV, 1958.

ROHLFS, Christian — Born on 22 December 1849 at Niendorf (Segeberg Dist., Holstein). Died on 8 January 1938 at Hagen. First attempts at art in 1864 after an accident. Spent 1869—1900 at Weimar, till 1874 as an art student, then as an independent artist. During 1901—27 taught at the Folkwang School, Hagen. Met Nolde at Soest in 1905 and 1906. In Munich in 1910—12, Hagen in 1912—27. During 1927—37 lived at Ascona. Returned to Hagen in 1937.
His graphic remains owned by the Folkwang Museum, Essen. The graphic material from the years 1908/09—26 comprise 177 wood- and linocuts, two lithographs and six stencils used as printing-blocks.
Lit: P. Vogt, *Christian Rohlfs, Oeuvre-Katalog der Druckgraphik*, n. p., 1950; P. Vogt, *Christian Rohlfs, Oeuvre-Katalog der Druckgraphik*, Recklinghausen, 1960 (with ample introduction); P. Vogt, *Christian Rohlfs, Aquarelle und Zeichnungen*, Recklinghausen, 1958 (with cat. of the watercolours and bibl.). *Ill. p. 105*

ROMIJN, Gustaaf Adriaan Maria — Born on 3 October 1922 at Nordwijkerhout, this Dutch artist lives today at Rotterdam. He studied architecture at Rotterdam and Maastricht. Otherwise a self-taught artist. After beginning as a sculptor, has worked since 1948 as a print-maker, since 1953 as a painter.
Lit: Cat. of the 2nd international exhibition of graphic art at Ljubljana in 1957; *Knaurs Lexikon abstrakter Malerei*, Munich and Zurich, 1957.

Rössing

Rohlfs

Romijn

ROUAULT, Georges — Born on 27 May 1871 in Paris. Died there on 13 February 1958. After an apprenticeship to a stained-glass artist and restorer of old church windows, became in 1891 a pupil of Gustave Moreau at the Ecole des Beaux-Arts. Met Léon Bloy in 1903. Acquaintance with Odilon Redon in 1907. In 1917 Ambroise Vollard became his dealer. From 1918—33, mainly commissioned by Vollard, appeared the well-known big sets of etchings done by a special method.
Lit: L. Venturi, *Georges Rouault,* 2nd ed., Paris, 1948; J. T. Soby, *Georges Rouault,* The Museum of Modern Art, 2nd ed., New York, 1947, Mayflower Books, (both have full bibls.); Pierre Courthion, *Georges Rouault,* London, 1962; As yet no complete cat. of the prints.
Ills pp. 117, 118

ROYEN, Peter — Born in 1923 in Amsterdam, this Dutch artist now lives in Switzerland at La Chaux-de-Fonds. Was represented at the 2nd international triennial of colour graphics at Grenchen in 1961.
Lit: Cat. of the international exhibition of graphic art at Grenchen in 1961.

Rouault

SAETTI, Bruno — Born on 21 February 1902 in Bologna, this painter and graphic artist studied at the Academy of his native city. Has lived since 1930 in Venice, teaching at the Academy since 1940. Colour lithographs mainly in the last few years.
Lit: VOLLMER IV, 1958; SERVOLINI, p. 721.

SANDIG, Armin — Born on 10 March 1929 at Hof (Saale). Self-taught. Living since 1951 at Hamburg as an independent artist. Took part in the exhibition of young German and French painters at Lucerne in 1958. City of Hamburg Lichtwark scholarship in 1961.
Lit: VOLLMER IV, 1958.

Royen

SANTOMASO, Giuseppe — Born on 26 September 1907 in Venice, where he was trained and lives today. In 1937 in Amsterdam and Paris, where he studied chiefly Braque, Matisse and Bonnard. Co-founder in Venice in 1946 of the *Nuova Sezessione,* the later Fronte nuovo delle Arti. Since 1947 *astratto-concreto* paintings. International prize for painting at the 1954 Venice Biennale. Graphic-art prize at Ljubljana in 1957.
Graphics: Etchings, aquatints and lithographs, often preceded by watercolour sketches.
Lit: VOLLMER IV; SERVOLINI, p. 732.

SAVIN, Maurice — The artist, who lives in Paris, was born on 17 October 1894 at Moras (Drôme). Studied first at Valence, then from 1913 at the Ecole des Arts Décoratifs in Paris. Also active since 1933 as a potter, since 1941 as a designer of embroidery cartoons. His graphic production comprises over 230 works.
Lit: VOLLMER IV, 1958; R. Nacenta, *School of Paris,* London, 1960.

Saetti

SCHIELE, Egon — Born on 12 June 1890 at Tulln (Danube). Died on 31 October 1918 at Vienna. From beginnings determined by the Vienna Academy and the art of Gustav Klimt, he developed from 1910 into the draughtsman of Austrian expressionism. In 1913 became a contributor to *Die Aktion,* a weekly of importance for German expressionism, edited from 1910 by Franz Pfemfert at Berlin. Schiele produced hundreds of drawings but only a scanty graphic œuvre comprising eleven works, of which few contemporary impressions exist.
Lit: O. Nirenstein, *Egon Schiele, Persönlichkeit und Werk,* Vienna, 1930; Complete cats. of the prints; A. Roessler, *Das graphische Werk von Egon Schiele,* Vienna, 1922; Klipstein and Kornfeld's stock cat. No 57, Bern, 1956; H. Schwarz, "Das graphische Werk von Egon Schiele" in *Philobiblon V,* 1, 1961.

Sandig

Schiele

Savin

Santomaso

Schlotter

Schmidt-Rottluff

Schreib

SCHLOTTER, Eberhard — Born on 3 June 1921 at Hildesheim, a sculptor's son. After being apprenticed to a painter, studied at the Munich Academy. Settled after the war at Darmstadt. President of the Darmstadt *Sezession* in 1955—56. Living since 1956 at Altea in Spain.
Lit: VOLLMER IV, 1958.

SCHMIDT-ROTTLUFF, Karl — Born on 1 December 1884 at Rottluff near Chemnitz. Went to Dresden in 1905 to study architecture, and as early as June of the same year had become a foundation member of the *Brücke* group, together with his slightly older fellow students Heckel, Kirchner and Bleyl. After the group's move to Berlin, suggested by Pechstein, Schmidt-Rottluff stayed on there. During 1931—35 he was a member of the Prussian Academy of Arts, and in 1947 accepted a professorship at the Berlin College of Fine Arts.
Graphics: His graphic production up to 1924 comprises over 300 woodcuts, 105 lithographs, and 70 line-engravings and etchings. Since 1924 his output of prints has remained small.
Lit: THIEME-BECKER XXX, 1936; VOLLMER IV, 1958; Rosa Schapire, *Karl Schmidt-Rottluffs graphisches Werk bis 1923*, Berlin, 1924; W. Grohmann, *Karl Schmidt-Rottluff*, Stuttgart, 1956 (with bibl.). *Ills pp. 83, 87*

SCHNEIDER, Gérard — Born on 28 April 1896 at Sainte-Croix (Vaud Canton), the artist grew up at Neuchâtel. In 1916 he went to study in Paris, where he took up permanent residence in 1922 and has lived as a French citizen since 1948. Pure abstract paintings since 1944. Represented in Venice and São Paulo and at the two documentas in 1955 and 1959, among other shows.
12 colour lithographs for poems by Robert Ganzo date from 1949.
Lit: VOLLMER IV, 1958; M. Seuphor, *A Dictionary of Abstract Painting*, London, 1958.

SCHOOFS, Rudolf — Born in 1932 at Goch on the Lower Rhine, the artist studied during 1952—55 at Krefeld under Georg Muche and remained his assistant till 1958. Since 1958 an instructor at the Cassel Werkschule.
Graphics: Engravings on copper and zinc.
Lit: Cat. of an exhibition of thirty engravings by Schoofs at the Galerie Brusberg, Hanover, in 1960; Cat. of exhibition of engravings by Schoofs in Dortmund and Wuppertal, 1962.

SCHREIB, Werner — Born in 1925 in Berlin, the artist attended the Werkkunstschulen at Kiel and Wiesbaden after the war, then continued by teaching himself, and studied in Paris intermittently under S. W. Hayter. Living since 1953 at Wiesbaden. Represented at documenta II, Cassel, in 1959, at the graphics exhibitions of Lugano and Tokyo and the 30th Venice Biennale in 1960.
Lit: VOLLMER IV, 1958.

SCHUMACHER, Emil — Lives at Hagen, Westphalia, where he was born on 29 August 1912. Studied at the art school in Dortmund, worked as a technical draughtsman during the war, and in 1947 became a foundation member of the *Junger Westen* artists' association. During 1959—60 a guest teacher at the Hamburg College of Fine Arts.
Lit: VOLLMER IV, 1958; A. Schulze Vellinghausen, "Emil Schumacher" in *Junge Künstler 58/59*, Cologne, 1958. *Ill. p. 225*

Schneider

Schoofs

Schumacher

SCHWITTERS, Kurt — Born on 20 June 1887 in Hanover. Lived at Little Langdale, Westmorland. Died on 8 January 1948 at Ambleside. Studied during 1909—14 at Dresden. Influenced after the war by Kandinsky and Franz Marc. In Hanover in 1919 invented a dadaism of his own, which he championed during 1919—24 through poems and articles in *Der Sturm*, and 1923—32 in his periodical *MERZ*. Emigrated to Norway in 1935, to England in 1940.
Lit: THIEME-BECKER XXX, 1936; VOLLMER IV, 1958.

Schwitters

SCOTT, William — Born on 15 February 1913 at Greenock, Renfrewshire, the artist has lived since 1931 in London. First studied at Belfast, then from 1931—36 in London. Longish visits to France and Italy in 1937—39. Journeys to Canada and the States in 1953 and 1954. Taught painting at the Bath Academy of Art in 1946—56.
Lit: VOLLMER IV, 1958.

SEEWALD, Richard — Born on 4 May 1889 at Arnswalde (Neumark). To Munich in 1909 to study architecture. Self-taught as a painter. Exhibited at the First German Autumn Salon at Berlin in 1913. Spent 1924—31 teaching at the Cologne Werkschulen. In 1931 moved to Ronco, Switzerland. A professor at the Munich Academy of Fine Arts during 1953—58. Back in Ronco since 1958. Besides illustrations to his own and other people's books, many portfolio works.
Lit: THIEME-BECKER XXX, 1936; VOLLMER IV, 1958; L. G. Buchheim, *Graphik des Deutschen Expressionismus*, Feldafing, 1959.

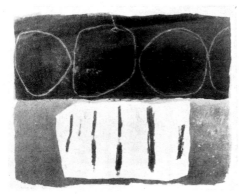
Scott

SEGALL, Lasar — Born on 8 July 1891 at Vilna, the son of a Torah copiest. Died on 2 August 1957 at São Paulo. Went early to study art at Berlin, and attended the Dresden Academy in 1910—11 at the same time as Otto Dix and George Grosz. During 1914—23 in Dresden one of the exponents of the social-revolutionary German expressionism of the war and post-war periods. In 1923 moved for good to Brasil. Became one of the founders and inspirers of modern Brasilian art.
From 1910—30 prints formed an essential part of his artistic output. Three albums with lithographs and etchings appeared in 1919 and 1921.
Lit: F. M. Bardi, *Lasar Segall*, Milan (as publ. of the São Paulo Museum), 1959 (with bibl.); THIEME-BECKER XXX, 1936; VOLLMER IV, 1958.

SEVERINI, Gino — Born on 7 April 1883 at Cortona, Arezzo. Now lives at Meudon near Paris. Went early to Rome, where in 1901 he met Umberto Boccione and Giacomo Balla, and in 1906 to Paris, where he got to know Modigliani, Max Jacob, and Braque, and became from 1909—13 one of the chief exponents of futurism. During 1916—21 his cubist period. In the 'twenties and 'thirties he championed a neo-classicism. Since then an abstracting tendency.
Graphics: Etchings during 1908—09. Lithographs in 1931. Colour lithographs of recent years.
Own writings: G. Severini, *Du cubisme au classicisme*, Paris, 1921; G. Severini, *Tutta la vita di un pittore*, Milan, 1946 (vol. 1 of an autobiography).
Lit: Pierre Courthion, *Gino Severini*, Milan, 1946 (1st edit. 1930); THIEME-BECKER XXX, 1936; VOLLMER IV, 1958. *Ill. p. 217*

Severini

SHAHN, Ben — Born on 12 September 1898 at Kovno on the Memel, the artist went to the United States in 1906 and lives today at Roosevelt, New Jersey. A trained lithographer, he studied, after his apprenticeship, in New York and in Paris at the Académie de la Grande Chaumière. Returned to the States in 1928. Murals during the 'thirties. Joint exhibition at the Museum of Modern Art, New York, in 1947. One-man shows in Venice and in England. His more recent works in the style of a "personal realism".
Lit: VOLLMER IV, 1958; *American Prints Today*, 1959 *Ill. p. 142*

Seewald

Segall

Shahn

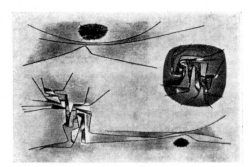
Singier

Siqueiros

Skodlerak

SINGIER, Gustave — Born on 11 February 1909 at Warneton in the Belgian province of West Flanders, the artist has lived in Paris since 1919. At first worked as an interior designer, but active since 1936 as an independent painter, helped on by Charles Walch. Co-founder of the Salon de Mai in 1943. Taught painting at the Académie Ranson during 1952—54. Also did designs for tapestries and stained-glass windows.
Graphics: Colour lithographs and colour etchings since 1951.
Lit: VOLLMER IV, 1958; BENEZIT VII, 1957; *Gustave Singier, Das graphische Werk*, Brunswick, 1958 (pub. as a cat. on the occasion of an exhibition at Brunswick: 29 works listed by Rolf Schmücking). *Ills pp. 227, 229*

SIQUEIROS, David Alfaro — Born on 29 December 1898 at Chihuahua in Mexico. Lives at Mexico City. From 1910—14 studied art in Mexico. Served in the revolutionary army during 1914—18. Military attaché at Paris from 1919. Study trips in Europe. Returned to Mexico in 1922. Murals. Collaboration with Orozco and Ribera.
Lit: VOLLMER I, 1953 (entered under Alfaro).

SKODLERAK, Horst — Born in 1920 at Jugnaten (Memel Territory), the artist studied during 1937—39 at the Königsberg Academy under Alfred Partikel. After the war, went to Schleswig-Holstein and now lives at Brodten near Lübeck as an independent artist.
Lit: VOLLMER IV, 1958; Cat. "Die Insel", Hamburg, 1959.

SONDERBORG, K. R. H. — Born in 1923 at Sonderborg on Alsen, the artist now lives at Paris. After a commercial training, worked till 1945 in Russia for a Hamburg firm. Studied painting under Ewald Becker-Carus at Hamburg in 1946. During 1947—49 a student at the Hamburg State Art School under Willem Grimm. Visited Italy in 1951. Studied at S. W. Hayter's Atelier 17 in Paris during 1953. City of Hamburg Lichtwark prize in 1955.
Lit: VOLLMER IV, 1958; W. Schmalenbach, "K. R. H. Sonderborg" in *Junge Künstler 58/59*, Cologne, 1958. *Ill. p. 237*

SOULAGES, Pierre — Born on 24 December 1919 at Rodez in southern France, the artist is self-taught and has lived in Paris since 1946 as an abstract painter. After his first exhibition at the Salon des Surindépendants in 1947, he soon achieved international success with his art. Visited Japan and the United States in 1958, thanks to two awards.
Graphics: Apart from a few colour lithographs, chiefly works printed from copper, with cut-out plates (1951—52 and 1957).
Lit: BENEZIT VII, 1957; VOLLMER IV, 1958; DORIVAL II, 1960. *Ill. p. 234*

SPACAL, Luigi — The artist lives at Trieste, where he was born on 15 June 1907. Studied at the art schools of Venice and Monza, and at the Brera Academy, Milan. International prize for graphics at the 29th Venice Biennale in 1958. Special show at the 4th international graphic-art exhibition at Ljubljana in 1961. His favourite graphic technique is woodcut.
Lit: VOLLMER IV, 1958; Cat. of the 4th international exhibition of graphic art at Ljubljana in 1961.

Sonderborg

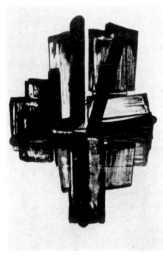
Soulages

Spacal

SPRINGER, Ferdinand — Born on 1 October 1907 at Berlin, son of the publisher Ferdinand Springer. Lives in Paris as a French citizen. After studying art history at Zurich under Heinrich Wölfflin and painting at Milan under Carlo Carrà, went to Paris, a pupil of Bissière there at the Académie Ranson. At S. W. Hayter's Atelier 17 in Paris during 1934—36. In 1939 to Grasse, 1942 to Switzerland. Returned to France after the war.
Lit: BENEZIT VIII, 1955; VOLLMER IV, 1958.

SRBINOVIC, Mladen — Born on 29 November 1925 at Susica near Gostivar in Yugoslavia, this painter and print-maker attended the Belgrade Academy of Art till 1950, and after further training as a painter became a teacher at the Belgrade Academy. In 1960 first prize for graphic art at Zagreb.
Lit: VOLLMER IV, 1958; Cat. of the 4th international exhibition of graphic art at Ljubljana in 1961.

STAEL, Nicolas de — Born on 5 January 1914 at St Petersburg into the Baltic military family de Staël-Holstein. Took his own life on 19 March 1955 at Antibes. Emigrated to Poland in 1919. After the early death of his parents, educated during 1922—30 at the Jesuit College in Brussels. Attended the Brussels Art Academy in 1932—33. Journeys to Holland, Paris, Spain and North Africa. From 1937 mainly in France: in Paris and intermittently at Tunis (with the Foreign Legion in 1939) and Nice. From 1952 in Provence.
In 1942 the first abstract pictures, 1944 friendship with Braque. In 1951 woodcuts, and the first *collages* in preparation for colour lithographs, 1953 independent *collages*, and in 1954 etchings.
Lit: BENEZIT VIII, 1955; VOLLMER IV, 1958; DORIVAL II, 1960.

STEWART, Reba — Young American artist who spent 1957 in Japan and came into notice as a contributor to *IGAS*.
Lit: *IGAS* 25/Sept. 1957.

SUGAI, Kumi — Born on 13 March 1919 at Kobe, Japan. Studied at the art school in Osaka and has lived since 1952 in Paris. Graphic awards: 1959 at Ljubljana, 1960 at Tokyo, 1961 at Grenchen.
Lit: Cat. of the 4th international exhibition of graphic art at Ljubljana in 1961; BENEZIT VIII, 1955; VOLLMER IV, 1958.

SUMMERS, Carol — Born in 1925 at Kingston, New York, the artsit is now living at New York. He got his B. A. at Bard College, then studied under Stefan Hirsch and Louis Schanker. Italian state scholarship for a visit to Italy. Tiffany and Guggenheim scholarships.
Lit: VOLLMER IV, 1958; *American Prints Today*, 1959.

Springer

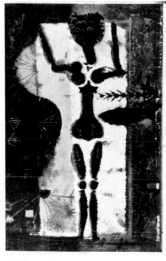

Srbinovič

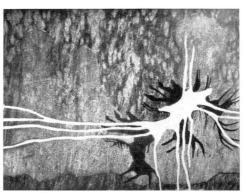

Stewart

Summers

Sugai

Stael

Sutherland

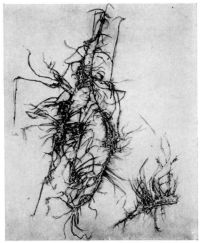

Takal

Tal Coat

SUTHERLAND, Graham Vivian — Born on 24 August 1903 in London, the artist lives at Trottiscliffe in Kent. Studied at the Goldsmiths' College School of Art during 1921—27. In 1927—29 taught print-making, in 1933—37 book illustration and composition, at the Chelsea School of Art. Sutherland found his personal style in 1935 and, with John Piper, is one of the representatives in Britain of a romantic-surreal art trend.
Lit: THIEME-BECKER XXXII, 1938; VOLLMER IV, 1958; D. Cooper, *The Work of Graham Sutherland*, London, 1961. *Ill. p. 198*

TAKAL, Peter — Born on 8 December 1905 at Bucharest. Now lives at New York. After school-days in Berlin, studied in Paris. Emigrated to the United States in 1939. Takal also composes chamber music and has made a name as a poet and prose writer.
Lit: VOLLMER IV, 1958; *American Prints Today*, 1959.

TAL COAT, Pierre — Born on 12 December 1905 at Clohars-Carnoët (Brittany). Lives in Paris. After beginnings as a sculptor, spent 1924—26 in Paris. Joined the *Forces Nouvelles* group there in 1931. During 1940—44 in Aix-en-Provence, from 1943 at Cézanne's Château Noir. Influence of Chinese art since 1947.
Lit: BENEZIT VIII, 1958; VOLLMER IV, 1958; DORIVAL II, 1960.

TAMAYO, Rufino — Born on 26 August 1899 at Oaxaxa, Mexico, of Red Indian descent. Studied from 1917 at the San Carlos Art Academy in Mexico, becoming a teacher there in 1933. From 1927 lived and worked alternately in Mexico City and New York. To Paris in 1951. Murals for a room at the UNESCO Building.
Tamayo's style combines elements of ancient Mexican and of modern European art.
Lit: THIEME-BECKER XXXII, 1938; R. Cogniat, *Rufino Tamayo*, Paris, 1951; BENEZIT VIII, 1955; VOLLMER IV, 1958.

TANGUY, Yves — Born on 5 January 1900 at Paris into a Breton family. Died in January 1955 at Woodbury, Connecticut. First approached painting as a self-taught artist — inspired by a picture of Chirico's — and joined the surrealists in 1925. Contributor to *La Révolution surréaliste*. Emigrated to the United States in 1939.
Lit: BENEZIT VIII, 1955; VOLLMER IV, 1958; *Encyclopedia of Painting*, London, 1956; J. T. Soby, *Yves Tanguy*, Museum of Modern Art, New York, Mayflower Books, n. d.; Cat. of the memorial exhibition in New York in 1955 (with bibl.).

TAPIES, Antonio — This Spanish painter lives at Barcelona, where he was born on 13 December 1923. Studied law till 1946. Self-taught as a painter. One of the founders of the review *Dau Al Set* at Barcelona in 1948. During 1950—51 at Paris on a French state scholarship. Took part in the first show of the *Dau Al Set* group at Barcelona in 1951. Since then represented at many international exhibitions in Europe and America.
Lit: Cat. of the "New Spanish Painting and Sculpture" exhibition at the Museum of Modern Art, New York, in 1960 (with bibl.). *Ill. p. 250*

Tamayo

Tapies

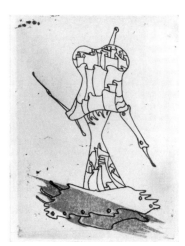

Tanguy

TERECHKOVITCH, Konstantin — Born on 1 May 1902 near Moscow, the artist went to Paris in 1920, where he became acquainted with Soutine and the Russian Ballet. In Bonnard's footsteps he developed into the "peintre de la réalité poétique".
Lit: F. Fels, C. Terechkovitch, Paris, 1928; THIEME-BECKER XXXII, 1938; VOLLMER IV, 1958.

TEUBER, Hermann — Born on 12 October 1894 in Dresden. Lives in Berlin. From 1919 to 1922 attended the Dresden School of Arts and Crafts. Spent 1922–26 studying at the Berlin Academy under Karl Hofer and Hans Meid (graphic art). Rome prize in 1936. In 1937 forbidden to exhibit. Appointed instructor in graphic art at the Berlin College of Fine Arts in 1950. City of Düsseldorf Cornelius prize in 1954.
Lit: VOLLMER IV, 1958.

THARRATS, Juan José — Born 1918 at Gerona in Catalonia, this Spanish artist now lives in Barcelona. Spent 1931–33 in France at Béziers. Moved with his family to Barcelona in 1935. First abstract pictures in 1946. Co-founder of the Dau Al Set group at Barcelona in 1948. Exhibited there with the Dau Al Set in 1951. Paris scholarship in 1953. During the following years represented at the big international shows in Europe and America.
Lit: Cat. of the "New Spanish Painting and Sculpture" exhibition at the Museum of Modern Art, New York, in 1960 (with bibl.).

TOULOUSE-LAUTREC, Henri-Marie-Raymond de — The artist, who was born on 24 November 1864 at Albi of an old line of counts, died on 9 September 1901 at Malromé. Made a cripple at an early age by two accidents during 1878–79, he went to Paris in 1881 to study art. After his first instruction from the animal painter Princeteau and a short period in Bonnat's studio, he worked during 1883–85 under Cormon, with whom he got to know Emile Bernard and Van Gogh, and also the art of Degas. From 1885 on he found his world in Montmartre. In 1893 he met Van de Velde on the occasion of an exhibition at Brussels, in 1895 Oscar Wilde and Aubrey Beardsley in London.
In 1891, soon after the early posters of Bonnard and Chéret, appeared the first ones by Toulouse-Lautrec. His first contribution to the Revue Blanche in 1892.
Lit: F. Jourdain, Toulouse-Lautrec, London, 1955; DELTEIL X and XI, 1920; J. Adhémar, Oeuvre graphique de Toulouse-Lautrec, Bibl. nat., Paris, 1951 (with additions and corrections to Delteil). *Ills pp. 25, 43, 45*

TOWN, Harold Barling — The artist lives at Toronto in Canada and was born there on 13 June 1924. After his studies, a member of the Painters Eleven Group at Toronto. Came into notice at the Venice Biennale of 1956 through his "single autographic prints". Prizes for graphic art at the international exhibitions in São Paulo (1957) and Lugano (1958).
Lit: Daval, Canadian Drawings and Prints, Toronto, 1952; VOLLMER IV, 1958.

TRIER, Hann — Born on 1 August 1915 at Düsseldorf-Kaiserswerth, the artist now lives in Berlin. Having grown up at Cologne from 1919, he studied in 1934–38 at the Düsseldorf Academy. A soldier and technical draughtsman during the Second World War. Spent 1952–55 in South America and the United States. During 1955–56 guest teacher, since 1957 professor, at the Berlin College of Fine Arts.
Books and catalogues illustrated with original prints have been published by the Galerie Der Spiegel, Cologne.
Lit: VOLLMER IV, 1958. *Ill. p. 243*

Terechkovitch

Teuber

Tharrats

Toulouse-Lautrec

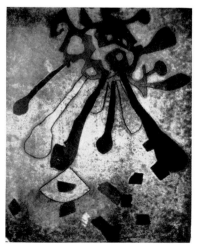
Town

Trier

Trökes

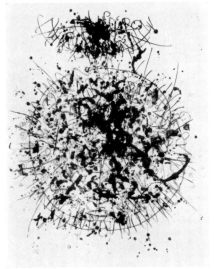

Turnbull

TROKES, Heinz — Born on 15 August 1913 at Hamborn in the Rhineland. Lived on the Spanish Balearic island of Ibiza. During 1933—36 a pupil of Johannes Itten, later (1940) of Hans Muche at Krefeld. Met Kandinsky in Paris in 1937. Spent 1940—49 in Berlin, 1950—52 in Paris, and 1952—56 on Ibiza. Appointed professor at the Hamburg College of Fine Arts in 1956. Gave up his professorship voluntarily in 1958 and returned to Ibiza. Since 1960 has taken a painting class at the Stuttgart Academy.
Lit: W. Grohmann, *Trökes*, Berlin, 1959; VOLLMER IV, 1958.   *Ill. p. 242*

TURNBULL, William — Born in 1922 at Dundee, Angus. Lives in London, where he teaches sculpture at the Central School of Arts and Crafts. Studied at the Slade School during 1946—48. Spent 1948—50 at Paris. Represented in 1952 at the 26th Venice Biennale. Like his approximate contemporary the sculptor Eduardo Paolozzi, influenced by Alberto Giacometti.
Lit: VOLLMER IV, 1958; *A Dictionary of Modern Sculpture*, London, 1962.

UBAC, Raoul — Born on 31 August 1910 at Malmédy, the artist went in 1929 to Paris, where he studied in the studios of Montparnasse. During 1932—39 worked chiefly as a photographer, under surrealist influence (Max Ernst and Man Ray). After 1943 came via drawing (pen, wash and gouache) to painting. First joint exhibition in Paris in 1950.
Lit: VOLLMER IV, 1958; DORIVAL II, 1960.   *Ill. p. 247*

UCHIMA, Ansei — Born in 1921 in America, the artist studied in Japan and was taken prisoner during the Second World War. Returned to America in 1959.
Lit: *IGAS* 41/Nov. 1960; Cat. of the "Japan's Modern Prints" exhibition, Chicago, 1960.

UTRILLO, Maurice — Born on 26 December 1883 in Paris, the son of the painter Suzanne Valadon. Died on 5 November 1955 at Dax. From 1902 on, with a longish break due to his stays at sanatoria for alcoholics during 1914—21, he painted his landscapes and street scenes of Paris, first under Pissarro's influence, subsequently in various manners developed by himself. Began to achieve success with exhibitions around 1920. Later also lived at Le Vésinet on the Seine, Le Lavandou, Dax, or by the Mediterranean.
Graphics: Lithographs and etchings (no catalogue yet).
Lit: THIEME-BECKER XXXIV, 1940; VOLLMER IV, 1958; DORIVAL I, 1959.

VALADON, Suzanne (really Marie-Clémentine) — Born on 23 September 1867 at Bessines near Limoges. Died in April 1938 in Paris. Suzanne Valadon was the mother of the painter Utrillo. When still a child she came to Paris, where Toulouse-Lautrec and Degas discovered the artistic talent of their young model and encouraged her to draw. Later she painted as well, exhibiting her pictures with the impressionists.
Graphics: Aquatints (1895), etchings (1904—05), drypoints (1908—10).
Lit: BENEZIT VIII, 1955; C. Roger-Marx, *Dix-huit planches originales de Suzanne Valadon (1895—1910)*, Paris, 1932.

Ubac

Uchima

Utrillo

Valadon

VALLOTTON, Félix — Born on 28 December 1865 at Lausanne. Died on 28 December 1925, a "Frenchman by choice from French Switzerland". Vallotton came to Paris as early as 1882, studied at the Académie Julian, and joined the nabis circle in 1893, contributing as a painter to their shows and as a draughtsman to the *Revue Blanche*.
Graphics: The work produced in Paris from 1882 on comprises 22 etchings, 55 lithographs and 145 woodcuts. Vallotton's woodcuts are precursors of the modern planar woodcut. The artist also made a name as a writer and art critic.
Lit: H. Hanloser-Bühler, *F. Vallotton et ses amis*, Paris, 1936; L. Godefroy, *l'Oeuvre gravée de Félix Vallotton*, Paris and Lausanne, 1932.

VASARELY, Victor — Born on 9 April 1908 at Pécs in Hungary. After studying at the Academy in Budapest, spent 1928—29 at the "Bauhaus" there. In Paris from 1930. Since 1947 the exponent of an "abstract, constructive and geometric art". The *Mouvement* manifesto in 1955.
Lit: Cat.-monograph of the Galerie Denise René, Paris, 1959 (with bibl. and list of exhibitions); cat. of Musée des Arts Décoratifs, Paris, 1963 (with bibl.). *Ill. p. 226*

VEDOVA, Emilio — Born on 9 August 1919 in Venice, the artist has been living there again since 1945. He trained himself at Rome, belonging in 1942 to the *Corrente* and after the war to the Fronte nuovo delle Arti and the Gruppo degli Otto.
Lit: L. Venturi, *Otto pittori italiani*, Rome, 1952.

VERTES, Marcel — Born in Budapest on 10 August 1895, this graphic artist and illustrator now lives in the United States. He was a pupil of the Hungarian painter Károly Ferenczy, and went in 1925 to Paris, where he soon became well-known through his portofolios of lithographs and colour etchings.
Lit: BENEZIT VIII, 1955; *Les Cahiers d'art-documents*, No. 27, Geneva, 1956.

VESPIGNANI, Renzo (Lorenzo) — Born in 1924 in Rome and living there now, the artist was a co-founder in 1949 of the Pittori del Portonaccio group, which champions a social neo-realism. Since 1944 also active as a graphic artist.
Lit: "Pittorio del Portonaccio" cat., Rome, 1949.

VIEILLARD, Roger — Born on 9 February 1907 at Le Mans. In 1911 the family moved to Paris, where Vieillard is still living. Studied during 1935—37 at S. W. Hayter's Atelier 17. Since then has worked chiefly as a line-engraver. After the war joint exhibitions of his works with Gromaire and Villon. During 1939—56 he produced, besides twelve illustrated books, about 150 individual prints.
Lit: *Les Cahiers d'art-documents*, No. 49, Geneva, 1957.

VILA-CASAS, Joan — Born in 1920 in Sabadell, where he studied at the art school. First exhibitions in Sabadell and Barcelona. Adherence to tachism at Paris in 1949. Sets of etchings listed in Gerald Cramer's stock cat. No. 12, Geneva, 1961.
Lit: Cat. of an exhibition of Spanish art at Hamburg in 1960. *Ill. p. 242*

Vallotton

Vasarely

Vedova

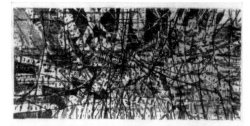

Vila-Casas

Vertès

Vieillard

Vespignani

Villon

VILLON, Jacques (Gaston Duchamp) — Born on 31 July 1875 at Damville (Eure). Died June 1963. Half-brother of the cubist sculptor Raymond Duchamp (1876–1918) and the painter Marcel Duchamp (founder of New York dadaism). Studied from 1894 at the Atelier Cormon. In 1911 a co-founder of the cubist *Section d'Or* group. First abstract period about 1930. Painting prize at the Venice Biennale in 1956.
Graphics: Began in 1900. About 175 etchings, some of them colour ones, up to 1910. His graphic production now comprises over 600 works.
Lit: P. Eluard, *Jacques Villon*, Paris, 1948; J. Auberty and C. Pérussaux, *Jacques Villon, Catalogue de son œuvre gravée*, Paris, 1950; *Jacques Villon, Oeuvre gravée*, cat. of the exhibition at Louis Carré's, Paris, 1954; *Laboureur / Villon*, cat. of an Antwerp exhibition in 1955 (some additions); Cat. of an exhibition of his engravings at the Bibl. nat., Paris, in 1959.   *Ill. p. 170*

VIVIANI, Giuseppe — Born on 18 December 1899 at Agnano (Pisa), this graphic artist now lives at Marina di Pisa. A follower of *pittura metafisica*, he has achieved a large graphic production using Morandi's stylistic means.
Lit: P. C. Santini, *L'opera grafica di Viviani*, Ivrea, 1958; A complete cat. by Piero Chiara is in preparation.   *Ill. p. 136*

VLAMINCK, Maurice — Born on 4 April 1876, of Flemish and Lorraine descent. Died in October 1958 at La Tourillière (Rueil-la-Gardelière). He was a painter and writer, and in his early days also a racing cyclist and musician. In 1900 he got to know Derain and in 1901 met the art of Van Gogh at the latter's memorial exhibition in Paris. During the following years he made the acquaintance of Matisse, Picasso and Apollinaire. In 1905–07 he and Derain were the principle exponents of fauvism. Spent 1908–14 under Cézanne's influence, from which he freed himself with a struggle after the war.
Graphics: In all about 105 single prints, among them 24 woodcuts belonging to the years 1905–14. From 1919–20 on chiefly etchings and lithographs, the latter mostly in the 'twenties. Besides the individual prints, about 20 books, in part illustrated with original graphics.
Own writings: Memoirs and writings on art as well as novels and poems.
Lit: M. Sauvage, *Vlaminck*, Geneva, 1956 (with bibl.); On the prints: A provisional list in the cat. of the Vlaminck collection of Dr S. Pollog (Zurich) exhibited at the Kunstmuseum, Bern, in 1961; A complete cat. of the graphics being prepared by Dr S. Pollog at Zurich.   *Ill. p. 124*

Viviani

VUILLARD, Edouard — Born on 11 November 1868 at Cuiseaux (Saône-et-Loire). Died on 21 June 1940 at La Boule. From 1888 studied at the Académie Julian in Paris, joining the nabis circle in 1889, along with Maurice Denis and Bonnard. First individual exhibition at the *Revue Blanche* gallery in 1891. Visited Hamburg, England and Holland in 1913. From 1908 taught at the Académie Ranson. A painter of still-lifes, portraits and murals.
Graphics: 60, mainly colour, lithographs produced between 1893 and 1934. The earliest belong to the incunabula of nabis graphic art. There exist seven etchings as well.
Lit: C. Roger-Marx, *Vuillard: His Life and Work*, London, 1946; C. Roger-Marx, *l'Oeuvre gravée de Vuillard*, London, 1948.   *Ill. p. 49*

WEBER, A. Paul — Born on 1 November 1893 at Arnstadt in Thuringia, the artist now lives at Schretstaken (Lauenburg Dist.) near Hamburg. Issuing from commercial art, he drew for the press during the First World War, and from 1919 on produced his book illustrations and the successions of cartoons criticizing the times that led to his arrest in 1937. After the war came further illustrations and sets of lithographs, which have been on view at many shows in Germany and in 1952 also at the 2nd international graphics exhibition of Lugano. Since 1940 the artist has worked for the Griffelkunst-Vereinigung, Hamburg-Langenhorn as well.
Lit: G. Ramseger, *A. Paul Weber, Graphik*, Oldenburg-Hamburg, 1956.

WEISSAUER, Rudolf — Born on 17 May 1924 at Munich, where he studied at the Academy in 1945–49 and is now a painter and print-maker. As a graphic artist, prefers lithography. Study trips through Europe, and to the United States and Mexico.
Lit: VOLLMER V, 1961.

Vlaminck

Vuillard

Weber

Weissauer

WENDLAND, Gerhard — Born on 29 October 1910 at Hanover, the artist attended the School of Arts and Crafts there till 1932, and took his journeyman's examination in 1933. After the war back at Hanover, first as an independent artist, in 1954—57 as an art teacher, from 1957 as an instructor at the Werkkunstschule. Appointment at the Nuremberg Academy in 1960. Represented at documenta II, Cassel in 1959.
Lit: Cat. of documenta II at Cassel in 1959; VOLLMER V, 1961.

WESTPFAHL, Conrad — Born on 23 November 1891 in Berlin. Lives today in Munich. Studied in Berlin, Munich and Paris in 1910—14. Soldier in 1914—18. After the war lived in Berlin till 1926. Spent 1926—33 in Paris and Provence, then, following a short spell in Berlin, 1934—39 in Athens. Munich since 1940.
Lit: Cat. of the 3rd international exhibition of graphic art at Ljubljana in 1959; VOLLMER V, 1961.

WHISTLER, James Abbott McNeil — Born on 10 July 1834 at Lowell, Mass. Died on 17 July 1903 in Chelsea. After early years in Russia and a spell at West Point Military Academy, he lived from 1855 on in Europe, chiefly in Paris and London. At Paris he studied under Gleyre and was a friend of Degas, Legros, Bracquemond and Fantin-Latour. Also knew Courbet, whom he visited at Trouville in 1864 and 1865. The etcher Seymour Haden was his brother-in-law.
Graphics: A set of 12 etchings *d'après nature* published by Delâtre at Paris in 1858. From 1859 date 16 etchings with Thames views and from 1879—80 the 40 prints of the two Venice sets — his weightiest contribution to the history of modern graphic art.
Lit: THIEME-BECKER XXXV, 1942 (with full bibl.); Graphic cats: F. Wedmore, *Whistler's Etchings*, London, 1886; T. R. Way, *The Cattalogue of Whistler's Lithographs*, London, 1905, New York, 1914 (new edit.); E. G. Kennedy, *The Etched Work of Whistler*, 4 vols, New York, 1910. *Ill. p. 11*

WILTHELM, Heinrich — Born on 17 November 1913 at Bochum, where he lives now, the artist studied during 1929—39 at the Folkwang School, Essen, and the Düsseldorf Academy under Mataré and Nauen. Since 1951 exclusively a graphic artist.
Lit: VOLLMER V, 1961.

WIND, Gerhard — Born on 22 January 1928 at Hamburg, the artist now lives at Düsseldorf. After being an apprentice book-seller, studied in 1952—54 under Kluth, Winter and Nay at the Hamburg State Art School, and in 1954 graphic techniques under Otto Coester at Düsseldorf. Collaborated at times in 1954 and 1956 with Joseph Fassbender. Rome prize (Villa Massimo) in 1958.
Lit: *Geh durch den Spiegel*, Ser. 15, Galerie Der Spiegel, Cologne, 1958; VOLLMER V, 1961.

WINTER, Fritz — Born on 22 September 1905 at Altenbögge, Westphalia, a miner's son. Lives at Diessen, Upper Bavaria. After working in the mines, spent 1927—30 studying at the Bauhaus under Paul Klee and Schlemmer. To Diessen in 1931. Military service and captivity during 1939—49. After the war belonged to the ZEN group. Prize at the Venice Biennale in 1952. Since 1955 teaching at the Cassel Werkakademie.
Lit: W. Haftmann, *Fritz Winter*, Bern, 1951, Munich 1957. *Ill. p. 236*

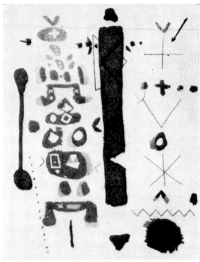

Wendland

Westphal

Wilthelm

Whistler

Winter

Wind

Wolff

Wols

Wunderlich

Yoshida

WOLFF, Gustav Heinrich — Born on 24 May 1886 at Zittau into a family (which he left early on) otherwise dwelling at Barmen. Lived before the First World War in Rome (1903) and Paris (1905–14), during it as a civilian internee on the Channel coast, and from 1918 mainly at Berlin, where from 1920–34 he produced in connection with his sculptures, besides a mass of drawings, his sets of woodcuts and broadsheets.
Lit: Cat. of the Wolff exhibition at the Museum für Kunst und Gewerbe, Hamburg, in 1957; A monograph with complete cat. of the sculpture and graphic works is being prepared by Frau A. Holthusen, Hamburg.

WOLS (Wolfgang Schulze) — Born on 27 May 1913 in Berlin. Died on 1 September 1951 in Paris. In 1919 the family moved to Dresden, where the young Wols occupied himself with music and photography. After studying briefly at the Bauhaus (in 1932, the school's last interim year in Berlin), went as a photographer to Spain and to France, living there till 1939 and from 1945 mainly in Paris. His paintings and drawings, done to begin with in his spare time, at first belong to the surrealist succession, later to *art informel*.
Graphics: Chiefly drypoints from the years 1942–51, in part book illustrations to Sartre, Kafka and Paulhan, among others.
Lit: C. Royen, *Art-document*, No. 35/36, 1953; Cat. of the prints by W. Grohmann in *Quadrum VI*, 1959 (52 works, 1942–51, listed with ills). *Ill. p. 223*

WUNDERLICH, Paul — Born in 1927 at Berlin, the artist studied at Hamburg during 1946–52 and taught graphic techniques at the Hamburg College of Fine Arts from 1952–60. German young-artists prize for graphics in 1960. Living at present in Paris.
Lit: Cat. of the "Acht Künstler aus Hamburg" exhibition at Cassel in 1961; VOLLMER V, 1961; H. Th. Flemming, "Paul Wunderlich" in *Junge Künstler* 1963/64, Cologne, 1963.

YOSHIDA, Masaji — Born on 3 May 1917 at Wakayama, Japan. Lives in Tokyo. Studied painting at the Tokyo Academy till 1941. Represented at many international exhibitions, most recently at Ljubljana in 1961.
Lit: Cat. of the 4th international exhibition of graphic art at Ljubljana in 1961.

ZADKINE, Ossip — Born on 14 July 1890 at Smolensk. His mother came from Scotland. In 1906 attended a school in the north of England. Went in 1908 to study sculpture in London and in 1909 to the Ecole des Beaux-Arts in Paris. An independent artist in Paris from 1911. In the French army during 1914–18. First exhibitions in Brussels and Paris in 1919, Brussels and London in 1927. Spent 1940–45 in the States. Taught at the Académie de la Grande Chaumière, Paris, from 1946 to 1953. Grand prize at the Venice Biennale in 1950.
Lit: THIEME-BECKER XXXVI, 1947; A. M. Hammacher, *Zadkine*, London, 1958; R. Cogniat, *Zadkine*, Paris, 1958. *Ill. p. 200*

ZAO WOU-KI — Born on 1 February 1920 at Peking. Lives in Paris. Spent 1934–40 studying at the art school in Hangchow, then taught there during 1941–47. To Paris in 1948. Since 1950 represented at the big international shows.
Lit: BENEZIT VIII, 1955 (under Wou-Ki); N. Jacometti, *Zao Wou-Ki, Catalogue raisonné de l'œuvre gravée et lithographiée 1914–1954*, Bern, 1955. *Ill. p. 194*

ZIMMERMANN, Mac — Born on 22 August 1912 at Stettin. Studied from 1930–33 at the Stettin Werkkunstschule. Went in 1934 as a press draughtsman to Hamburg, and in 1938 to Berlin. Living since 1949 in Munich. City of Berlin art prize in 1950. Now a professor at the Berlin Academy of Fine Arts.
Lit: B. Degenhart, *Mac Zimmermann, Skizzenbuch*, Munich, 1955; VOLLMER V, 1961.

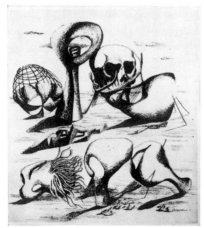

Zimmermann

Zadkine

Zao Wou-Ki

LIST OF ILLUSTRATIONS ACCOMPANYING THE BIOGRAPHIES

ABRAMO, Livio. *Paraguay*, 1958, woodcut.

ADAM, Henri-Georges. *Woman*, 1951, line-engraving.

AFRO (Basaldella, Afro). *Composition*, 1953, lithograph.

APPEL, Karel. *Funny Sight, c.* 1960, colour lithograph.

ARMITAGE, Kenneth. *Two seated Figures*, 1960, colour lithograph.

ARP, Hans. *Siamese Leaf, c.* 1949, woodcut (Bolliger 32).

ATLAN, Jean. *Composition 1 (The Simoom)*, 1957, colour lithograph (*L'Oeuvre gravée* 132).

BARGHEER, Eduard. *Men and Boats on the Shore*, 1952, etching.

BARLACH, Ernst. *The Conqueror, c.* 1924, lithograph (Schult 226).

BARTOLINI, Luigi. *Behind the Window, c.* 1957, colour etching.

BASKIN, Leonard. *The Poet Laureate*, 1955, woodcut.

BAUMEISTER, Willi. *Faust*, 1952, lithograph.

BAZAINE, Jean. *Mountain Landscape*, 1960, colour lithograph (Maeght 806).

BECK, Gustav Kurt. *Forms*, 1958, colour linocut.

BECKMANN, Max. *Self-portrait with graver*, 1916, etching (Glaser 82).

BERGMAN, Anna-Eva. *Composition*, 1953, colour etching.

BERKE, Hubert. *Nora*, 1959, colour lithograph.

BIROLLI, Renato. *Venetian Lagoon*, 1954, colour lithograph.

BISSIERE, Roger. *Abstract Composition*, 1957, colour etching (Pub. as annual gift of the Kestner-Gesellschaft, Hanover).

BOCCIONI, Umberto. *Mother at her Knitting*, 1907, etching.

BONNARD, Pierre. *Study from the Nude, c.* 1925, lithograph (Mourlot 84).

BOUSSINGAULT, Jean-Louis. *The Omnibus*, ill. to Léon Paul Fargue, *D'après Paris*, 1930.

BOZZOLINI, Silvano. *Precipitations*, 1958, colour woodcut (*L'Oeuvre gravée* 164).

BRAQUE, *Georges*. Colour woodcut for Erik Satie's lyrical comedy *Le Piège de Méduse*, 1921 (Hofmann I).

BRAUND, Allin. *Stonehenge*, 1960, etching.

BRUNING, Peter. *Etching in Black*, 1959.

BRYEN, Camille. *Festival*, 1957, colour lithograph (*L'Oeuvre gravée* 111).

BUFFET, Bernard. *Semaphore, c.* 1959, drypoint.

CAMARO, Alexander. *February*, 1959, colour serigraph.

CAMPENDONK, Heinrich. *Seated Harlequin*, 1922, woodcut (Engels 59).

CAMPIGLI, Massimo. Lithograph for André Gide, *Theseus*, 1948.

CAPOGROSSI, Guerna Giuseppe. *Planes*, 1958, colour lithograph.

CARRA, Carlo. *Sea-coast*, 1924, etching.

CARZOU, Jean. *Salome*, 1959, colour lithograph.

CASORATI, Felice. *Boy in the Studio*, 1946, lithograph.

CASTELLANI, Leonardo. *Houses at Tavoleto*, 1956, etching.

CAVAEL, Rolf. *Composition*, 1958, colour lithograph.

CHADWICK, Lynn. *Dancing Figures*, 1952, lithograph.

CHAGALL, Marc. *Madonna with Fish*, 1951, lithograph (Meyer-Bolliger 114).

CHESNEY, Lee. *Rocks and Sea*, 1958, drypoint.

CHIRICO, Giorgio de. *My ancient Youth, c.* 1930, lithograph.

CLARKE, Geoffrey. *Study for a sculpture*, 1956, colour aquatint.

CLAVE, Antoni. *The Circus, c.* 1952, colour lithograph.

CLERICI, Fabrizio. *Turtle, c.* 1954, colour lithograph.

CLIFFE, Henry. *Circe*, 1958, colour lithograph.

CONSTANT (C. Nieuwenhuys). *Lithograph in Black*, 1948.

CORINTH, Lovis. *Self-portrait*, 1919, etching (Schwarz 380).

CORNEILLE (Cornelius van Beverloo). *Earth and Stars*, 1958, colour lithograph (*L'Oeuvre gravée* 213).

COURTIN, Pierre. *Red Springtime*, 1956, etching on zinc (Pub. Berggruen).

CRAWFORD, Ralston. *Third Avenue Elevated*, No. 2, 1952, colour lithograph.

CRIPPA, Roberto. *Totem*, 1956, colour lithograph.

CRODEL, Carl. *Squirrel, c.* 1950, colour lithograph.

DAHMEN, Karl Fred. *September*, 1959, colour lithograph.

DALI, Salvador. *Figures, c.* 1940, etching.

DAUBIGNY, Charles-François. *Apple-trees near Auvers*, 1877, etching (Delteil XIII, 126).

DAVIS, Stuart. Detail study for *Cliché, c.* 1958, colour lithograph.

DAY, Worden. *Prismatic Presences*, 1957, colour relief-print.

DEBENJAC, Riko. *Caryatid from the Karst*, 1957, colour aquatint.

DELAUNAY, Robert. *Window on the City*, 1910/26, lithograph.

DENIS, Maurice. *Allegory, c.* 1900, colour lithograph.

DERAIN, André. One of the 40 lithographs for V. Muselli, *Les Travaux et les jeux*, Paris, 1929.

DIX, Otto. *Old Fisherman*, 1948, lithograph (Karsch 141).

DOMINGUEZ, Oskar. *Homage to Manolete*, 1955, colour lithograph (*L'Oeuvre gravée* 61)

DRENKHAHN, Reinhard. *Lobster*, 1956, colour etching.

DUBUFFET, Jean. *Head, c.* 1956, colour lithograph.

DUFY, Raoul. One of the 110 etchings for E. Monfort, *La belle enfant*, A. Vollard, Paris, 1930.

DUNOYER DE SEGONZAC, André. *Portrait of Colette*, 1930, etching.

EDMONDSON, Leonard. *Escarpment*, 1956, colour etching.

EGLAU, Otto. *Nets on the Seashore*, 1956, colour etching.

ELENBAAS, Valdemar Hansen. *Rope-dancers*, 1958, colour lithograph.

ENSOR, James. *King Plague*, 1895, etching (Delteil XIX, 100).

EPPLE, Bernhard. *Sound Figure*, 1961, line-engraving on nickel-zinc.

ERNI, Hans. *Colts*, 1957, colour lithograph (*L'Oeuvre gravée* 124).

ERNST, Max. One of the three etchings for Benjamin Péret, *La Brebis galante*, Paris, 1949.

ESTEVE, Maurice. *Aladdin*, 1958, colour lithograph *(L'Oeuvre gravée* 186).

EVANS, Merlyn. From *Suite verticale*, 1957, aquatint, London, 1958.

FASSBENDER, Joseph. *Abstract Composition*, 1952, colour lithograph.

FAZZINI, Pericle. *Horse and Rider, c.* 1955, lithograph.

FEININGER, Lyonel. *Manhattan*, 1955, lithograph.

FELIXMULLER, Conrad. *The Fisherman*, 1924, woodcut.

FIEBIGER, Helmut. *Child and Cat*, 1953, colour linocut.

FIETZ, Gerhard. *L 1*, 1959, colour lithograph.

FINK, Herbert. *The great Pond, c.* 1960, etching and line-engraving (IGAS 41/1960).

FISCHER, Hans. *The Man with Seven Heads*, 1958, etching.

FLOCON, Albert. Line-engraving for Flocon, *Traité du burin*, Paris, 1952.

FRASCONI, Antonio. *The frozen Strait*, 1958, colour woodcut.

FREUNDLICH, Otto. Zincograph from the portfolio *The Signs*, Cologne, 1920.

FRIEDLAENDER, Johnny. *Bird in the Circle, c.* 1960, etching (Schmücking 71).

FUHR, Xaver. *Gothic, c.* 1951, lithograph.

GAUGUIN, Paul. Cover for the periodical *Le Sourire*, 1899/1900, woodcut (Guérin 76).

GEIGER, Rupprecht. Colour serigraph, 1958.

GENIN, Robert. Lithograph from *Skizzen und Erinnerungen*, Berlin, 1920.

GENTILINI, Franco. *Cathedral and Wind-instrumentalist, c.* 1955, colour lithograph.

GIACOMETTI, Alberto. Etching for Gilbert Laly, *La Folie Tristan*, Paris, 1959.

GILLES, Werner. *The Fisherman*, 1957, colour lithograph.

GILLET, Roger Edgar. *No-man's-land*, 1958, colour lithograph (*L'Oeuvre gravée* 156).

GISCHIA, Léon. *Castilian Hour*, 1960, colour lithograph (*L'Oeuvre gravée* 284).

GOLLER, Oskar. *Judgment*, 1953, colour lithograph.

GOTSCH, Friedrich Karl. *Pura, Ticino*, 1959, colour lithograph.

GRAMATE, Walter. *Self-portrait*, 1921, colour lithograph.

GRESKO, Georg. *Wayside Crucifix*, 1956, colour lithograph.

GRIESHABER, HAP. *Nursing Mother*, 1955, colour woodcut (Boeck 237).

GRIMM, Willem. *Twelfth Night*, 1948, woodcut.

GRIS, Juan. One of the five lithographs for Armand Salacrou's one-act play *Le Casseur d'assiettes*, Paris, 1924.

GROCHOWIAK, Thomas. *Striving upwards*, 1961, lithograph.

GROMAIRE, Marcel. Etching for H. Hertz, *Vers un monde volage*, Paris, 1926.

GROSS, Anthony. *Forge, c.* 1956, etching.

GROSSMANN, Rudolf. *The Poet*, 1918, etching.

GROSZ, George. *Night Spot*, 1916, lithograph.

GULINO, Nunzio, *Rope-dancer at Urbino*, 1958, etching.

GUTTUSO, Renato. *Women Carriers*, 1956, colour lithograph.

HAAGE, Sixten. *Printing-press*, 1960, colour woodcut.

HAASE, Volkmar. *Circling*, 1959, colour lithograph.

HAASS, Terry, *Docks*, 1959/60, colour etching.

HAJEK, Otto Herbert. *Abstract Composition*, 1960, lithograph.

HAMAGUCHI, Yozo. *Jug, Grapes and Lemon*, 1957, aquatint.

HANSEN, Karl Heinz. *Sick Dog*, 1957, woodcut.

HARTUNG, Hans. *Abstract Composition*, 1957, etching.

HARTUNG, Karl. *Two Figures before an Easel*, 1949, lithograph.

HAYTER, Stanley William. *Struggle*, 1936, line-engraving and etching.

HECK, Erich. *Annular Cells*, 1960, woodcut.

HECKEL, Erich. *Sunrise (On the Seashore)*, 1914, woodcut.

HEGENBARTH, Josef. *The seven Swabians*, lithograph.

HEILIGER, Bernhard. *Two seated Figures*, 1949, lithograph.

HELDT, Werner. *View from a Window, with Grand Piano*, 1949, lithograph.

HERKENRATH, Peter. *Zincograph II*, 1961.

HEYBOER, Anton. Colour drypoint on zinc, *c.* 1958 (not yet listed in the Spiegel cat.).

HINTSCHICH, Gerhard. *Southern Houses*, 1958, lithograph.

HOEHME, Gerhard. One of the set of six colour etchings *Between Red and Black* (Edition Rothe, Heidelberg, 1960).

HOFER, Karl. *Farmstead, c.* 1925, lithograph.

IHLE, John Livingston. *The Animal Kingdom, c.* 1957, etching (IGAS 27/1958).

ITEM, Georges. *Camargue Landscape II*, c. 1955, etching (IGAS 13/1955).

JAENISCH, Hans. *The Spirit of the Island*, 1959, colour lithograph.

JANSSEN, Horst. *The Anatomy Lesson of Dr Tulp*, 1958, etching.

JANSSON, Vide. *Blooming Blue*, 1960, colour woodcut.

JAWLENSKY, Alexei von. *Woman's Head*, c. 1912, lithograph.

JONGKIND, Johan Barthold. *The Mouth of Honfleur Harbour*, 1864, etching and drypoint (Delteil I, 11).

JORN, Asger. *Composition with small Figures*, 1944, colour lithograph.

JUKITA, Fumiaki. Colour woodcut, c. 1958.

KANDINSKY, Wassily. Etching IX from *Kleine Welten*, 1922.

KAUS, Max. *Portrait of a Man*, c. 1920, woodcut.

KINERT, Albert. *The Island II*, 1959, colour linocut.

KIRCHNER, Ernst Ludwig. *Sailing-boats near Fehmarn*, 1912/13, (Schiefler 213).

KLEE, Paul. *Height*, 1928, etching (Soby 37).

KLEINSCHMIDT, Paul. *Fortune-teller*, c. 1920, drypoint.

KLIEMANN, Carl-Heinz. *Double Portrait*, 1957, etching.

KLINGER, Max. *Disgrace*, 1887, etching, line-engraving and aquatint (Singer 165). No. 9 of the series *A Love-affair*.

KOGAN, Moissey. *Two standing female Nudes*, c. 1922, woodcut.

KOHLER, Max Ernst. *Large Bird*, 1958, colour etching.

KOHN, Misch. *Three Kings*, 1957, aquatint and relief-print (Zigrosser 128).

KOKOSCHKA, Oskar. Lithograph for Oskar Kokoschka, *Der gefesselte Columbus*, Berlin, 1921 (Arntz 28).

KOLLWITZ, Käthe. *Self-portrait*, 1924, lithograph (Klipstein 198).

KONOW, Jürgen von. *Summer Evening*, 1954/55, line-engraving and etching.

KOROMPAY, Giovanni. *Shipyard*, 1960, etching.

KRUCK, Christian. *Black Nude*, 1960, colour lithograph.

KUBIN, Alfred. *Bull in Mountain Pasture-land*, 1921, lithograph.

KUGLER, Rudolf. *Harbour Town*, 1951, colour etching.

LABOUREUR, Jean-Emile. *Girl at the Greengrocer's*, 1922, line-engraving.

LA FRESNAYE, Roger de. *The Oarsman*, 1914, lithograph.

LARDERA, Berto. *The Miracle*, 1956, colour lithograph.

LASANSKY, Mauricio. *Vision*, 1956, colour etching (Zigrosser 29).

LAURENCIN, Marie. *Gerda*, c. 1920, lithograph.

LAURENS, Henri. One of the 58 woodcuts for Lucien de Samosate, *Loukios ou l'âne*, Paris, 1946.

LEGER, Fernand. *Composition with two Figures*, 1920, lithograph. From the second portfolio series *Die Schaffenden*.

LEHMBRUCK, Wilhelm. *Macbeth II*, 1918, etching.

LEMCKE, Dietmar. *Mill in Majorca*, 1953, colour etching.

LE MOAL, Jean. *Spring II*, 1959, colour lithograph (*L'Oeuvre gravée* 221).

LETICIA, Anna. *Horses*, 1958, line-engraving.

LHOTE, André. *Sailor and Girl from Martinique*, 1930, colour lithograph.

LICATA, Riccardo. *Composition II*, c. 1955, etching.

LIMA, José. *Abstraction II*, 1958, aquatint.

LIPMAN-WULF, Peter. Colour woodcut, c. 1958.

LUCEBERT. One of 12 lithographs in black pub. by the Galerie Der Spiegel, Cologne, 1958.

LURCAT, Jean. *Blood and Life*, c. 1951, colour lithograph (Guilde de la Gravure).

MACCARI, Mino. *Penetration*, c. 1950, etching.

MAGNELLI, Alberto. *Composition L I*, 1958, colour lithograph (*L'Oeuvre gravée* 185).

MAILLOL, Aristide. *The Wave*, c. 1895, woodcut (Rewald 5). According to Rewald executed between 1893 and 1900.

MAKI, Haku. *Work No. 2*, 1957, woodcut.

MANESSIER, Alfred. One of the 12 colour lithographs for St John of the Cross, *Les Cantiques spirituels*, Paris, 1958.

MANET, Edouard. *The Granddaughter*, 1862, etching (Guérin 25 II).

MANZU, Giacomo. Etching for Virgil, *Georgics*, Milan, 1948.

MARC, Franz. *Birth of the Wolves*, 1913, woodcut (Schardt VII, 1913, 3).

MARCKS, Gerhard. *Persons of high Rank*, 1922, woodcut.

MARCOUSSIS, Louis. Etching for Tristan Tzara, *Indicateur des chemins de cœur, Poèmes*, Paris, 1928.

MARINI, Marino. *Horse and Rider*, 1952, lithograph in black.

MASCHERINI, Marcello. *Faun II*, 1956, colour lithograph.

MASEREEL, Frans. *Abandoned Child*, 1933, woodcut. From the portfolio *Expiations*, Paris, 1933.

MASSON, André. *Mont Sainte-Victoire*, 1956, etching.

MATARE, Ewald. *Horse advancing (towards the right)*, 1951, colour woodcut (Peters 229 III).

MATISSE, Henri. *Woman in a Deck-chair*, 1906, linocut (Lieberman 67).

MATTA, Roberto. *The Pianist*, 1956, colour lithograph (*L'Oeuvre gravée* 77).

MEEKER, Dean Jackson. *The Surgeon*, 1957, colour engraving in a mixed technique.

MEIDNER, Ludwig. *Self-portrait*, c. 1922, etching.

MEISTERMANN, Georg. *Jelly-fish*, 1953, colour lithograph (Pub. by the Galerie Der Spiegel, Cologne, 1954).

MENZEL, Adolf von. *Woman reading the Newspaper*, 1886, etching (Bock 1159).

MEYBODEN, Hans. *In the Window*, 1952, etching.

MILLET, Jean-François. *Peasant with Dung-barrow*, 1855, etching (Delteil I, 11 IV).

MIRO, Joan. *Woman in the Night*, 1940. One of the *Constellations* series pub. as stencils by Pierre Matisse, New York, 1959, after gouaches painted by Miró in 1940 at Varengeville on the Normandy coast. 50 copies of the publ. contain an etching and two colour lithographs.

MODERSOHN-BECKER, Paula. *Landscape under Trees*, c. 1900, etching.

MOORE, Henry. *Figures on a blue Ground*, 1957, colour lithograph.

MORANDI, Giorgio. *Big round Still-life with Flask and three Objects*, 1946, etching.

MORTENSEN, Richard. One of the 25 serigraphs from the portfolio *The fifth Canto* (Pub. 1960 by Denise René and the Galerie Der Spiegel).

MUELLER, Otto. *Double Portrait (Otto and Maschka)*, (Karsch 125 in the cat. of the exhibition at Nierendorf's in 1960). No. 3 of the portfolio *Otto Mueller, Ten Lithographs*, J. B. Neumann, Berlin, Autumn 1922.

MUMPRECHT, Rudolf. *Beauty taken by Surprise*, 1960, colour monotype.

MUNCH, Edvard. *The Day after*, 1895, drypoint and aquatint (Schiefler 15 IV).

MUNAKATA, Shiko. Woodcut from the series *Willow in Green and Blossoms in Red*, 1955.

MUSIC, Zoran Antonio. *Blue Nets*, 1956, colour etching (*L'Oeuvre gravée* 89).

NAUEN, Heinrich. *Landscape with Pond and bare deciduous Tree (Dilborn Park)*, c. 1920, etching.

NAY, Ernst Wilhelm. Colour etching, 1957 (Pub. Galerie Der Spiegel, Cologne).

NELE, Eva Renée. *Etching with cut-out Form*, 1959.

NESCH, Rolf. *Landing-stage*, 1932, metal print.

NIELSEN, Palle. One of the 35 linocuts for *Orfeus og Eurydike*, Copenhagen, 1959.

NOLDE, Emil. *Sailing-boat*, 1910, woodcut (Schiefler 37).

OBER, Hermann. *Percussion*, c. 1960, relief-print.

O'HARA, Frederik. *The Hunt*, 1957, colour lithograph (IGAS 1957/24).

OHMAE, Hiroshi. *Brave and noble*, 1957, colour woodcut with Japan lacquer (IGAS 1958/27).

ORLOWSKI, Hans. *Jenny*, 1956, woodcut.

OROZCO, José Clemente. *The Flag*, c. 1934, lithograph.

OSTROWER, Fayga. *Aquatint No. 5831*, 1958.

PANKOK, Otto. *The Fisherman*, 1942, woodcut.

PASCIN, Jules. *In the Salon*, c. 1925, woodcut.

PECHSTEIN, Max. *Head of a Fisherman*, 1922, etching.

PEDROSO D'HORTA, Arnaldo. *Woodcut D*, 1958.

PEREZ, Rossine. *Fable*, 1958, aquatint.

PERRIN, Brian. *Litton Dale*, c. 1958, etching and aquatint.

PETERDI, Gabor. *Apocalypse*, 1952, etching and drypoint on zinc.

PIAUBERT, Jean. *Composition*, colour lithograph.

PICASSO, Pablo. *The Sleeper*, 1947, lithograph: tusche on zinc (Mourlot 81).

PIGNON, Edouard. *Olive-trees*, c. 1950, colour lithograph (Guide de la Gravure 79).

PIOTROWICZ, Edmund. *On the Ship*, 1958, drypoint.

PISIS, Filippo de. *Flowers*, c. 1944, lithograph.

PISSARRO, Camille. *Boulevard Montmartre*, c. 1899 (Delteil XVII, 191).

PLATIEL, Roger. *Three Figures*, 1957, etching and line-engraving on copper. Individual prints in two or three colours.

POLIAKOFF, Serge. *Composition*, 1960, colour lithograph (Pub. 1960 as annual gift of the Hamburg Art Club).

POZZATI, Rudy. *Trees in Autumn Light*, 1959, colour etching (IGAS 33/1959).

PRAMPOLINI, Enrico. *Figure in Movement*, 1923, lithograph from Bauhaus Portfolio IV.

PRASSINOS, Mario. *Abstract Composition*, 1957, etching.

PRUDENZIATO, Angelo. *Light in the Night*, 1958, aquatint.

PURRMANN, Hans. *Bathers*, between 1915 and 1920, etching.

REDON, Odilon. *Vision*, 1879, lithograph. No. 8 of the portfolio *In the Dream* (Mellerio 34).

REINER, Imre. *Blossoms and Husks*, 1955, colour lithograph (IGAS 16/1955).

RESTEK, Josip. *Composition*, 1958, colour lithograph.

RICHARDS, Ceri. *The Pianist*, 1959, colour lithograph.

RICHIER, Germaine. One of the 24 etchings for René de Solier, *Contre terre*, Lausanne, 1958.

RODEL, Karl. *Harvest*, 1947, colour lithograph.

ROSSING, Karl. *Melancholy*, 1935, wood-engraving.

ROHLFS, Christian. *The Expulsion from Paradise*, c. 1917, woodcut (Vogt 103).

ROMIJN, Gustaaf Adriaan Maria. *Tug-boats*, 1956, colour woodcut (IGAS 19/1956).

ROUAULT, Georges. *Watteau*, 1929. One of the six lithographs for Rouault's poems *Paysages légendaires*, Paris, 1929.

ROYEN, Peter. *Abstract Composition*, 1959, colour etching.

SAETTI, Bruno. *Landscape with Sun*, 1957, colour lithograph.

SANDIG, Armin. *H. Figure*, 1959, etching.

SANTOMASO, Giuseppe. *Tempo di Spagna*, 1959, colour lithograph.

SAVIN, Maurice. *Siesta*, 1951, colour lithograph (Guilde de la Gravure 64).

SCHIELE, Egon. *Portrait of the Griechenbeisl Innkeeper Franz Hauer*, 1914, drypoint (Schwarz 4).

SCHLOTTER, Eberhard. *The Window*, c. 1960, etching.

SCHMIDT-ROTTLUFF, Karl. *Beach with Bathing-cabins*, 1915, etching (Schapire 14).

SCHNEIDER, Gérard. *Composition*, 1958, colour etching.

SCHOOFS, Rudolf. Engraving on zinc and copper, 1960.

SCHREIB, Werner. *Lunar Rock*, 1958, etching.

SCHUMACHER, Emil. *Composition*, 1959, colour etching (Edition Rothe, Heidelberg).

SCHWITTERS, Kurt. Woodcut, 1919. Pub. as an original woodcut together with prints by Barlach, Feininger, Heckel, Klee, and other artists in the *Kestnerbuch*, ed. Paul Erich Küppers, Böhme, Hanover (1919).

SCOTT, William. *Arran*, 1960, colour lithograph (Edition Abstracta, Freiburg im Breisgau, Cat. X/5).

SEEWALD, Richard. *Herdsman*, 1918, woodcut finished in watercolour.

SEGALL, Lasar. *Recollection of Vilna*, 1917, etching.

SEVERINI, Gino. *Still-life*, 1957, colour lithograph (*L'Oeuvre gravée* 159).

SHAHN, Ben. *"Where there is a sword there is no book"*, serigraph.

SINGIER, Gustave. *Soleil-Eclosion*, 1957 (*L'Oeuvre gravée* 119).

SIQUEIROS, David Alfaro. *Portrait of Moisés Sáenz*, 1931, lithograph.

SKODLERAK, Horst. *Landscape with Lighthouse and two Apples*, 1955, lithograph.

SONDERBORG, K. R. H. Etching, 1958 (Pub. Michael Hertz, Bremen).

SOULAGES, Pierre. Colour lithograph. Pub. Berggruen. Appeared in Pierre Soulages, *Gouaches et gravures*, 1957.

SPACAL, Luigi. *Old Houses*, 1958, colour woodcut.

SPRINGER, Ferdinand. *The Tree*, 1956, line-engraving and aquatint.

SRBINOVIC, Mladen. *Fortuna*, 1959, colour lithograph.

STAEL, Nicolas de. *Study in Blue*, 1954, colour lithograph.

STEWART, Reba. *Mountain Range*, 1957, colour lithograph (IGAS 25/1957).

SUGAI, Kumi. *Blue-black*, 1960, colour lithograph (*L'Oeuvre gravée* 270).

SUMMERS, Carol. *Gethsemane*, 1958, colour lithograph.

SUTHERLAND, Graham Vivian. *Owl and Trussing*, 1955, colour lithograph.

TAKAL, Peter. *Growth*, 1958, drypoint.

TAL COAT, Pierre. *Written on the Rock*, 1956, colour lithograph (Maeght 505).

TAMAYO, Rufino. *Wolf and Moon*, 1955, colour lithograph.

TANGUY, Yves. Colour etching from vol. 2 of Tristan Tzara, *L'Antitête*, 1949 (vol. 1 ill. by Max Ernst, vol. 3 by Miró).

TAPIES, Antonio. *No. 3*, 1959, lithograph.

TERECHKOVITCH, Konstantin. *The Wind*, 1955, colour lithograph (*L'Oeuvre gravée* 5).

TEUBER, Hermann. *Riding-school*, lithograph.

THARRATS, Juan José. *Composition*, 1957, colour lithograph (IGAS 25/1957).

TOULOUSE-LAUTREC, Henri-Marie-Raymond de. *Yvette Guilbert? (Lender?)*, c. 1895, lithograph (Delteil X, 157). One of the 13 lithographs of the series *Portraits of Actors and Actresses*.

TOWN, Harold Barling. *La Mer houleuse (The rolling Sea)*, 1958, colour lithograph.

TRIER, Hann. Colour engraving, 1957.

TROKES, Heinz. *Abstract composition*, 1956, lithograph.

TURNBULL, William. *Head II*, 1956, lithograph.

UBAC, Raoul. One of the six lithographs after slate engravings for Yves Bonnefoy, *Pierre écrite*, Maeght, Paris, 1958.

UCHIMA, Ansei. *An Emotion*, 1960, colour woodcut (IGAS 41/1960).

UTRILLO, Maurice. *La Place du Tertre*, 1924, lithograph.

VALADON, Suzanne. *Studies from the Nude*, 1896, etching.

VALLOTTON, Félix. *The Violin*, 1896 (Godefroy 171). From the series *Six Musical Instruments*.

VASARELY, Victor. Colour serigraph, c. 1955.

VEDOVA, Emilio. One of the six lithographs from the portfolio *Presences* (Edition Abstracta, Freiburg im Breisgau, 1960).

VERTES, Marcel. *Plighting*, c. 1930, lithograph.

VESPIGNANI, Renzo. *Lorry*, 1957, colour lithograph (IGAS 27/1958).

VIEILLARD, Roger. *The Horse in the Night*, 1946, line-engraving.

VILA-CASAS, Joan. *Abstract composition*, c. 1959, etching.

VILLON, Jacques. *Portrait of an Actor*, 1913, drypoint.

VIVIANI, Giuseppe. *Table with Lamprey*, c. 1938, etching.

VLAMINCK, Maurice. *Houses at Bougival*, c. 1909, woodcut.

VUILLARD, Edouard. *Interior with Sofa (In the Evening)*, (Roger-Marx 62 III).

WEBER, A. Paul. *The good Misnian*, 1932/55, lithograph (Ramseger 79).

WEISSAUER, Rudolf. *The Road*, 1960, lithograph.

WENDLAND, Gerhard. Etching from the series *The One and the Other*, 1959.

WESTPFAHL, Conrad. *Mother*, 1953, lithograph.

WHISTLER, James Abbott McNeil. *San Biagio*, 1879/80, etching (Wedmore 163).

WILTHELM, Heinrich. *Before Troy*, 1959, colour lithograph.

WIND, Gerhard. Colour serigraph, c. 1960.

WINTER, Fritz. *Black before Red*, c. 1958, colour lithograph.

WOLFF, Gustav Heinrich. *Europa*, 1924, woodcut.

WOLS. *Bulbous Plant*, 1942/49, drypoint (Grohmann XXXI).

WUNDERLICH, Paul. *Dr Aisen*, 1959, colour lithograph.

YOSHIDA, Masaji. *Novel Growth*, c. 1958, colour woodcut (IGAS 30/1958).

ZADKINE, Ossip. Lithograph from the series *The Labours of Hercules* (Pub. Galerie Czwiklitzer, Cologne).

ZAO WOU-KI. *Red Sun*, c. 1951, colour lithograph (Guilde de la Gravure 81; Jacometti 26).

ZIMMERMANN, Mac. *Burlesque*, c. 1950, etching.

LIST OF PLATES

Picture titles in foreign languages have been translated into English, except for a few that cannot be rendered concisely without ambiguity. The measurements (inches before centimetres) are those of the picture area or, for illustrations, those of the book. Work on big sets of illustrations often extended over many years, as with Chagall's *Bible* or Rouault's *Miserere*, and in such cases this has been noted, to substantiate the dating. The technical methods, interesting in relation to modern graphic art, of several of its predecessors (Doré, Menzel) or precursors (Manet) have also once again been mentioned briefly in their place.

7 JOSEPH VON FUHRICH, *Genovefa fills her Murderers with Compassion*. Etching, 9¹/₄ × 12⁵/₈ (23.6 × 32). No. 9 of *Illustrations to Genovefa*, 1832.
An Austrian born in Bohemia, Joseph von Führich (1800–76) represented the Nazarene movement in Vienna. He also became well-known chiefly as a draughtsman and etcher through his sets of illustrations, done in a style that developed under the influence of Dürer and Raphael. The 15 prints, etched by Führich himself, for Tieckes *Genovefa* date from 1824–25 (H. Wörndle, *Werkverzeichnis* 200).

7 GUSTAVE DORE, *The Wolves and the Sheep*. Woodcut, 9¹/₄ × 7¹/₂ (23.6 × 19). From *Fables de La Fontaine*, Paris, 1868 (Béraldi VI, Doré 151).
Like Menzel in Germany, Doré (1832–83) is among the artists who, instead of giving their woodcutter pencil drawings for their later book illustrations, did brush sketches, which were often transferred to the block photographically and in some cases executed in a tonal woodcut technique. With Doré photographic transfer began in 1862.

8 ADOLF VON MENZEL, *Zieten*, 1850. Woodcut, 10¹/₂ × 8⁵/₈ (26.5 × 21.8). No. 3 of 12 woodcuts *From King Frederick's Time*, Berlin, 1856 (Bock 1067).

8 ADOLF VON MENZEL, *Martha and Eve on their way to the judge*. Woodcut, 6³/₈ × 6 (16.1 × 15.1). No. 15 of thirty woodcuts for Heinrich von Kleist, *Der zerbrochene Krug*, Berlin, 1877 (Bock 1110).
An example of the tonal woodcut technique used by Menzel at this time. The preparatory drawings done with pencil or pen "with the aid of wash, because on this occasion tonal woodcut had to be employed". For nine compositions illustrating Kleist, Menzel had his preliminary drawings transferred to the wooden block photographically.

9 JOHAN BARTHOLD JONGKIND, *Dutch Canal near Rotterdam*, 1875. Etching, 5⁷/₈ × 9 (14.8 × 22.8) (Delteil I, 19).

9 CHARLES-FRANCOIS DAUBIGNY, *The Heavy Shower*, c. 1851. Etching, 5³/₈ × 9¹/₈ (13.6 × 23.2) (Delteil XIII, 85).

10 EDVARD MUNCH, *Woman*, 1895. Aquatint and drypoint, 11¹/₄ × 13 (28.5 × 33) (Schiefler 21 B V).

10 MAX KLINGER, *Forsaken*, 1884. Etching and aquatint, 12³/₈ × 17⁵/₈ (31.5 × 44.9). No. 5 of the cycle *Life*, op. VIII (Singer 131).

11 JAMES WHISTLER, *San Giorgio*, c. 1880. Etching, 8¹/₄ × 11⁷/₈ (20.9 × 30.2). From the series *Twenty-six Etchings* (Wedmore 167).

11 CAMILLE PISSARRO, *Landscape under Trees at l'Hermitage, Pontoise*, 1879. Aquatint, 8⁵/₈ × 10⁵/₈ (21.9 × 26.9) (Delteil XVII, 16 V).

12 JEAN-FRANCOIS MILLET, *Woman carding Wool*, c. 1856. Etching, 10¹/₈ × 6⁷/₈ (25.8 × 17.6) (Delteil I, 15).

12 EDOUARD MANET, *The Race*, 1864. Lithograph, 14³/₈ × 20¹/₈ (36.5 × 51) (Guérin 72). In earlier cats. dated later: Moreau-Nélaton, c. 1872; Rosenthal, between 1874 and 1877.

21 EDOUARD MANET, *The Chair*, 1875. Autograph, 11³/₈ × 10⁷/₈ (29 × 27.6) (Guérin 86 d).
For *Le Corbeau* (The Raven), *poème d'Edgar Poe*, Lesclides, 1875, translated by Stéphan Mallarmé and illustrated with five drawings by Manet. Drawn by the artist in autographic ink on transfer-paper and then transferred to the stone.

25 HENRI DE TOULOUSE-LAUTREC, *Woman Spectator*, 1893. Lithograph, 10³/₈ × 7¹/₈ (26.5 × 18.2) (Delteil X, 37).

34 PAUL GAUGUIN, *Women, Animals and Foliage*, c. 1899. Woodcut, 6³/₈ × 12 (16.3 × 30.5) (Guérin 59).

35 EMIL NOLDE, *Captives*, 1906. Woodcut, 6¹/₂ × 8⁷/₈ (16.6 × 22.6) (Schiefler 13 III).

39 EDVARD MUNCH, *Female Nude*, 1897. Woodcut, 15¹/₄ × 6⁷/₈ (38.8 × 17.5) (Schiefler 99, Cat. of the Oslo exhibition in 1946: No. 8). The print listed by Schiefler as a unique example is a two-colour print, pulled from a block sawn in two figure reddish-brown against a black background, 16¹/₂ × 12³/₄ (42 × 32.4). The impression reproduced here, from the Hamburg Kunsthalle, is one of a number of partial prints of the figure in black. There are quite a lot of colour woodcuts from sawn blocks by Munch: cf. Page 55.

43 HENRI DE TOULOUSE-LAUTREC, *The Englishman at the Moulin Rouge*, 1892. Colour lithograph, 18¹/₂ × 14⁵/₈ (47 × 37.2) (Delteil X, 12).

45 HENRI DE TOULOUSE-LAUTREC, *Au petit lever*, 1896. Colour lithograph, 20¹/₂ × 15³/₄ (52 × 40) (Delteil XI, 187). From the portfolio *Elles*.

47 PIERRE BONNARD, *The little Laundress*, 1896. Colour lithograph, 11³/₄ × 7¹/₂ (30 × 19) (Roger-Marx 42).

49 EDOUARD VUILLARD, *Interior with hanging Lamp*, 1899. Colour lithograph, 13³/₄ × 11 (35 × 28) (Roger-Marx 35 III). From the series of 12 lithographs *Landscapes and Interiors*, pub. in 1899 by Ambroise Vollard.

51 JAMES ENSOR, *Masks*, 1921. Colour lithograph, 8¹/₄ × 6¹/₈ (21 × 15.3). Title-page of *Scènes de la vie du Christ*, Galerie G. Giroux, Brussels, 1921, an album of 32 touched-up lithographs.
These colour lithographs were made after a series of 36 coloured-pencil drawings done in 1912. Strictly speaking they are reproductions and have therefore not been included in the catalogues of the original prints.

53 EDVARD MUNCH, *Anxiety*, 1896. Lithograph in two colours, 16¹/₂ × 15¹/₈ (42 × 38.5) (Schiefler 61 b II). Bi-colour print from two stones.

55 EDVARD MUNCH, *Moonlight*, 1896. Woodcut, 16¼×18⅜ (41.2 × 46.7) (Schiefler 81 A b).
Third state of the first version. Print in three colours taken from two blocks, one of them sawn into several pieces. The first block carries the drawing; with the parts of the other block the tones are overprinted.

57 EDVARD MUNCH, *To the Wood*, 1915. Colour woodcut, 20⅛ × 25⅜ (51 × 64.6) (Schiefler 444).
The example mentioned by Schiefler as in the Hudtwalcker collection has belonged since 1954 to the Hamburg Kunsthalle.

59 ODILON REDON, *He falls towards the Abyss*, c. 1895. Lithograph, 11 × 8¾ (28 × 21.4) (Mellerio 150).
No. 17 of the third series for Gustave Flaubert, *Tentation de Saint-Antoine*.
The 24 lithographs of this series were printed in 1896 for Vollard in an edition of 50 examples. Not until 1938 did an edition in book form appear, published by Vollard. The text illustrations of this edition, not listed by Mellerio, were done around 1910.

60 EMIL NOLDE, *Two Demons*, 1906. Etching and tone-biting, 7⅝ × 5¾ (19.3 × 14.7) (Schiefler 58 II).

67 ERNST LUDWIG KIRCHNER, *Three Women in Conversation*, 1906/07. Colour woodcut, 15⅜ × 13⅝ (39 × 34.5) (Schiefler 71).

69 ERNST LUDWIG KIRCHNER, *Still-life*, c. 1908. Colour lithograph, 14⅛ × 13 (36 × 33) (Schiefler 49). Printed in colour from four stones.

71 ERNST LUDWIG KIRCHNER, *Girl*, 1918. Colour woodcut, 15¾ × 14¾ (40 × 37.5) (Schiefler 353 b). Printed in colour from two blocks.

73 ERNST LUDWIG KIRCHNER, *Woman in the Night*, 1919. Colour woodcut, 22⅝ × 13¾ (57.5 × 35) (Schiefler 389). Printed in colour from a block sawn in two.

75 ERICH HECKEL, *Woman reclining*, 1910. Colour woodcut, 15¾ × 11¾ (40 × 29.8).

77 ERICH HECKEL, *Men leading Horses (The white Horses)*, 1912. Colour woodcut, 12¼ × 12⅜ (31 × 31.5).

79 EMIL NOLDE, *Mill by the Water*, 1926. Colour lithograph, 25¼ × 31½ (64 × 80). Printed from one black and four colour plates (too late for Schiefler).
A proof-impression shown at the Hamburg Art Club's Nolde exhibition in April 1927.

81 EMIL NOLDE, *Fisher Children*, 1926. Colour lithograph in red, 25⅝ × 31½ (65 × 80) (too late for Schiefler).
An impression shown at the Hamburg Art Club's Nolde exhibition in April 1927.
The print at the Hamburg Kunsthalle reproduced here is an impression taken from two stones inked with different reds. There are other versions at Seebüll and in the Sprengel collection, Hanover (exhibited in 1955 at the Kestner-Museum and dated 1928 in the cat.).

83 KARL SCHMIDT-ROTTLUFF, *The Road to Emmaus*, 1918. Woodcut, 15⅝ × 19⅝ (39.7 × 49.9) (Schapire 212).

84 MAX PECHSTEIN, *Clerong (Man's Head)*, 1917. Woodcut, 9⅝ × 7⅞ (24.5 × 20) (Fechter 119).

85 ERICH HECKEL, *Straight Canal, Ostend*, 1915. Woodcut, 14⅝ × 10⅝ (37.3 × 27).

86 ERNST LUDWIG KIRCHNER, *Müller and Scherer*, 1922. Drypoint, 11¾ × 9⅞ (30 × 25) (Schiefler 469).
Two Swiss artists who both died young in the same year, 1927. Obituaries by Kirchner in the *Kunstblatt*, 1927.

87 KARL SCHMIDT-ROTTLUFF, *Bathers*, 1920. Line-engraving, 15½ × 13⅛ (39.5 × 33.2) (Schapire 46).

88 EMIL NOLDE, *Hamburg, Inner Harbour*, 1910. Etching, 12¼ × 16⅛ (31 × 41) (Schiefler 144 II).

90 FRANS MASEREEL, *Sack-heavers*, 1933. Woodcut, 9⅞ × 7½ (25 × 19). From the portfolio *Expiations*, Paris, 1933.

93 PAULA MODERSOHN-BECKER, *The Goose-girl*, c. 1900. Etching, 9⅞ × 8 (25.1 × 20.3) (Pauli 6).

94 LOVIS CORINTH, *Urfeld Village*, 1920. Drypoint, 7⅜ × 9¾ (18.7 × 24.8) (Schwarz 432 III). No. 3 of the portfolio *By the Walchensee*. Pub. Fritz Gurlitt, Berlin, 1920.

94 LOVIS CORINTH, *Building the Ark*, 1923. Lithograph, 19⅝ × 25⅝ (50 × 65) (Müller 816). One of a projected series *The Flood*.

95 ERNST BARLACH, *Raging Barbarian*, c. 1916/17. Lithograph, 11 × 15⅝ (28 × 39.8) (Schult 91).

95 ERNST BARLACH, *Woman halfway down the Cellar Stairs*, 1912. Lithograph, 8¾ × 10 (22.3 × 25.4) (Schult 16). No. 1 of the portfolio for Barlach's play *Der tote Tag*, Berlin, 1912.

96 KARL HOFER, *Sleeping Woman*, c. 1930. Lithograph, about 10⅝ × 9⅞ (27 × 25).

97 KATHE KOLLWITZ, *Woman meditating*, 1920. Lithograph, 21¼ × 14¾ (54 × 37.5) (Klipstein 147 II).

98 ALFRED KUBIN, *Horse-pond*, 1920. Lithograph, 8¾ × 13 (21.1 × 33) (Raabe 127 b). From the *Alfred Kubin Portfolio*, Vienna, 1920.

98 OTTO DIX, *Funeral*, 1922. Etching, 10⅞ × 13⅝ (27.5 × 34.5) (No. 48 in the list of the complete graphic works from 1913—60 compiled by Florian Karsch for the cat. of the exhibition at the Galerie Meta Nierendorf, Berlin, in 1961). No. 6 of the series of six etchings *Death and Resurrection*, pub. by the artist, Dresden, 1922.

99 GEORGE GROSZ, *Street Corner*, 1915. Lithograph, 19⅛ × 13¾ (48.5 × 35). One of the nine lithographs from the first Grosz portfolio, Berlin, 1916.

100 OSKAR KOKOSCHKA, *The Concert* I (half-length portrait with folded arms, from the front), 1921. Red-chalk lithograph, 27⅛ × 18¼ (69 × 46.5) (Arntz 123).

101 OSKAR KOKOSCHKA, *Portrait of Walter Hasenclever*, 1918. Lithograph, 24 × 16½ (61 × 42) (Arntz 102).

102 MAX BECKMANN, *Road (Landscape with Balloon)*, 1918. Etching, 9 × 11⅜ (23 × 29) (Glaser 115). From the portfolio of 19 etchings *Faces*. Pub. by Piper as the thirteenth printing of the Marées Society.

103 MAX BECKMANN, *The Fall*, 1946. Lithograph, 11¾×10¼ (30 × 26.2). From the portfolio *Day and Dream*, pub. Curt Valentin, New York, 1946.

104 MAX BECKMANN, *Group Portrait (Edenbar)*, 1923. Woodcut, 19½ × 19½ (49.5 × 49.5) (Too late for Glaser).

105 CHRISTIAN ROHLFS, *Return of the Prodigal Son*, 1916. Woodcut, 18⅞ × 13¾ (48 × 35) (Vogt 99).

106 OTTO MUELLER, *A squatting and a lying Nude on the Dunes*. Colour lithograph, 11⅝ × 18½ (29.5 × 39.2) (Karsch 140). The Hamburg Kunsthalle also has the painted version of this composition. The date is uncertain: about 1920. Buchheim's monograph with a complete cat. was not available to us.

107 OTTO MUELLER, *Two Gypsies*, 1927. Colour lithograph, 27³/₄ × 19⁵/₈ (70.5 × 50) (Karsch 145). One of the nine lithographs of the so-called "Gypsy Portfolio", printed by Lange, Breslau Academy, 1927.

109 EWALD MATARE, *Three Cows* (one above the other), 1948. Colour woodcut, 20 × 15 (50.7 × 38) (Peters 311).

110 GERHARD MARCKS, *Renunciation*, 1926. Woodcut, 10¹/₄ × 8¹/₂ (26 × 21.5).

110 OTTO PANKOK, *Seated Gypsy*, 1936. Woodcut, 19³/₈ × 20³/₈ (49.2 × 51.6).

111 PABLO PICASSO, *From a Centaur's Life*, 1947. Etching. One of the four etchings for Ramón Raventos, *Dos contes*, Paris and Barcelona, 1947. Book size, 13³/₈×10¹/₄ (34×26). A French edition of the same year contains four other etchings.

111 PABLO PICASSO, *Pan*, 1948. Lithograph, 25⁵/₈ × 20¹/₈ (65 × 51) (Mourlot 111). Executed at Vallauris on 10 March 1948, at the same time as the *Big Owl* and five other music-making *Fauns*. Tusche on zinc.

112 PABLO PICASSO, *David and Bathsheba*, 1949. Lithograph, 25³/₄ × 19¹/₂ (65.5 × 49.5) (Mourlot 109 *bis*). During the years 1947–49 Picasso copied Cranach's Berlin picture in ten different states on a zinc plate. A zinc-plate impression of the sixth state was transferred to stone in April 1949, and worked over with pen and scraper. Our reproduction is of such a print taken from the stone.

113 PABLO PICASSO, *Woman with green Hair (Woman with Hairnet)*, 1949. Colour lithograph, 25⁵/₈ × 19⁵/₈ (65 × 50) (Mourlot 178 II). Print taken from a zinc plate dated 18. 4. 1949.

115 PABLO PICASSO, *Fauns and Goat*, 1959. Colour linocut, 24³/₈ × 29¹/₂ (62 × 75). No 31 of the series of 45 linocuts from the years 1958–60.

117 GEORGES ROUAULT, *The hard Business of Living*. Aquatint etching, 18⁷/₈ × 14¹/₈ (48 × 36). No. 12 of the series *Miserere*, Paris, 1948. As part of the 100 engravings originally planned for Ambroise Vollard, to have made up two portfolios (*Miserere* and *Guerre*), about 65 big plates were completed in the years 1916–27. Not until 1948 did 58 prints from them appear under the general title *Miserere*. The models (paintings, gouaches and wash drawings) were transferred photomechanically to copper-plates, which the artist then worked over by various methods (aquatint, drypoint, roulette).

118 GEORGES ROUAULT, *Man's Head*, 1926. Aquatint etching, about 13¹/₂ × 9⁷/₈ (34.4 × 25). From the series of 4 prints for *Les Fleurs du mal* (not yet published). Same technique as the *Miserere* engravings.

119 MARC CHAGALL, *Abraham mourning Sarah*, 1956. Etching and drypoint, 11¹/₂ × 9¹/₂ (29.3 × 24). No. 3 from *La Bible*, Tériade, Paris, 1956 (Meyer-Bolliger 98).
Work on the 105 illustrations to the Old Testament, commissioned by Vollard, began in 1931. By 1939, 66 engravings were ready; the remaining 39 were not completed till 1952–56. The Abraham cycle was done between 1931 and 1939.

120 MARC CHAGALL, *Nude at the Window*, 1953–54. Lithograph, 16¹/₄ × 22¹/₂ (41.4 × 57) (Cain-Mourlot, *Chagall Lithographe* 90).

120 MARC CHAGALL, *The three Acrobats*, 1926. Etching and aquatint, 13⁵/₈ × 14⁵/₈ (34.6 × 37.2) (Meyer-Bolliger 75).

121 MARC CHAGALL, *The Women on the Ifrit's Back*, 1948. Colour lithograph, 17¹/₈ × 13¹/₈ (43.5 × 33.2) (Cain-Mourlot, *Chagall Lithographe* 42).

No. 7 of the 12 (or 13) colour lithographs for four tales from *The Arabian Night*, done during 1946–56 in the United States and pub. as an album in 1948 by Pantheon Books.

123 ROBERT DELAUNAY, *Saint-Séverin*, 1909 (1926). Lithograph, 22⁵/₈ × 16⁷/₈ (57.5 × 43). Titled and dated in the stone: St Séverin 1909. Done in 1926 after a work dating from 1909 (information supplied by Mme Sonia Delaunay-Terk).

124 MAURICE VLAMINCK, *Women's Head*, c. 1906. Woodcut, 12³/₈ × 9 (31.5 × 22.8) (Cat. of the Bern exhibition in 1961: No. 4).

125 HENRI MATISSE, *Woman combing her Hair*, c. 1950. Linocut, 9³/₈ × 7³/₄ (23.8 × 19.7). Ill. 17 in the album *Henri Matisse, gravures récentes*, Berggruen, Paris, 1952.

126 HENRI MATISSE, *Seated Girl with Goldfish Bowl*, 1929. Etching, 8¹/₂ × 6 (21.7 × 15.3) (Lieberman 53).

127 HENRI MATISSE, *Girl Dancer at the Mirror*, 1927. Lithograph, 15³/₄ × 11 (40 × 28).

128 RAOUL DUFY, *Epsom Racecourse*, 1930. Colour lithograph, 12³/₄ × 17¹/₂ (32.3 × 44.6).

129 ANDRE DERAIN, *Woman's Face supported by her left Hand*, c. 1927. Lithograph.

130 ANDRE DUNOYER DE SEGONZAC, *Colette at her Desk*, c. 1930. One of the 35 etchings for Colette, *La Treille muscate*. Paris, 1932. Book size, 13 × 10¹/₄ (33 × 26). Done, together with other portraits of Colette, in 1929–30 at Saint-Tropez.

131 ALBERTO GIACOMETTI, *Interior with hanging Lamp*, 1957. Lithograph, 23 × 15 (58.5 × 38) (No. 48 in the Klipstein and Kornfeld exhibition cat. of 1959).

132 JEAN CARZOU, *Railway Tracks*, c. 1958. Colour lithograph, 12⁵/₈ × 9⁷/₈ (32 × 25).

133 BERNARD BUFFET, *Ram's Head*, c. 1958. Colour lithograph, 19⁵/₈ × 26³/₄ (50 × 68).

134 GIORGIO DE CHIRICO, *Two Figures*, c. 1930. Colour lithograph, about 16¹/₈ × 12¹/₄ (41 × 31).

135 CARLO CARRA, *The Landlady*, 1924. Etching, 11⁷/₈ × 8⁵/₈ (30.3 × 21.8).

136 GIUSEPPE VIVIANI, *Still-life with Duck, Fig-leaves and Campanile*, 1937. Etching.

136 GIORGIO MORANDI, *House behind Trees*, 1927. Etching, 9 × 11¹/₄ (23 × 28.5).

137 MASSIMO CAMPIGLI, *Women out walking*, 1957. Colour lithograph, 18¹/₂ × 14 (47 × 35.5) (*L'Oeuvre gravée* 130).

139 LEONARD BASKIN, *The Anatomist*, 1952. Woodcut, 13¹/₂ × 10⁷/₈ (34.4 × 27.5).

140 MISCH KOHN, *Oedipus*, 1959. Aquatint on zinc, 19⁵/₈ × 15¹/₂ (50 × 39.4) (Zigrosser 155).

141 MAURICIO LASANSKY, *My Son*, 1947. Colour etching, 16³/₄ × 13³/₄ (42.5 × 35) (Zigrosser 76).

142 ANTONIO FRASCONI, *Don Quixote*, 1949. Colour woodcut.

142 BEN SHAHN — LEONARD BASKIN, *Beatitudes*, c. 1954. Colour woodcut, 10¹/₄ × 15¹/₈ (26 × 38.5). Drawn by Shahn, cut by Baskin.

146 HEINRICH CAMPENDONK, *Woman by the Stove*, 1918. Woodcut, 8¹/₂ × 8 (21.5 × 20.2) (Engels 41).

147 FRANZ MARC, *Expiation*, 1912. Woodcut, 7⁷/₈ × 10¹/₈ (20 × 25.8) (Schardt VII, 1912, 4).

148 LYONEL FEININGER, *Vessels alongside the Quay*, 1918. Woodcut, 6³/₄ × 9⁷/₈ (17.3 × 25).

149 LYONEL FEININGER, *Village*, 1920. Woodcut, 8¹/₄ × 13¹/₄ (21.1 × 33.6).

169 JUAN GRIS, *L'Apero*, 1921. Lithograph, 12¹/₄ × 8⁵/₈ (31 × 22). A print from Max Jacob, *Ne coupez pas, Mademoiselle*, Paris, 1921.

169 GEORGES BRAQUE, *Small Cubist Guitar*. Etching, 5¹/₂ × 7⁷/₈ (14 × 20) (Hofmann 2). Executed 1909; first print 1910; edition pub. Maeght, 1954 (25 examples).

170 JACQUES VILLON, *The Ploughman*, 1951. Etching, 9¹/₄ × 14 (23.5 × 35.5).

170 GEORGES BRAQUE, *The Nest, (Bird IX)*, 1955. Etching 8⁷/₈ × 13³/₈ (22.5 × 34) (Hofmann 66).

171 GEORGES BRAQUE, *Helios VI (Hera)*, 1948. Colour lithograph, 18¹/₂ × 16¹/₈ (47 × 41) (Hofmann 29).

173 FERNAND LEGER, *The Dove*, c. 1950. Colour lithograph, 16¹/₈ × 13 (41 × 33).

175 ANDRE MASSON, *Lovers on a Leaf*, 1954. Colour etching, 12 × 10¹/₈ (30.5 × 25.5).

177 JOAN MIRO, *L'Oiseau fusée*, 1952. Colour etching, 13⁵/₈ × 17⁵/₈ (34.5 × 44.7) (Maeght 1702).

179 WASSILY KANDINSKY, *Composition with Group of Figures*, 1912/13. Woodcut, 5⁷/₈ × 7¹/₄ (14.9 × 18.5). One of the series *Klänge* (Sounds), prose-poems with black-and-white and colour woodcuts printed from the block, Munich, 1913.

180 WASSILY KANDINSKY, *Abstract Composition*, 1912/13. Woodcut, 8¹/₂ × 8⁵/₈ (21.7 × 22). One of the *Klänge* series (like 179).

181 WASSILY KANDINSKY, *Abstract Composition*, 1922. Colour lithograph, 10¹/₄ × 10¹/₈ (26 × 25.5). No. 4 of the series *Kleine Welten* (Small Worlds), 12 original prints (4 etchings, 4 colour lithographs, 4 woodcuts, 2 of them in colour), Berlin, 1922.

183 FRANZ MARC, *Birth of the Horses*, 1913. Colour woodcut, 8¹/₂ × 5³/₄ (21.5 × 14.5) (Schardt VII, 1913, 5).

185 PAUL KLEE, *Tightrope-walker*, 1921. Colour lithograph, 17¹/₈ × 10¹/₂ (43.5 × 26.8) (Soby 27).

186 PAUL KLEE, *Death for an Idea*, 1915. Lithograph (Soby, text ill. X/XI).

187 PAUL KLEE, *Old Man calculating*, 1929, Etching, 11³/₄ × 9¹/₂ (30 × 24) (Soby 38).

188 ROLF NESCH, *Dance*, 1955/56. Colour metal print, 22¹/₂ × 16 (57 × 40.5). Part of a triptych owned by the artist. Colour print taken in one operation from a ground-plate plus variously inked additional parts and little bits of wire-gauze laid close together (information from the artist for a cat.).

189 ROLF NESCH, *Rosa Rosita Rosensparre*, 1952/53. Colour metal print, 23 × 16³/₈ (58.5 × 41.5). Taken in two operations from variously inked components and bits of variously meshed wire-gauze (information from the artist for a cat.). After an example at the Hamburg Kunsthalle.

191 WERNER GILLES, *Ophelia*, 1947. Lithograph, 15 × 20¹/₂ (38 × 52). At first grey, the paper of the original later turned yellow through the action of light.

192 WERNER GILLES, *Moonlight Night*, 1919. Woodcut, 6³/₄ × 5⁷/₈ (17 × 15).

193 HAP GRIESHABER, *Eros II (Narcissist)*, 1953. Colour woodcut, 14⁵/₈ × 18³/₈ (37 × 46.8) (Boeck 212).

194 ZAO WOU-KI, *Hydrangeas*, 1953. Colour lithograph, 17³/₈ × 23¹/₈ (44 × 58.8) (Jacometti 66).

194 MAX ERNST, *Masks*, c. 1951. Colour lithograph, 13×19⁵/₈ (33 × 50) (Guilde de la Gravure 76).

195 HENRI LAURENS, *Seated female Nude*, 1950. Colour lithograph, 19¹/₈ × 10³/₄ (48.7 × 27.4).

196 HENRY MOORE, *Confined Statues*, 1951. Colour lithograph, 13¹/₄ × 9¹/₂ (33.5 × 24). One of the eight colour lithographs for André Gide's French translation of Goethe's *Prometheus*, Paris, 1951.

197 LYNN CHADWICK, *Two Watchers*, 1960. Colour lithograph, 15 × 10 (38 × 25.4).

198 GRAHAM VIVIAN SUTHERLAND, *Predatory Form II*, 1953. Colour lithograph, 29¹/₂ × 20¹/₂ (75 × 52.2).

199 CERI RICHARDS, *The golden Fish*, 1959. Colour lithograph, 30 × 19⁵/₈ (76.3 × 50). From a series of six prints for piano music by Debussy. Pub. St George's Gallery, London.

200 OSSIP ZADKINE, *Rural Festivity*, 1960. Colour lithograph, 24⁵/₈ × 16⁵/₈ (62.6 × 42.3) (*L'Oeuvre gravée* 267).

201 MARINO MARINI, *Horses (Acrobat with Horses)*, c. 1952. Colour lithograph, 19¹/₈ × 13 (48.5 × 32) (Guilde de la Gravure).

217 GINO SEVERINI, *Composition*, c. 1954. Colour lithograph, 14³/₄ × 11¹/₈ (37.5 × 28.4) (Guilde de la Gravure).

218 HANS ARP, *Leaf-Torso*, 1960. Colour lithograph, 25⁵/₈ × 18¹/₈ (65 × 46). Annual gift of the Hamburg Art Club.

219 WILLI BAUMEISTER, *Mycenae*, c. 1944. Colour serigraph, 11¹/₄ × 17 (28.5 × 40.6).

219 GEORG MEISTERMANN, *Fire Dove*, 1953. Colour serigraph, 13³/₄ × 17 (35 × 43.2) (Galerie Der Spiegel cat., 16).

220 HENRI-GEORGES ADAM, *December*, 1952. Etching, 24⁵/₈ × 18⁷/₈ (62.5 × 48). Produced by means of cut-out plates, a method Adam first used in 1952.

221 JOHNNY FRIEDLAENDER, *Fishes II*, 1955. Etching in three colours, 22 × 15³/₄ (56 × 40) (Schmücking 32).

223 WOLS, *Face*. Etching, 4¹/₂ × 3³/₄ (11.5 × 9.5) (Grohmann XXV in *Quadrum 6*, 1959). Dates from 1942. Pub. in 1945 as an illustration to Camille Bryen, *Baleine-Ville*.

223 WOLS, *Thistle*. Etching, 4³/₄ × 3⁷/₈ (12 × 10) (Grohmann XXX). Dates from between 1942 and 1949.

224 PIERRE COURTIN, *Boundary-marks*, 1959. Etching on zinc, 19¹/₈ × 9¹/₂ (48.5 × 24). Pub. Berggruen, Paris.

225 EMIL SCHUMACHER. One of seven etchings from the portfolio *Poetry in Black-and-white*, Edition Abstracta, Freiburg im Breisgau, 1958. Page size, 18⁷/₈ × 14¹/₈ (48 × 36).

226 VICTOR VASARELY. Multi-colour serigraph, 13 × 6⁵/₈ (33 × 16.8). Pub. as a supplement to the exhibition cat. of the Galerie Der Spiegel, Cologne, 25/1961.

227 GUSTAVE SINGIER, *Noontide Hour*, 1957. Colour lithograph, 15 × 18³/₄ (38 × 47.5) (*L'Oeuvre gravée* 139 — Schmücking, Brunswick cat., 23).

229 GUSTAVE SINGIER, *Provençal Interior II*, 1951. Colour lithograph, 18¹/₄ × 11⁵/₈ (46.3 × 29.5) (Guilde de la Gravure — Schmücking, Brunswick cat., 1 II).

230 JEAN BAZAINE, *Chicago*, 1953. Colour lithograph, 25⁵/₈ × 19³/₄ (65.2 × 50.2). Detail of a bigger composition (Maeght 1101).

231 ALFRED MANESSIER, *February in Holland, c.* 1954. Colour lithograph, 17¹/₈ × 25⁵/₈ (43.5 × 65) (*L'Oeuvre gravée* 96).

233 ROGER BISSIERE, *Abstract Composition, c.* 1956. Colour lithograph, 18¹/₂ × 13¹/₄ (47 × 33.8).

234 PIERRE SOULAGES, *Composition, c.* 1957. Etching in two colours, 23³/₈ × 17¹/₈ (59.5 × 43.5).

235 HANS HARTUNG, *Abstract Composition*, 1954. Etching in two colours, 20¹/₄ × 15³/₈ (52 × 39).

236 MAURICE ESTEVE, *Matinailles*, 1956. Colour lithograph, 17³/₄ × 22 (45 × 56) (*L'Oeuvre gravée* 70).

236 FRITZ WINTER, *Abstract Composition, c.* 1952. Colour lithograph, 20¹/₈ × 26³/₄ (51 × 68).

237 K. R. H. SONDERBORG, *Composition*, 1958. Colour etching, 16³/₄ × 22¹/₈ (42.7 × 56.2).

237 JOSEPH FASSBENDER, *Composition*, 1957. ("The Offenbach Print"). Lithograph, 21⁵/₈ × 30³/₈ (55 × 77).

238 GABOR PETERDI, *Germination I*, 1951. Etching, line-engraving and aquatint on zinc in eight colours, 16³/₈ × 20⁵/₈ (41.5 × 52.5).

239 STANLEY WILLIAM HAYTER, *Leçon d'Anatomie*, 1954. 16¹/₈ × 12¹/₄ (41 × 31) (*L'Oeuvre gravée* 1955, 26).

241 GABOR PETERDI, *Stormy Sky*, 1959. Drypoint, 22⁵/₈ × 31¹/₂ (57.5 × 80).

241 STANLEY WILLIAM HAYTER, *Composition with five Figures*, 1946. Line-engraving and soft-ground etching in four colours, 14³/₄ × 23⁷/₈ (37.5 × 60.5).

242 HEINZ TROKES, *Night*, 1957. Colour lithograph, 15 × 19¹/₄ (38 × 49).

242 JOAN VILA-CASAS, *Composition, c.* 1959. Etching, 9⁷/₈ × 19³/₄ (25 × 50).

243 HANN TRIER. Etching in three colours, 1957, 12⁵/₈ × 6¹/₈ (32 × 15.5). Pub. Galerie Der Spiegel, Cologne.

244 HANS JAENISCH, *Reflection*, 1959. Lithograph in three colours, 18⁷/₈ × 13³/₄ (48 × 35). Pub. Edition Rothe, Heidelberg.

245 SERGE POLIAKOFF, *Composition I, c.* 1955. Colour lithograph, 22¹/₂ × 17¹/₈ (57 × 43.5) (*L'Oeuvre gravée* 69).

247 RAOUL UBAC. One of the slate engravings for André Frénaud, *Poèmes du petit vieux*. This print reproduced in *Derrière le miroir*, 1958 (ed. Livres et Gravures). Ubac's process also used in illustrating Yves Bonnefoy's poems *Pierre écrite*, 1958, from which our small illustration in the Biographies section comes. For the book, the artist lithographed his slate engravings.

248 JEAN DUBUFFET, *Work and Play*, 1953. Colour lithograph, 12 × 7 (30.4 × 17.7).

249 JEAN DUBUFFET, *Jelly-fishes*, 1959. Lithograph, 20⁷/₈ × 16¹/₄ (53 × 41.3). No. 9 from Album X of *Les Phénomènes*, Berggruen, Paris.

250 ANTONIO TAPIES, *Composition, c.* 1959. Lithograph, 24³/₄ × 35³/₈ (63 × 90).

250 ANTON HEYBOER, *Composition*, 1959. Colour drypoint on zinc, 12¹/₄ × 17³/₄ (31 × 45) (No. 19 in the cat. *Geh durch den Spiegel*, 1960).

ACKNOWLEDGEMENTS

The author and publishers wish to express their thanks to all artists, galleries and collectors who have provided originals and photographs. The reproductions appear by permission of:

A. A. B., Brussels, for works by Ensor; the Barlach-Gesellschaft; Dr Beckmann; Cosmopress, Geneva, for works by Klee; S. P. A. D. E. M., Paris and Cosmopress, Geneva, for works by Adam, Bonnard, Boussigault, Denis, Dufy, Dunoyer, Ensor, Ernst, Freundlich, Gauguin, Genin, Gromaire, La Fresnaye, Léger, Maillol, Matisse, Pascin, Picasso, Redon, Rouault, Utrillo, Valadon, Vallotton, Vertes, Vlaminck, Vuillard, Wols; Professor Dix; Julia Feininger; Professor Grieshaber; Mr Roman Norbert Ketterer, Stuttgart, for works by Campendonk, Heckel, Hofer, Kirchner, Pechstein, Schmidt-Rottluff; the Welz Gallery, Salzburg, for works by Kokoschka; Marlborough Fine Art Limited, London, for works by Armitage, Baumeister, Chadwick, Moore, Sutherland; Otto Stangl Gallery, Munich, for works by Marc; Springer Gallery, Berlin, for works by Trökes; Forlaget Norsk, Oslo, for works by Munch; Professor Jaenisch; Nina Kandinsky; Dr Kollwitz; Professor Mataré; Mr Müller-Herbig; Professor Meistermann; Ernst W. Nay; Pierre Soulages; Stiftung Emil Nolde, Seebüll.